The Private Pilot's Licence Course

Air Law, Operational Procedures and Communications
JAR Edition

Jeremy M Pratt

ISBN 874783 71 3

Published by

Airplan Flight Equipment Ltd

This book is intended to be a guide to the aviation law and radiotelephony elements of the UK PPL course. This book is **NOT** to be taken as a definitive interpretation of any aviation law, regulation, rule, procedure or information. In the UK the main 'competent authority' regarding interpretation and applicability of rules, regulations and procedures is the Civil Aviation Authority, to whom such questions should be addressed in the first instance. More so than any other aspect of flying, rules, regulations and procedures change on a regular basis. It is good airmanship and sound aviation practice to regularly up-date and check your knowledge of RT and Air Law rules, regulations and procedures.

Originally published as:
The Private Pilot's Licence Course Air Law and Radiotelephony

First Edition 1995
Reprinted with revisions 1996
Reprinted with revisions 1997
Reprinted with revisions 1998
Reprinted with revisions 1999
Second edition 2000
Reprinted with revisions 2000
Reprinted with revisions 2001

The Private Pilot's Licence Course
Air Law, Operational Procedures and Communications

ISBN 1 874783 71 3

Airplan Flight Equipment Ltd,
1a Ringway Trading Estate, Shadowmoss Road, Manchester M22 5LH
Tel: 0161-499 0023   Fax: 0161-499 0298   enquiries@afeonline.com
www.afeonline.com

contents

Air Law introduction

Air Law

contents

contents

contents

contents

contents

contents

editorial

Acknowledgments

As always, this book would not have been possible without the invaluable assistance of many people and organisations:

Air Accident Investigation Branch

Aviation Picture Library

Civil Aviation Authority:

Mr W A Beal, Chief RTF Examiner

Chart Room

Geoff Leach, Deputy Head Dangerous Goods Office

Safety Promotion Section

Special thanks to:

Dave Beech (head of section) Bill Walker & Nic Smith of Airspace Policy 1

Paul Cooper

Jon Davidson

Steve Dickinson

Peggy Follis

Harry Hargreaves

Roger Hyde

Jeff Lloyd

Peter R March

Chris Mathews

John Nelson

Popular Flying Association

Martin Robinson – AOPA

Rob Taylor – GDi studio

Mike Vines

AUTHOR: JEREMY M PRATT

Jeremy Pratt took his first flying lesson aged 14, paid for by weekend and holiday jobs at his local airfield cleaning aircraft and working in the hanger. Later he also worked in the air/ground station of the airfield and in the operations department of an air taxi company. He completed his PPL after being awarded an Esso/Air League scholarship and became a flying instructor at the age of 19. Since then he has taught students for the Private Pilots Licence and associated ratings and also applicants for professional flying licences. He has flown as a commercial pilot in a variety of roles and has also flown microlights, gliders and helicopters. He stays current by instructing and flying around Europe for business and pleasure.

He has been Managing Director of Airplan Flight Equipment since 1985, is author of the 'Pilot's Guide' series, the 'Questions and Answers' series; and has also co-authored, compiled and contributed to, a number of aviation books and publications.

TECHNICAL ADVISORS:

Bill Stitt – Chief Flying Instructor of Essex Flying School, Bill has been a flying instructor for over 25 years and is a delegated flight examiner. He has been training instructors for over 20 years and he is married to a flying instructor: their daughter also flies!

Phillip G Mathews – Chief Flying Instructor of Cotswold Aviation Services, Phil has over 10,000 hours experience of flying light aircraft. He gained his PPL at the age of 17 and went on to achieve an ATPL through the 'self-improver' route. Phil also runs his own business teaching applicants for the PPL and IMC rating technical exams and flies as a commercial pilot.

John Dale – John worked in Air Traffic Control for the RAF for over 12 years. He now works as an Air Traffic Control Officer in the Tower and Approach sections at Manchester International Airport. John gained his PPL 20 years ago, and now holds a commercial licence and instructor ratings. He specialises in Instrument Rating training and also flies twins up to business jets.

Kevin Edmunds – Kevin gained his PPL at the age of 17 through an RAF flying scholarship. He went on to join the air traffic service and is today an ATCO at Manchester International Airport, as well as being an active commercial pilot and flying instructor. Kevin has run RT courses for 21 years and is an RT examiner. He also runs courses for, and examines, candidates for the aeronautical radio station operator's Certificate of Competence.

Air Law introduction

The rules are there for the guidance of the wise, and the protection of the foolish

Oh no...not law!

It's not an unnatural reaction. Many people are attracted to flying in the first place by the notion of the freedom of the skies; in the context of flight, restrictions and regulations can seem tiresome. But in actual fact, 'aviation law' is generally much more concerned with common-sense practicalities than obscure legal technicalities. Matters such as the rules of the air, altimeter settings, the distinction between VFR and IFR flight, licence privileges and so on are relevant to the pilot every time an aircraft gets airborne, and they're not the sort of things you can stop and look up whilst you are flying the aeroplane. For this reason, aviation law is the first written paper an aspiring pilot has to take, and it must be passed before first solo.

Other aspects of aviation law relate to subjects such as the operation of aircraft, the organisation of air traffic services, airspace classifications, aircraft documentation and the like. Despite sounding rather daunting, many of these regulations are merely enshrining in law aspects of aviation which really amount to no more than natural common sense and good practice – or 'airmanship' as it's usually known in an aviation context. For example, it's pretty self-evident that pilots need to carry out certain essential checks and procedures before getting airborne. In aviation law, this requirement is formalised in 'Pre-flight action by commander of aircraft'. Similarly, pilots should obviously not allow their aircraft to be a menace to others ("Endangering safety of any person or property"); the design, maintenance and operation of aircraft should be to a certain standard ('Certificate of airworthiness to be in force') and so on. In fact, what at first sight might look like a mass of complex legislation and regulations turns out to be mostly rules and procedures based on nothing more than sound practice and many years of operating experience – often acquired the hard way. It's interesting to note that those who head-up the legislative departments of the Civil Aviation Authority tend to be pilots rather than lawyers.

However, the undeniable fact is that we live in increasingly litigious times. The era has gone when a pilot could fly anywhere he chose, beat-up airfields and his friend's houses, land where he liked and expect to receive a warm reception. The aeroplane has long since ceased to be a novelty; anti-social behaviour is not generally appreciated now, and the errant pilot is far more likely to find a decidedly unfriendly reception committee waiting when he lands. Most people would agree that this change, in itself, is not a bad thing. The fact remains that, in aviation, breaking the law is first and foremost a matter of compromising your own safety and the safety of others. The rules *ARE* there for a reason.

Throughout this book the 'pilot' is mostly referred to by means of the pronoun 'he'. This has been done purely to avoid the cumbersome and repetitive use of 'he or she'. I ask for the understanding of the reader in what is obviously an unsatisfactory situation for all.

One final detail. Perhaps more than any other aspect of flying an aeroplane, the 'small print' of aviation law changes frequently. It pays to keep up-to-date with the latest regulations and procedures if you want to enjoy safe and trouble-free aviating.

Air Law introduction to 2nd Edition

As it says overleaf, perhaps more than any other aspect of flying an aeroplane, aviation law changes frequently. As the publisher it has always been our philosophy to keep the print runs for the air law books as low as economically possible, so that we can incorporate changes to aviation law as soon as possible into the printed work. A glance at the editions page near the front of the book will show that on average we make one such update and revision a year, for matters as fundamental as licence privileges, or as minor as a reference to an airfield that has now closed. Such is the way of aviation rules and procedures and as publisher we accept that as part of the territory.

However, the last few months have seen nothing less than a seismic change in the rules that govern pilots – especially those concerning licensing and licence privileges, which has meant not just a revised Air Law book, but a completely re-written volume. The introduction of the JAR PPL has also meant a complete shift in the examination philosophy. The Air Law and Operational Procedures exam for the JAR PPL is now as much about ICAO definitions and recommended procedures as it is about the law as it affects a pilot with a licence issued by the CAA.

The difference between the two is crucial.

A recommendation or definition in an ICAO document, or a proposal in a JAR text, is exactly that – a recommendation or proposal. It has no basis in national law until the country involved (in the case the UK) has gone through the process of law making and it has reached the statute books. Therefore, you cannot assume that because a particular procedure or recommendation is contained in an ICAO or JAR document, it is UK law. Thus it is that the Air Law examination may require knowledge of an ICAO recommendation which is at variance to the relevant UK law.

To simplify the situation, where knowledge of an ICAO definition or recommendation is required, but it is markedly different to UK law (or no UK equivalent exists), the relevant information is clearly marked in a shaded box.

The moral of this is that the law can, and does, change with a disturbing frequency, and there is no reason to think that this will alter in the future. It is highly improbable that the rules and procedures as you learn them to pass the Air law exam will be completely unchanged in six months time, let alone six years. The only solution to is keep up-to-date with changes and new regulations as they happen. Just as the author and publisher of this book have to accept this as part of the territory of the business we are in, so you – the pilot – must accept it as part of the responsibility of holding a pilot's licence. And the first step is to simply accept that change is inevitable; after that the process of keeping up-to-date becomes that much more acceptable.

It is also worth noting that Air Law and Communications procedures are often inextricably linked, which is why we have put both subjects within the same book Before sitting the Air law exam you are highly recommended to work through the Communications section, and *vice versa*. To help you locate information, the index has been combined so that for any subject you can find at a glance both the Air law and Communications reference.

Air Law is the first technical exam for the PPL course, and can be daunting at first sight. Take heart – you're not alone. Read on and good luck!

Jeremy M Pratt

April 2000

Legislation

▶ **Basis of Aviation Law**

▶ **Aviation Law Documentation**

▶ **Revision**

Air Law

▶ Basis of Aviation Law

Aviation law in most countries is based upon the rules and procedures set out by the International Civil Aviation Organisation (ICAO). ICAO was established in 1944 to standardise the operating procedures and navigational practices of international aviation. This led to the articles of the Convention on International Civil Aviation (sometimes known as the Chicago Convention) and these articles are the principles on which aviation regulations and procedures are based. While they are not the most fascinating way to start a study of air law, these articles are in the syllabus and questions about them may be in the examination, so you are strongly advised not to skip past them! In the following, where the term 'state' is used, this relates to those states that have contracted to the Chicago Convention. The state of registry is the state on whose register an aircraft is entered.

Article 1 – Sovereignty

Every state has complete and exclusive sovereignty over airspace above its territory.

Article 2 – Territory

The territory of a state is the land areas and adjacent territorial waters under the sovereignty, protection or mandate of the state.

Article 5 – Non-Scheduled Flights Over State's Territory

The aircraft of states, other than scheduled international air services, have the right to make flights across state's territories and to make stops without obtaining prior permission, although the state may require the aircraft to make a landing. For flights over inaccessible regions or those without adequate air navigation facilities the state may require aircraft to follow prescribed routes, or obtain special permission for such flights.

The Convention on International Civil Aviation (Chicago Convention)

Article 10 – Landing at Customs Airports

If a state requires crossing aircraft to make a landing, the state can require that landing to be at a designated customs airport. Similarly departure from the territory can be required to be from a designated customs airport.

Article 11 – Applicability of Air Regulations

The laws and regulations of a state applicable to the arrival and departure of aircraft engaged in international air navigation, or to the operation of such aircraft while within its territory, shall apply to the aircraft of all contracting states.

Article 12 – Rules of the Air

Every aircraft flying over a state's territory, and every aircraft carrying a territory's nationality mark – wherever it is – must comply with that territory's rules of the air. Each state shall keep its own rules of the air as uniform as possible with those established under the convention, the duty to ensure compliance with these rules rests with the contracting state. Over the high seas, the rules established under the Convention apply.

Article 13 – Entry and Clearance Regulations

A state's laws and regulations regarding the admission and departure of passengers, crew or cargo from aircraft shall be complied with on arrival, upon departure and whilst within the territory of that state.

Article 16 – Search of Aircraft

The authorities of each state shall have the right to search the aircraft of other states on landing or departure, without unreasonable delay, and to inspect certificates and other documents prescribed by this Convention.

Article 22 – Facilitation of Formalities

Each state shall adopt all practical measures to expedite navigation by aircraft between state's territories, and to prevent unnecessary delay to aircraft, crews, passengers and cargo.

Article 23 – Customs and Immigration Procedures

Each state undertakes to establish customs and immigration procedures affecting international air navigation in accordance with the practices established by the Convention.

Article 24 – Customs Duty

Aircraft flying to, from or across, the territory of a state shall be admitted temporarily free of duty. Fuel, oil, spare parts, regular equipment and aircraft stores retained on board are also exempt customs duty, inspection fees or similar charges.

Article 29 – Documents Carried in Aircraft

Every aircraft engaged in international navigation shall carry the following documents:

Its Certificate of Registration

Its Certificate of Airworthiness

Crew licences

Journey logbook

Radio licence

A list of passenger names, places of embarkation and destination

A cargo manifest

Note: It is an international standard that before an international flight the Pilot-In-Command must ensure that the aircraft is airworthy, that it is duly registered and that all relevant certificates are on board the aircraft.

Article 30 – Aircraft Radio Equipment

Aircraft of a state flying in or over the territory of another state shall only carry radios licensed and used in accordance with the regulations of the state in which the aircraft is registered. The radio(s) may only be used by members of the flight crew issued with a licence for that purpose by the state in which the aircraft is registered.

Article 31 – Certificates of Airworthiness

Every aircraft engaged in international navigation must have a valid Certificate of Airworthiness issued by the state in which it is registered.

Article 32 – Licences of Personnel

The pilot and crew of every aircraft engaged in international navigation must have certificates of competency and licences issued or validated by the state in which the aircraft is registered. For the purposes of flight over its own territory, each state reserves the right to refuse to recognise certificates of competency or licences granted to any of its nationals by another state.

Article 33 – Recognition of Certificates and Licences

Certificates of Airworthiness, certificates of competency and licences issued or validated by the state in which the aircraft is registered, shall be recognised as valid by other states. The requirements for issue of those Certificates of Airworthiness, certificates of competency and licences must be equal to or above the minimum standards established by the Convention.

Article 34 – Journey Logbooks

Every aircraft engaged in international navigation will have a journey logbook which must be maintained with details of the aircraft, its crew and each journey, in a form described by the Convention.

Article 35 – Cargo Restrictions

No munitions or implements of war may be carried in or over the territory of a state except with the permission of that state. Each state must determine what constitutes munitions or implements of war giving consideration to the recommendations of the International Civil Aviation Organisation (ICAO). Each state reserves the right to regulate or prohibit the carriage of articles other than munitions or implements of war, provided this does not interfere with the operation, navigation or safety of aircraft.

Article 36 – Photographic Apparatus

Each state may prohibit or regulate the use of photographic apparatus in aircraft over its territory.

Article 37 – Adoption of International Standards and Procedures

Each state shall collaborate in securing the highest practical uniformity in air navigation; regulations, standards, procedures and organisation in relation to aircraft; personnel; airways and auxiliary services.

Article 39 – Endorsement of Certificates and Licenses

An aircraft or part which was the subject of an international standard of airworthiness or performance, and which failed to satisfy that standard at the time of certification, shall have endorsed on or attached to its airworthiness certificate complete details regarding that failure. Any licence holder who does not satisfy international standards relating to that licence or certificate shall have attached to or endorsed on that licence information regarding the particulars in which he does not satisfy those standards.

Article 40 – Validity of Endorsed Certificates and Licenses

No aircraft or personnel with endorsed licences or certificates will engage in international navigation except with the permission of the state or states whose territory is entered. The registration or use of any such aircraft or part, in a state other than that in which it was originally certified, will be at the discretion of the state into which the aircraft or part is imported.

These principles have been used to produce a series of ICAO documents known as 'Annexes', which contain the detail of recommended regulations and procedures. The annexes of most relevance are:

Annex 1	Personnel Licensing
Annex 2	Rules of the Air
Annex 3	Meteorological Services for International Air Navigation
Annex 6	Operation of Aircraft
Annex 7	Aircraft Nationality and Navigation Marks
Annex 8	Airworthiness of Aircraft
Annex 9	Facilitation
Annex 11	Air Traffic Services
Annex 12	Search and Rescue Services
Annex 13 (!)	Aircraft Accident Investigation
Annex 14	Aerodromes
Annex 15	Aeronautical Information Services
Annex 17	Security
Annex 18	Transport of Dangerous Goods by Air

An ICAO annex (in this case annex 11 – Air Traffic Services)

Members of ICAO may interpret an annex in accordance with their particular circumstances, and enact a rule or law which is different from an ICAO procedure if they choose to. Such differences are listed by country in the appropriate annex. This process is known as "filing a difference". As you might expect, this can lead to some significant variations in aviation laws and procedures between different countries, although the rules of the air (described in the following chapter) are by-and-large internationally recognised.

The most recent development in air law has been the work of the Joint Aviation Authorities (JAA), an organisation seeking to introduce uniform standards to harmonise European aviation rules, procedures, licensing and airworthiness standards. The new rules are known as 'JARs' – Joint Aviation Requirements – and many will have a profound effect on aviation procedures. Some JARs have now come into force in the UK, in particular those involving pilot licensing, and these are known collectively as JAR-FCL (Flight Crew Licensing). These will be described later. Further JARs regarding operational procedures (JAR-OPS) are expected to come into force in due course and you are strongly advised to keep abreast of on-going changes to aviation law which can be expected to occur at a faster-than-usual rate over the next few years.

▶ Aviation Law Documentation

In the UK, the regulation of aviation is primarily the responsibility of the Civil Aviation Authority (CAA). It is the CAA which drafts and communicates aviation rules and regulations, and information concerning UK aviation law can be found in a number of official documents:

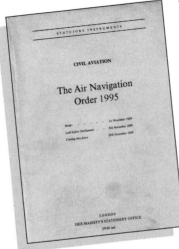

– The *Air Navigation Order*. Usually referred to as the 'ANO', this contains the legal documents enacting civil aviation legislation.

TOP> The Air Navigation Order is the principal reference for aviation legislation in the UK

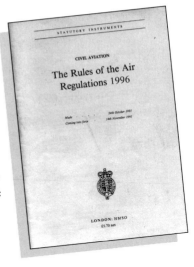

RIGHT> The Rules of the Air are the aviation equivalent of the 'Highway Code'

–The *Rules of the Air*. These rules are the nearest aviation equivalent of the 'Highway Code', setting down rights of way, air traffic control procedures, etc.

BOTTOM> The AIP contains information about airfields, airspace, restrictions and procedures etc.

–The *Aeronautical Information Publication*. The AIP (also known as the "Air Pilot") contains essential information regarding national procedures and aerodromes, airspace, radio facilities, meteorological services, search and rescue and many other items. By its nature the AIP requires constant updating; this is done by the re-issue of pages for the AIP and by NOTAMs *(q.v.)*

– *NOTAMs* (Notices to Airmen) contain information regarding temporary or permanent changes of information in the AIP.

Legislation

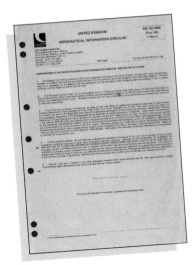

– *Aeronautical Information Circulars*. AICs are published monthly and contain advice on operational and administrative matters of importance to pilots and aircraft operators.

AICs contain information on administrative and safety matters.

The CAA also issues a number of publications containing information on specific areas of aviation law, rules and procedures.

It is important to appreciate that whilst the JAR air law syllabus concentrates on ICAO and JAR procedures, actual UK law is brought into force by an Act of Parliament (such as the Air Navigation Order), which might not be the same. This leaves a situation where you might be expected to know a particular ICAO procedure or definition to pass the air law examination, but in practice be bound by a UK law which is different. In this book, where there is a significant difference between an ICAO procedure and the applicable UK law, or there is no UK equivalent, the ICAO procedure or definition will be clearly marked as such.

PINK -

▶ Revision

Revision questions are printed at the end of each chapter in this book. The aim of the revision questions is to enable you to test your knowledge of the chapter subject, and to help you retain the principal elements of each subject.

Attempt the revision questions once you are satisfied that you have understood and learnt the main points of each chapter. You should aim for a success rate of around 80%.

1 What is the definition of the 'territory' of a state?

2 Can a state require a crossing aircraft to make a landing?

3 Can duty be charged on fuel, oil, spare parts, regular equipment and aircraft stores retained on board when an aircraft stops in a state's territory?

4 Who is responsible for ensuring that the relevant documents are carried on an international flight?

5 Under ICAO recommendations, which of the following documents must be carried on an international flight:

   – Certificate of Registration

   – Certificate of Compliance

   – Certificate of Regulation

6 Does an aircraft or person with an endorsed licence or certificate require the permission of the state or states whose territory is entered if engaging in international navigation?

7 What does 'ANO' stand for?

8 Which CAA document contains information regarding aerodromes, airspace, radio facilities, meteorological services, search and rescue, etc.?

9 How often are AICs published?

Answers at LAW183

Rules of the Air

▶ The Rules of the Air – General

▶ Rules for Avoiding Collisions

▶ Rights of Way In Flight

▶ Flight in the Vicinity of Aerodromes

▶ Order of Landing

▶ Take-off and Landing on Runways

▶ Landing and Take-off

▶ Rights of Way on the Ground

▶ Aerobatics

▶ Right-Hand Traffic Rule

▶ Simulated Instrument Flight

▶ The Low Flying Rules

▶ Visual Flight Rules (VFR)

▶ Distress, Difficulty and Urgency Signals

▶ Ground-to-Air Visual Signals

▶ Aerodrome Lighting

▶ Runways

▶ Light Signals

▶ Visual Signals Visible to an Aircraft on the Ground

▶ Taxiway Signals and Markings

▶ Marshalling Signals

▶ Movements at Aerodromes

▶ Use of Aerodromes

▶ Aerodrome Traffic Zones

▶ Notification of Arrival and Departure

▶ Aviation Fuel

▶ Closure of Airfields

▶ Interception of Aircraft

▶ Revision

▶ The Rules of the Air – General

ICAO Annex 2 covers international standards of the Rules of the Air. Within the UK, the Rules of the Air are set out in the 'Rules of the Air Regulations', which gives them the status of law and cover such items as rights of way, lights and signals (on aircraft and aerodromes) and a variety of other factors affecting the safety of aircraft. As such, they could be likened to a sort of airborne highway code. In accordance with Article 12 of the Convention on International Civil Aviation, the UK rules of the air apply to all UK-registered aircraft wherever they may be, and to all aircraft within the UK. They can only be disregarded under limited and highly specific circumstances:

– to avoid immediate danger

– to comply with the law of a country other than the UK which the aircraft is within

– to allow pilots in the UK armed forces to comply with military flying regulations.

If a pilot departs from a rule to avoid immediate danger, the circumstances must be reported to the CAA in writing within ten days.

▶ Rules for Avoiding Collisions

It is ultimately the duty of the aircraft commander to take all possible measures to avoid a collision, even when an aircraft is operating under an air-traffic control clearance. There are five general principles:

– an aircraft must not fly so close to another as to create the danger of a collision.

– aircraft must not fly in formation unless the commanders have agreed to do so. In

this context, it is important to appreciate that formation flying is **extremely dangerous** unless you have had proper training and a prior briefing. Formation flying is one of those aspects of aviation that is most definitely *not* as easy as good pilots make it look. Unfortunately a number of untrained pilots have discovered this fact the hard way.

Aircraft must not fly in formation unless the commanders have agreed to do so. Even then, formation flying is not for the untrained

– a flying machine towing a glider is considered to be a single aircraft commanded by the commander of the flying machine.

– an aircraft which has to give way must avoid passing over, under or ahead of the other aircraft unless well clear.

– an aircraft which has right of way should maintain course and speed. Obviously if this creates a risk of collision (e.g. the other aircraft does not give way) the commander must act to avoid a collision.

▶Rights of Way In Flight

If the aircraft are of different classes, the rule of precedence applies:

1. Balloons

2. Gliders

3. Airships

The order of priority in the air

4. Flying Machines

Powered aircraft must give way to aircraft towing gliders or objects.

Foot launched powered flying machines (FLPFMs) must give way to all other aircraft. A 'flying machine' essentially means a heavier than air, power driven aircraft – e.g. aeroplanes, helicopters and gyroplanes.

All other aircraft give way to balloons

– Converging. If the converging aircraft are of the same class, the aircraft on the right has right of way. This rule can be simply remembered as "On the Right, In the Right". Remember that the aircraft giving way should avoid passing over or under the aircraft that has right of way, or passing ahead of it unless well clear (see 'Rules for Avoiding Collisions').

Where two aircraft are converging, the aircraft on the right has right of way ("on the right in the right")

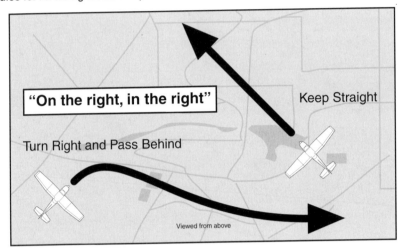

– Approaching head-on. Each aircraft must alter heading to the right.

Where two aircraft are approaching head-on, each aircraft shall alter course to the right

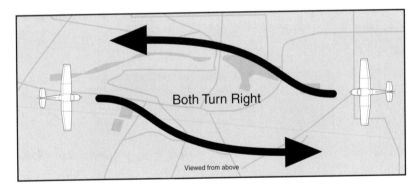

– Overtaking. The aircraft which is being overtaken has right of way. The overtaking aircraft must keep clear by altering heading to the right. The overtaking aircraft must continue to keep well clear of the other aircraft, regardless of the change in relative positions in the two.

An aircraft overtaking another in the air shall alter course to the right

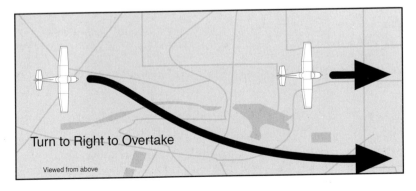

A glider overtaking another glider in the UK can alter its heading to the left or right.

> ICAO definition: An overtaking situation exists while the overtaking aircraft is approaching another from the rear within an angle of less than 70° from the plane of symmetry (extended centreline) of the aircraft being overtaken.

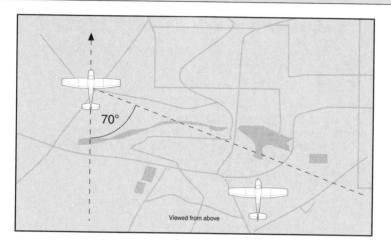

Viewed from above

When deciding on avoiding action, remember the old adage that **constant bearing means constant danger.** In other words, if the other aircraft remains at the same spot on your windscreen or window, there is a serious risk of collision. The subject of collision avoidance is also discussed in detail in the 'Flying Training' section of the PPL course (Book1).

▶ Flight in the Vicinity of Aerodromes

Unless an Air Traffic Control (ATC) unit authorises otherwise, a flying machine, glider or airship in the vicinity of an aerodrome must:

– conform to the traffic pattern formed by landing aircraft or keep well clear of the pattern.

– make all turns to the left unless ground signals indicate otherwise. Left-hand circuits are standard unless otherwise specifically stated or indicated.

▶ Order of Landing

An aircraft landing or on final approach has right of way over other aircraft in flight and on the surface. Where two or more flying machines, gliders or airships are making simultaneous approaches, the lower aircraft has right of way, except that:

– an aircraft must not cut in front of, or overtake, an aircraft already on final approach.

– if ATC has given an order of priority to land, aircraft must approach in that order.

– if the commander of an aircraft is aware that another aircraft is making an emergency landing, he must give way. If this situation occurs at night, he must not make a further attempt to land until further permission has been given.

▶ Take-off and Landing on Runways

Take-offs and landings should be in the direction indicated by ground signals or into wind if there are no signals, unless good aviation procedure dictates otherwise.

Normally only one aircraft may land on a runway at a time. An aircraft may land on a runway before the aircraft ahead has vacated if they are authorised to do so by an ATC unit. This is known as a 'land after' instruction and is discussed in the RT section.

After landing an aircraft must move clear of the runway as soon as possible, unless an ATC unit authorises otherwise.

▶ Landing and Take-off

Where landings and take-offs are **not** confined to a runway, the following rules apply:

– an aircraft taking-off must leave on its left an aircraft which has taken off or is about to take-off.

– an aircraft landing must leave on its left an aircraft which has landed, is about to land or about to take-off. When the landing is completed, the aircraft must turn left (after the pilot in command has checked that this will not endanger or inconvenience any other traffic).

– after landing the flying machine must move clear of the landing area as soon as possible unless otherwise authorised by an ATC unit.

Aircraft are expected to turn left after landing, in the absence of an instruction to the contrary

After landing
Turn to the LEFT

Land to the right

Rights of Way on Landing

▶Rights of Way on the Ground

The following rules of precedence apply:

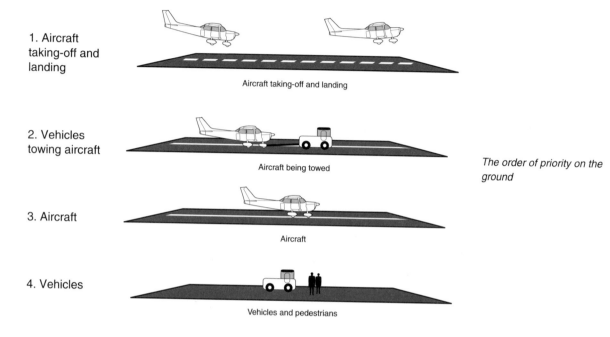

1. Aircraft taking-off and landing

Aircraft taking-off and landing

2. Vehicles towing aircraft

Aircraft being towed

3. Aircraft

Aircraft

4. Vehicles

Vehicles and pedestrians

The order of priority on the ground

As with the rules for avoiding collisions in the air, even when an aircraft is operating under an air-traffic control clearance it is still ultimately the duty of the aircraft commander to take all possible measures to avoid a collision.

– Converging. Where two aircraft are converging, the aircraft on the right has right of way ("on the right, in the right") and the other aircraft must give way.

Where two aircraft are converging the aircraft on the right has right of way ("on the right in the right")

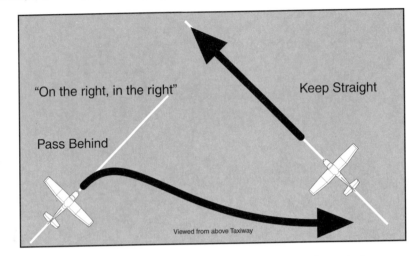

– Head-on. Where two aircraft are approaching head-on, each must alter course to the right.

Where two aircraft are approaching head-on, each aircraft shall alter course to the right

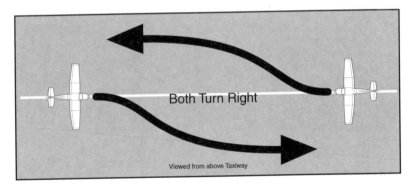

– Overtaking. When overtaking, the overtaking aircraft must avoid the other by turning left. *Note that this is different from the rule regarding airborne overtaking.*

An aircraft overtaking another on the ground must alter course to the left

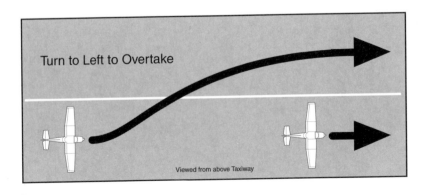

▶Aerobatics

No aerobatic manoeuvre may be flown over the congested area of any city, town or settlement. Aerobatics may only be carried out in controlled airspace with the permission of the appropriate ATC unit.

'Aerobatic manoeuvres' include spins, loops, rolls, stall turns, inverted flight and similar manoeuvres.

Aerobatics must be flown over open countryside – and preferably at a safe height

The 'congested area' of a city, town or settlement is defined as any area which is substantially used for residential, industrial, commercial or recreational purposes. This is an important definition, which will be referred to again with regard to the low-flying rules.

If the aircraft has a transponder (used to display a set of numbers of a controller's radar screen, and described more fully in the RT section), this should be set to the code 7004 from five minutes before commencing aerobatics until the cessation of aerobatic manoeuvres.

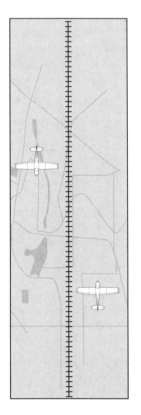

The 'Right-Hand Traffic' rule

▶Right-Hand Traffic Rule

When an aircraft is following a ground line-feature in the UK, such as the coastline, a road, a railway, a canal or river, etc., it must keep that feature on its left unless it is flying in controlled airspace and has been otherwise instructed by an appropriate ATC unit. This rule means that if two aircraft are following the same line-feature but in different directions, they should be on opposite sides of the line feature.

▶Simulated Instrument Flight

If an aircraft is to fly in simulated instrument-flight conditions (e.g. with screens fitted or with IFR goggles worn to restrict the external vision of the pilot) certain conditions must be met:

– the aircraft must be fitted with dual controls.

– a safety pilot must be carried in the second control seat.*

– if the safety pilot does not have a complete field of vision forward and to each side, a third person (a 'competent observer') must be carried. The competent observer must be able to see the area blind to the safety pilot and to be able to communicate with the safety pilot.

*Note that a student pilot cannot qualify as a safety pilot.

▶The Low Flying Rules

The rules regarding minimum height to fly at are set out in Rule 5 of the Rules of the Air. Rule 5 contains three main criteria, often referred to as the "three provisions":

The three basic provisions of the low flying rules

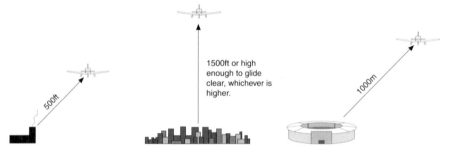

Minimum Separation

– *500ft Provision*

An aircraft must not fly closer than 500ft to any person, vessel, vehicle or structure.

– *1500ft Provision*

When flying over the congested area of any city, town or settlement, an aircraft must fly high enough to land clear of the area without danger to persons or property if the engine fails; **or** fly not less than 1500ft above the highest fixed object within 600m of the aircraft – whichever is higher.

– *1000m Provision*

An aircraft must not fly over or within 1000m of an organised open-air gathering of more than 1000 people; **or** lower than a height which would allow it to land clear of the gathering if the engine failed – whichever is higher.

Each of these provisions is subject to various exceptions and provisos, which need to be understood in detail if the pilot is to comply with Rule 5 at all times. Unfortunately, the provisions of this rule are often misunderstood by pilots – and occasionally such misunderstandings have an unfortunate habit of leading to prosecution. It makes sense to look at Rule 5 in more detail.

Nothing in Rule 5 prohibits an aircraft from flying in such a way as to save life. However, this exception applies to flights such as those undertaken in support of search and rescue operations, etc. It does *not* apply to low flying carried out in order to stay in visual contact with the ground.

None of the Rule 5 provisions apply to an aircraft taking off, landing, or practising approaches to land at a Government (military) aerodrome or a licensed aerodrome in accordance with 'normal aviation practice'. If practising approaches at a licensed or military aerodrome, the aircraft must use airspace normally used for landings and take-offs at the aerodrome to qualify for exemption from Rule 5.

Practice approaches at an unlicensed airfield *are* subject to Rule 5 and so, for practical purposes, are prohibited. This might appear to prohibit a go-around from an approach to land at an unlicensed airfield, since in most cases the aircraft will breach at least one of the Rule 5 criteria during such a manoeuvre. However, the CAA has stated that an approach to an unlicensed airfield need not end in a landing if the approach is made to assess turbulence or crosswind, inspect the surface condition, or to check for obstructions and slope. However, the 1500ft provision does apply to aircraft taking off and landing at an unlicensed aerodrome. The terms 'licensed' and 'unlicensed' in relation to an aerodrome are described more fully later in this chapter. Certain provisions of Rule 5 may also be waived by the CAA in relation to air races, air displays, etc. Aircraft are exempt from the 500ft provision when taking-off or landing in accordance with normal aviation practice. Gliders are exempt when hill-soaring, and some aircraft operations (crop spraying, oil pollution control, picking up and releasing tow ropes, banners, etc.) can also be exempted.

When flying to an unlicensed airfield (such as this private strip), the rule 5 provisions apply more strictly than when flying at a military or licensed airfield

The 1500ft provision introduces the concept of a **congested area**. The congested area of a city, town or settlement is defined by the CAA as being any area which is substantially used for residential, industrial, commercial or recreational purposes. What constitutes a city or town is probably quite obvious, but what constitutes a settlement is more difficult. The CAA does not offer a strict definition, and indeed the word can be interpreted very broadly. All in all, you might think that the scope of the 1500ft provision is very wide, and you would probably be right. The current view of the CAA appears to be that any area depicted on the CAA 1:500 000 charts as a built-up area qualifies as a congested area. Similarly, any settlement with clearly defined boundaries is also a congested area. Pilots should therefore observe the 1500ft/land-clear minima when flying over any such built-up area.

The CAA view is that any built-up area large enough to be shown on an aeronautical chart, even the smallest hamlet (represented by small yellow circles) constitutes a 'congested area'

Ensuring that you can meet the general requirement to land clear is the responsibility of the pilot in command, *not* ATC. If ATC offers a clearance which would not enable you to meet the land-clear requirement, you should not accept it. For the purposes of the land-clear requirement, playing fields and recreational areas, etc. are *not* acceptable landing sites.

The requirement to remain at least 1500ft above the highest fixed object within 600m over a congested area does not apply on routes which have been notified for the purposes of Rule 5, or when flying on a Special VFR clearance. However the land-clear requirement still applies.

This is obviously a 'congested area'. Remember that playing fields etc. are not acceptable areas to 'land clear' in the terms of rule 5. Complying with Rule 5 is the responsibility of the pilot in command, regardless of any ATC clearance

A helicopter must not fly below a height that will allow it to land without danger to persons or property if an engine fails. Helicopters are also subject to the rule requiring them to be at least 1500ft above the highest fixed object within 600m over a congested area. Over a specified area of central London, a helicopter must not fly below a height that would allow it to land clear of the area if an engine failed.

The CAA maintains that prosecutions for low flying are only made in cases where pilots are displaying bad airmanship or a disregard for normal aviation practice. Low flying poses a number of dangers, not just to the pilot and aircraft but also to those on the ground. In addition, very few people on the ground appreciate the sight and sound of an aircraft involved in illegal low flying, and such actions (especially near an airfield or airstrip) can only strengthen the hand of those who seek to restrict our freedom to fly.

"An aircraft shall not fly closer than 500 feet to any person, vessel, vehicle or structure"

Illegal low flying is one of the most commonly prosecuted offences involving private pilots, and it is very rare for a pilot to defend such a prosecution successfully. So, if you choose to do a low-level 'beat up' of your home airfield, it's no use claiming later that it was just a normal missed approach– it's all been tried before. Quite apart from the obvious dangers, accurate low flying is also a lot harder than it looks. For example, military fast-jet pilots may fly low only after intensive training; they have regular currency checks and are subject to strict rules. There are definite limits on how low they may go, and they are subject to penalties if they transgress.

All in all, the legal and safety risks of low flying make it just not worthwhile. A pilot seeking to add some thrills to his flying is much better advised to find a flying school offering an aerobatics course. Aerobatics are safer, more interesting and more fun, and will add much more to flying skill and knowledge.

►Visual Flight Rules (VFR)

In essence, an aircraft can be controlled by the pilot either by reference to the view outside the window or, if this is not possible, by sole reference to the flight instruments. The basic licence for which you are training means conducting nearly all flights in accordance with Visual Flight Rules – known as VFR. In principle, flying VFR means being able to control the aircraft, navigate and avoid collisions by external reference – and it follows that this is only possible if the weather conditions, such as cloud base and visibility, are good enough to give the pilot adequate external reference. It is therefore an essential requirement for VFR flight that the weather conditions meet a criteria known as Visual Meteorological Conditions (VMC).

> ICAO Definition: Visual Meteorological Conditions (VMC) – meteorological conditions expressed in terms of visibility, distance from cloud and ceiling, <u>equal to or better than</u> a specified minima.

Put simply, to fly VFR the aircraft must be in VMC. The specified minima for VMC is discussed in a later chapter.

►Distress, Difficulty and Urgency Signals

If a flight has a problem, it makes sense to tell others about it, so that they can either offer assistance or keep out of your way! However, now is a good place to say that in the event of an emergency, the pilot's number one priority always is to fly the aeroplane and deal with the problem. Getting involved with a long radio conversation about non-essential information, such as pilot qualifications or how many people you have on board, may distract you from that primary task – don't do it! An aircraft commander can make one or more of the following signals to indicate a problem.

To indicate a **distress** situation, where the aircraft is threatened by grave and imminent danger and requires immediate assistance:

– By RT, the word **"Mayday"**.

– By visual signalling, the Morse code SOS(• • • – – – • • •); a series of red pyrotechnic lights, or a red parachute flare.

– By sound signalling, the Morse code SOS (• • • – – – • • •); or the continuous sounding of any sound apparatus.

To give notice of **difficulties** which compel the aircraft to land, but it does not require immediate assistance:

– a series of white pyrotechnic lights

– the repeated switching on and off of the aircraft's landing lights

– the irregular switching on and off of the aircraft's navigation lights

Note: the procedure for notifying a 'difficulty' is not generally applicable outside the UK

To give notice of an **urgency** situation regarding the aircraft itself, or something or somebody in sight of the aircraft:

– by RT, the words **"Pan Pan"**

– by visual signalling, the Morse code XXX(– • • – – • • – – • • –)

– by sound signalling, the Morse code XXX (– • • – – • • – – • • –)

Additionally, the aircraft's transponder (described later) can be used to indicate to the existence of a problem. The three standard emergency codes are:

7700 *Distress*

7600 *Radio communications failure*

7500 *Unlawful interference (i.e. hijack)*

▶ Ground-to-Air Visual Signals

The *signals square* on an airfield is a 12-metre square within which signals to an aircraft in flight are placed. The signals square is normally located close to the control tower or ATSU, presumably so that no-one has to walk too far to change the signals! ATSU (Air Traffic Service Unit) is a generic term for any organisation providing some type of Air Traffic Service – whether it is a set of fully qualified Air Traffic Controllers with radar and hi-tec gadgets, or a part-time radio operator with a cat and a kettle! Ground-to-Air signals are primarily intended for the guidance of an aircraft arriving at an aerodrome. Aerodromes not accepting non-radio aircraft do not have to display a signals square – which is why you will not see one outside the tower at London Heathrow, for instance – and military airfields used as Relief Landing Grounds also do not have them.

A typical signals square at a general aviation airfield – in this case Halfpenny Green

Rules of the Air

Take-off and land
in the direction of
the shaft of the T

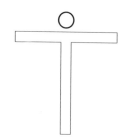

Direction of take-off
and landing are not
necessarily the same

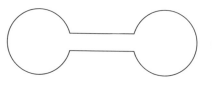

All ground movement
confined to paved or
hard surfaces

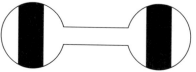

Take-off and landing
must take place on
the runway, but
ground movement is
not confined to paved
or hard surfaces

*Ground signals which may
be displayed within the
signals square*

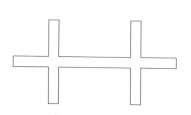

Gliding in progress

Helicopters
may only land or
take-off within the
designated area

LAW23

Right-hand circuit in force

Due to the state of the manoeuvring area, pilots should exercise special care when landing

Ground signals which may be displayed within the signals square

Landing prohibited

Light aircraft may take-off and land either on the runway or the designated area

Rules of the Air

There may be other ground signals, outside the signals area, visible to an aircraft in flight. These might include:

Aerodrome name/identity

Helicopter landing area

Light aircraft landing/take-off area

Tow-rope/banner dropping area

Glider take-off/landing area

Windsocks

Helicopters
section of the manoeuvring area to be used only for the take-off and landing of helicopters

Light aircraft
section of the manoeuvring area to be used only for the take-off and landing of light aircraft

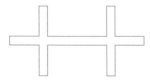

Gliders
An area to be used only for the taking-off and landing of gliders

Runway
Placed at the left-hand side of a runway (when viewed from the direction of landing) indicates the runway to be used

Ground signals which may be displayed outside the signals square

Tow rope dropping area
Tow ropes and articles towed by aircraft are to be dropped only in the area in which the cross is placed

At military aerodromes, additional signals may be displayed:

LANDING DANGEROUS

Runway is non-usable

EMERGENCY USE ONLY

The runway is fit for emergency use only (such runways may be temporarily obstructed)

Additional ground signals which may be seen at military aerodromes

LAND IN EMERGENCY ONLY

This board is displayed in the signals square

LIGHT AIRCRAFT LANDING AREA

A red 'L' in the signals square indicates that light aircraft may land in a special grass area, marked with white-coloured markings. Taxying on the grass is permitted

▶ **Aerodrome Lighting**

Aerodrome Beacon (ABn). A civil aerodrome may display an aerodrome beacon, which will be either alternating green/white or flashing white. These are becoming quite rare in the UK.

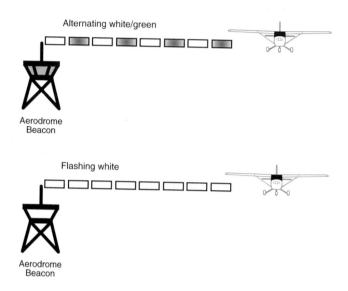

Aerodrome Beacons may be flashing white, or alternating white/green

Identification Beacon (IBn). A light flashing the two-letter Morse-code identifier for the aerodrome every twelve seconds. At a civil aerodrome the light is green; at a military aerodrome it is red.

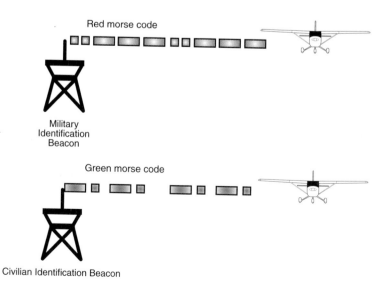

Identification Beacons at civilian airfields flash green Morse identification letters; at military airfields they are red.

Obstructions on and near an aerodrome may be marked by red obstruction lights.

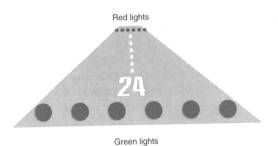

Runway lights positioned to mark the useable portion of the runway

Lights marking the runway threshold (the beginning of the runway) are fixed unidirectional lights showing green in the direction of the approach to the runway. Lights marking the end of the runway are fixed unidirectional lights showing red in the direction of the runway.

Runways may also have *approach-slope indicators*. These are lighting systems which help the pilot judge the approach angle of descent to the runway. The exact approach angle set on these systems depends on the airfield, runway and local topography, but it is normally in the region of 3° (which is a little shallower than the normal approach angle for a light aircraft). The lighting units are essentially set in concrete next to the runway (so they are not easily adjustable) and are usually one of two types:

As the name implies, the PAPI system tends to give rather more accurate guidance; one reason is that there is an immediate shift from white to red and vice versa, rather than the transitional pink colour often seen when using VASIs.

Visual Approach Slope Indicators (VASIs)

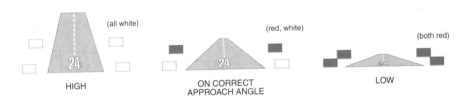

Precision Approach Path Indicator (PAPI)

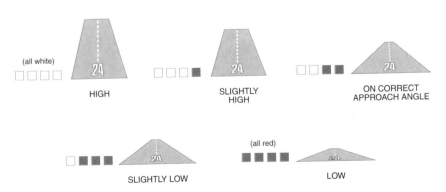

▶Runways

In general, runway markings are white in colour. Two or more white crosses signify a section of runway or taxiway unfit for the movement of aircraft.

The runway threshold will usually be marked with a two-figure number indicating the take-off/landing direction (magnetic) to the nearest 10°. So for example, Runway 24 has a magnetic direction of 240° magnetic or thereabouts. In the opposite direction, the runway number will always be the reciprocal – that is 180° different. In this instance the reciprocal of 24 is 06. Where parallel runways are in use, a letter is added to the runway designator (L = Left, C = Centre, R = Right)

The threshold of a paved runway may also be marked by white 'piano keys'.

A runway threshold can be *displaced*, either temporarily or permanently. Such displacement may be to prevent all aircraft movements in the area, or only to prevent landings (take-offs still being permitted in that area).

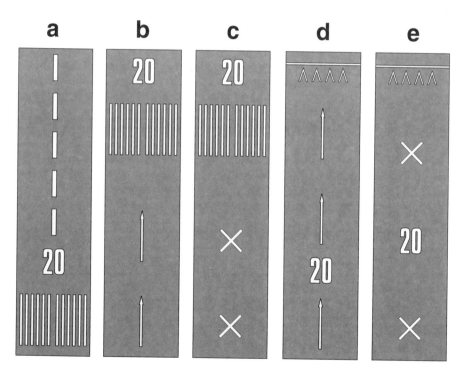

a) Most major runways have 'piano key' threshold markings. The number indicates the magnetic runway direction in tens of degrees – in this case 200°

b) A displaced threshold. The displaced area is suitable for the movement (but not landing) of aircraft

c) A displaced threshold where the displaced area is unfit for the movement of aircraft (indicated by the white crosses)

d) A temporarily (6 months or less) displaced threshold. The displaced area is suitable for the movement (but not landing) of aircraft

e) A temporarily displaced threshold. The displaced area is unfit for the movement of aircraft (as indicated by the white crosses)

All paved runways should have centre-line markings. Unpaved runways, or runways where there is insufficient contrast between the surface and the runway edge, may have white strips to delineate the edge.

If an airfield is listed in the UK Aeronautical Information Publication (AIP) its runways will probably have been measured and inspected by CAA personnel. The resulting measurements allow the runway dimensions to be described in precise terms.

The length of runway available for the take-off run is called (conveniently enough) the *Take-Off Run Available* (*TORA*). This distance often coincides with actual length of the runway itself.

Beyond the end of TORA may be a *stopway*. A stopway is an area of ground where the aircraft can be safely brought to a halt in an emergency. The stopway should be clear of obstructions that could damage the aircraft

The area beyond the TORA over which the aircraft can climb to 50ft is called the *clearway*. The clearway will include the stopway and any additional surface cleared of obstructions over which the aircraft can safely climb. As a general rule, the clearway will only extend as far as the airfield boundary and in any case the maximum clearway accounted for is no more than 50% of the TORA distance.

The TORA plus the stopway distance is known as the *Emergency Distance Available* (*EDA*)

The TORA plus the clearway distance (which includes the stopway) is known as the *Take-Off Distance Available* (*TODA*). The calculated take-off distance required should never be more than the TODA for a safe take-off to be made.

The length of runway available for the landing run is called the *Landing Distance Available* (*LDA*). The LDA is calculated assuming that the landing aircraft arrives over the runway threshold at 50ft. If there is some obstacle high enough to endanger a landing aircraft in the area approaching the landing runway, the runway threshold will be *displaced* and the LDA will be reduced accordingly. A displaced threshold allows the landing aircraft to make an approach high enough to clear obstacles in the approach path. The calculated landing distance required should never be more than the LDA for a safe landing to be made.

The TORA, TODA, EDA and LDA for a runway will be listed in the AIP, and this document (as updated and amended) is the primary reference for runway length information. Commercially produced flight guides will also list some or all of these distances, as well as containing information for airfields not listed in the AIP.

The definitions of the runway and surrounds

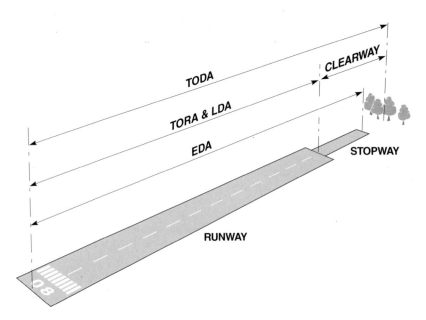

Rules of the Air

If the runway surface is wet, braking action will be less effective and an aircraft will need a longer distance to come to a halt. For this reason there are five standard terms to describe runway conditions:

Description	Runway condition
Dry	The surface is not affected by water, slush, snow or ice
Damp	The surface shows a change of colour due to moisture
Wet	The surface is soaked but no significant patches of standing water are visible
Water Patches	Significant patches of standing water are visible
Flooded	Extensive standing water is visible

JAR definition: A runway that has water patches or is flooded is considered to be *contaminated*.

►Light Signals

To communicate with a non-radio aircraft, an ATSU can make light signals which have the following meanings.

Light Signal	FROM AN AERODROME	
	to Aircraft in Flight	to Aircraft on Ground
STEADY RED	Give way to other aircraft and continue circling	Stop
RED PYROTECHNIC LIGHT OR RED FLARE	Do not land; wait for permission	–
RED FLASHES	Do not land; aerodrome not available for landing	Move clear of landing area
GREEN FLASHES	Return to aerodrome; wait for permission to land	To an aircraft: You may move on the manoeuvring area and apron. To a vehicle: you may move on the manoeuvring area
STEADY GREEN	You may land	You may take-off
WHITE FLASHES	Land at this aerodrome after receiving continuous green light and then, after receiving green flashes, proceed to apron	Return to starting point on the aerodrome

Although the days when every aircraft carried pyrotechnic lights are long gone, an aircraft can in principle (and if suitably equipped) make certain light signals, which have the following meanings:

Light Signal	From an aircraft in flight to an aerodrome
RED PYROTECHNIC LIGHT OR RED FLARE	Immediate assistance is requested
STEADY GREEN GREEN FLASHES OR PYROTECHNIC	**By night:** May I land? **By day:** May I land in a direction different from that indicated by the landing T?
WHITE FLASHES WHITE PYROTECHNIC LIGHTS SWITCHING ON AND OFF LANDING LIGHTS OR IRREGULAR FLASHING OF THE NAVIGATION LIGHTS	I am compelled to land

ICAO procedure: If an aircraft is in or about to enter a prohibited, restricted or danger area, a series of bursting green and red lights or stars may be fired from the ground at 10 second intervals (note: this procedure is no longer applicable in the UK)

▶Visual Signals Visible to an Aircraft on the Ground

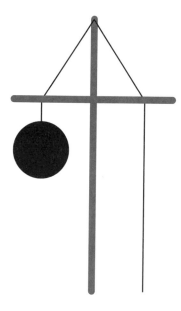

Runway 03 Left in use

Point at which pilots should report

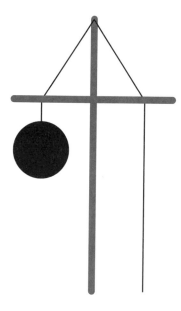

Direction of take-off and landing not necessarily the same

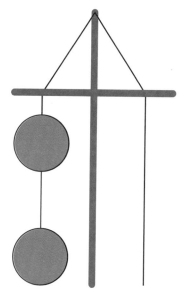

Gliding in progress

Visual signals visible to an aircraft on the ground

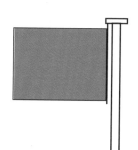

Left-hand circuit in force

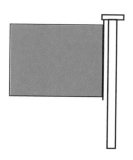

Right-hand circuit in force

Visual signals visible to an
aircraft on the ground

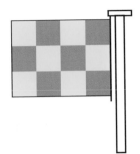

Air traffic control in operation

The 'Black C' indicates the
point at which pilots
should report

Typical ground signals at
a small airfield (Bodmin).
Note the markings in the
signals square, the point
to which pilots report, and
the runway in use – 03

▶Taxiway Signals and Markings

In general, taxiway markings are yellow in colour. At larger airfields a taxiway will be given a designator letter, to which various signs on the airfield (and published diagrams) will refer. Runways are referred to by their two-figure designator.

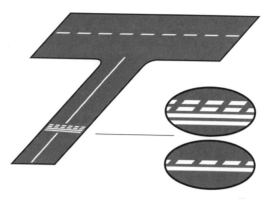

Holding point markings across a taxiway. The lines may be single or double, but the broken line is always on the runway side

The holding point for a runway will be shown by yellow markings across the taxiway itself:

and possibly on boards at the side of the taxiway:

Taxiway holding point boards. The numbers are the runway designator, the letter is the designation of the holding point.

You should *never* pass the holding point for an active runway without an ATC clearance where appropriate, nor without having visually checked that the runway and the approach area are clear of other aircraft. Incidentally, at major airfields there may be other holding points marked with the word CAT (e.g. CAT II, CAT III). These are holding points used when certain types of instrument approach are being flown, and will not usually concern you unless ATC gives a specific instruction in relation to a CAT holding point.

Typical taxiway boards at a larger airfield (Bristol)

A sign having white letters on a red background is a mandatory instruction sign. These normally mark points which should not be passed without ATC authorisation.

A No Entry sign

Inbound destination signs. These will direct you to a specific part of the aerodrome. The abbreviations used are:

APRON

STANDS – aircraft parking stands

GA – general aviation apron

FUEL

TERM – gate position for aircraft loading/unloading

CIVIL

MIL – area reserved for military aircraft

PAX – area reserved for passenger handling

CARGO

INTL – area for handling international flights

FBO – Fixed Base Operator (often the handling agent for GA flights at a larger airfield)

HELI – Helicopter parking

The boundary of the airfield, or an area unfit for the movement of aircraft, is delineated by orange and white striped markers.

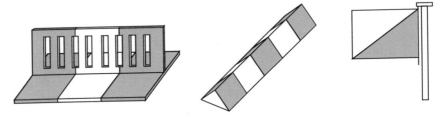

Boundary markers

Area unfit for the movement of aircraft

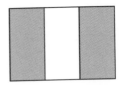

Aerodrome boundary

▶ Marshalling Signals

Whilst taxying or parking, the pilot may receive *marshalling* signals. These signals are provided for the **guidance** of the pilot and, according to the Rules of the Air, a pilot is not required to obey marshalling signals if in his opinion it is unsafe to do so. As always, the general maxim is that it is the pilot in command (PIC) who is responsible for the safety of the aircraft and passengers, and in matters of safety the pilot in command has the final say.

Right or left arm down, the other moved across body and extended to indicate position of the next marshaller.

Proceed under the guidance of another marshaller

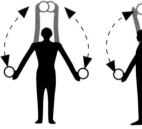

Arms repeatedly moved upward and backward.

Move ahead

Right arm down, left arm repeatedly moved upward and backward. The speed of movement indicates the rate of turn.

Open up starboard engine or turn to port

Left arm down, left arm repeatedly moved upward and backward. The speed of movement indicates the rate of turn.

Open up port engine or turn to starboard

Marshalling signals to a fixed-wing aircraft

Arms repeatedly crossed above the head. The speed of the arm movement indicates the urgency.

Stop

A circular motion of the right hand at head level, with the left arm pointing at the appropriate engine.

Start engine

Air Law

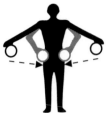

Arms extended, palms facing inwards, then swung from the extended position inwards.

Chocks inserted

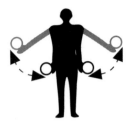

Arms down, palms facing outwards, then swung outwards.

Chocks away

Marshalling signals to a fixed-wing aircraft

Either arm and hand placed level with the chest, then moved across with the palm downward.

Cut engine(s)

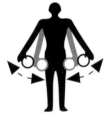

Arms placed down, palms towards the ground, then moved up and down several times.

Slow down

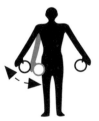

Arms placed down, palms towards the ground, then either right or left arm moved up and down indicating that the engines on the left or right side, should be slowed down.

Slow down engines on indicated side

Arms placed above the head in a vertical position.

This bay

Rules of the Air

Raise arm, with fist clenched, horizontally in front of the body, then extend fingers.

Release brakes

Raise arm and hand, with fingers extended, horizontally in front of body, then clench fist.

Engage brakes

Left hand over head with fingers extended, to indicate the number of the engine to be started, and a circular motion of the right hand at head level.

Start engine(s)

Point left arm down, move right arm down from overhead vertical position to horizontal forward position, repeating right arm movement.

Back aircraft tail to starboard

Marshalling signals to a fixed-wing aircraft

Point right arm down, move left arm down from overhead vertical position to horizontal forward position, repeating left arm movement.

Back aircraft tail to port

The right arm raised at the elbow with arm facing forward.

All clear. Marshalling finished

There are also designated marshalling signals to a helicopter:

Arms placed horizontally. **Hover**

Arms moved down and crossed in front of the body. **Land**

Left arm extended horizontally forward, then right arm making a horizontal slicing movement below left arm. **Release load**

Marshalling signals to a helicopter

Arms horizontal with the palms up, beckoning upwards.
The speed of the arm movement indicates the rate of ascent. **Move upwards**

Arms horizontal with the palms down, beckoning downwards.
The speed of the arm movement indicates the rate of descent. **Move downwards**

Either arm horizontally sideways, then the other arm moved in front of the body to that side, in the direction of the movement, indicating that the helicopter should move horizontally to the left or right side, as the case may be, repeated several times. **Move horizontally**

Arms placed down with the palms facing forward, then repeatedly swept up to shoulder level. **Move back**

Additionally the pilot can make the following signals to a marshaller:

Raise arm and hand with fingers extended horizontally in front of the face, then clench fist.

Brakes engaged

Raise arm with fist clenched horizontally in front of face, then extend fingers.

Brakes released

Arms extended palms facing outwards, move hands inwards to cross infront of face.

Insert chocks

Signals from a pilot to a marshaller

Hands crossed in front of face, palms facing outwards, move arms outwards.

Remove chocks

Raise the number of fingers on one hand indicating the number of the engine to be started. For this purpose the aircraft engines are numbered from the aircraft's left.

Ready to start engines

▶Movements at Aerodromes

An aircraft must not taxi on the apron or manoeuvring area of an aerodrome without the permission of the ATC or AFIS (Aerodrome Flight Information Service) unit (if there is one) or the aerodrome authority. A couple of definitions:

– the *apron* is the part of an aerodrome where aircraft can load and unload passengers and cargo, refuel and park. Occasionally referred to as the *pan* at a military airfield.

– the *manoeuvring area* is the part of the aerodrome provided for the take-off and landing and movement of aircraft, excluding the apron and any maintenance area.

> ICAO definitions:
>
> Aerodrome – a defined area of land or water (including any buildings, installations and equipment) to be used wholly or partially for the arrival, surface movement and departure of aircraft.
>
> Aircraft stand – a designated area of an apron used for the parking of an aircraft.
>
> Landing Area – the part of the movement area intended for the take-off or landing of aircraft.
>
> Movement Area – the part of an aerodrome used by aircraft taking-off, landing and taxying, including the apron (note: this is not the same as the manoeuvring area).

Except where a public right of way exists, a person or vehicle must not go onto any part of an aerodrome without the permission of the person in charge of the aerodrome. A vehicle or person must not go onto, or move on, the manoeuvring area of an aerodrome which has an ATC or AFIS unit except with the permission of that unit.

▶Use of Aerodromes

The licensed aerodromes of the UK are listed in the AD section of the UK AIP. Civil aircraft may not land at any aerodrome not listed in the AIP except in an emergency, or if special permission has been obtained from the aerodrome operator. Aerodromes can be classed as one of three types:

– **Government** aerodromes. These are essentially military aerodromes occupied by the RAF, RN or Army, or some visiting force such as the United States Air Force (USAF).

– **Licensed** aerodromes. These are aerodromes which meet certain minimum standards in respect of equipment and facilities, Rescue and Fire Fighting Services (RFFS), obstacles on and near the aerodrome and so on. Suitable aerodrome are issued with a licence by the CAA and are subject to regular inspection to ensure they continue to meet the required standards.

– **Unlicensed** aerodromes. These are typically aerodromes which either do not meet the necessary criteria for a licensed airfield, or whose normal operations do not justify them becoming licensed. In some cases a licensed airfield may become unlicensed at certain times, e.g. when the Rescue and Fire Fighting Services are not available. It is important to remember that the 1500ft/land-clear provisions of Rule 5 (low flying) apply to flight after take-off and before landing at an unlicensed airfield.

LEFT> This grass airfield (Bodmin) is licensed

RIGHT> This grass airfield (Old Warden, home of the Shuttleworth Collection) is unlicensed

Remember, some airfields may be unlicensed during certain hours even if they are open

It is quite common for an operator to stipulate that an aerodrome may only be used subject to 'PPR' – which stands for "Prior Permission Required". You should assume that PPR means telephoning your intended destination before departure and receiving specific permission to use the airfield– although in rare cases written permission may be required. Do not assume that PPR can be obtained via the radio. When flying to any government (e.g. military) aerodrome, prior permission **must** always be obtained before take-off. The filing of a full flight plan (described later in this book) does not constitute obtaining PPR. If an aerodrome is notified as being PPR, it is for good reason – not simply to discourage visitors. Sometimes the nature of the airfield or its activities make a telephone briefing necessary. In any case, an aircraft arriving at a PPR airfield without having obtained the necessary PPR is unlikely to receive a warm welcome, and it would be a shame to fly all the way to your intended destination only to find that they do not want you there! Do remember that in the case of an aerodrome which is not listed in the AIP– e.g. an unlicensed airfield – obtaining the permission of the operator to use the strip beforehand is a legal requirement.

Obtaining PPR where necessary is most important. Leaving aside the obvious discourtesy, the consequences of not doing so can be anything from rather amusing to outright dangerous. In respect of Government aerodromes, there was an incident in which a helicopter landed at a military airfield without permission whilst a security exercise was in progress. The occupants of the helicopter spent several uncomfortable hours with the military police until their identities had been confirmed. Several less entertaining incidents have occurred involving aircraft arriving unannounced, and without permission, at private airstrips. In doing so they endanger themselves (many unlicensed airfields and strips are used for other activities when not required for aviation purposes, and therefore may not be safe for

aircraft at all times) and may also seriously damage relations between the operator and local residents. This naturally threatens the future of the very airstrip they are using.

For practical purposes, check the AD section of the AIP or a flight guide for information on PPR, licensed/unlicensed status, opening hours and other such information. If in doubt, *always* assume that PPR (by telephone) applies.

You can usually assume that a private strip is unlicensed, and that PPR applies

▶Aerodrome Traffic Zones

Many UK aerodromes have an Aerodrome Traffic Zone (ATZ) surrounding the aerodrome, which is established to protect aircraft operating around the airfield from transiting aircraft. The dimensions of an ATZ are:

Vertically   Surface to 2000ft 'Above Aerodrome Level' (AAL)

Horizontally   A circle centred on the mid-point of the longest runway, with a radius of 2nm (where the longest runway is 1850m or shorter) or 2.5nm (where the longest runway is longer than 1850m).

AERODROME TRAFFIC ZONE (ATZ)

The standard dimensions of an ATZ

2000ft

2nm

* If the runway is more than 1850m long,
the ATZ has a radius of 2.5nm

Some ATZs, which would normally have a radius of 2nm, have been extended to 2.5nm. These exceptions are notified in the AIP.

An ATZ is active at the following times:

AERODROME	ATZ ACTIVE
Government aerodrome	During the notified hours
Aerodrome with an ATC unit or	During the notified hours of watch of the aerodrome unit
Licensed aerodrome with air/ground radio station	During the notified hours of watch of the air/ground radio station

An ATZ (for Seething aerodrome) as marked on a CAA chart. ATZs that are wholly within controlled airspace are not shown

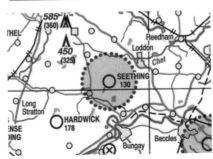

AIRFIELD	PRINCIPLE RUNWAY	RUNWAY LENGTH	ATZ RADIUS	WINTER HOURS	SUMMER HOURS	CONTACT FREQUENCY
Benbecula Civil N5728.86 W00721.78 19	06/24	1651	2	0930-1615 Mon-Fri 0930-1215 Sat	0830-1515 Mon-Fri 0830-1115 Sat	ATC 119.200
Benson Government N5136.95 W00105.66 226	01/19	1823	2	H24	H24	ATC 120.900
BEVERLEY/Linley Hill Civil N5353.90 W00021.61 3	12/30	708	2	0900-SS	0800-SS	A/G 123.050
Biggin Hill Civil N5119.82 E00002.04 600	03		2	0730-2100 Mon-Fri 0900-2000 Sat, Sun & PH	0630-2000 Mon-Fri 0800-1900 Sat, Sun & PH	ATC 129.400
Birmingham Civil N5227.34 W00144.94 325	15/33	2255	2.5	H24	H24	ATC 131.325

A sample page from the AIP showing ATZ hours of operation

In relation to government aerodromes, the notified hours are listed in the GEN section of the AIP.

The notified hours of watch of ATC units, aerodrome flight information units and air/ground stations may be found in the AD section of the AIP.

An aircraft must not fly within an active ATZ unless the commander has the permission of the ATC unit, or has contacted any other type of ATSU. In the case of a government (military) aerodrome, it is important to appreciate that even if the ATSU cannot be contacted, the ATZ is active during the hours notified in the AIP. This is usually H24, i.e. 24 hours a day. Of course, even if the aerodrome ATZ is not active, there may be traffic operating from the aerodrome, and the pilot must still exercise caution.

Some offshore installations (oil and gas rigs, etc.) have ATZs, which extend from mean sea level to 2000ft AMSL and have radii of 1.5nm from the installation.

▶Notification of Arrival and Departure

When an aircraft is expected at an aerodrome, the commander must inform that aerodrome as soon as possible if the destination is changed or the arrival will be delayed by more than 45 minutes (note that this applies if, for example, you have received PPR by telephone from your intended destination). Wherever possible, the commander must report on arrival and before departure to the appropriate authority at an aerodrome. These duties are known as *booking in* and *booking out* respectively. Notification of arrival, or delay to an expected arrival, is particularly important. If you fail to do this, the aerodrome authority may well begin *overdue action* to try to find you. At the very least this may involve the ATSU in a good deal of tedious telephoning of other airfields along your route. If your flight cannot be traced, full-scale Search And Rescue (SAR) operations maybe initiated. If this type of operation is initiated merely because you changed your plan without informing your destination, you are unlikely to be 'flavour of the month' once you are traced.

▶ Aviation Fuel

No person in charge of an aviation fuel installation (including a refuelling vehicle) at an aerodrome will allow fuel to be used in an aircraft if they know or suspect that it is not fit for use. The CAA lays down requirements for the storage and supply of aviation fuel at aerodromes, including a requirement for the daily inspection of a fuel sample from the storage facility.

Aviation fuel installations carry special markings to indicate the type of fuel available:

The marking of an aviation fuel installation Note that at a military airfield, you may see the NATO designations F18 used for AVGAS and F34 or AVTUR used for JET A-1

Blue White Red   White Black

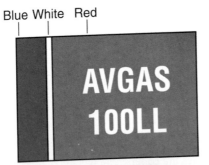
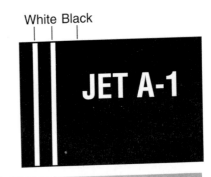

All fuelling installations should clearly indicate the type of fuel they dispense. Check BEFORE allowing the aircraft to be refuelled

▶ Closure of Airfields

An air traffic controller can close a CAA or public licensed aerodrome in the following circumstances:

– if the landing area is unfit.

– the closure has been publicised by NOTAM or Supplements.

– when essential facilities have failed.

Note that an air traffic controller does *not* have the authority to close an airfield for weather reasons alone: the pilot is responsible for observing the appropriate weather minima. In an emergency, a pilot will be allowed to land regardless of the condition of the aerodrome or its facilities.

▶Interception of Aircraft

The interception of a civilian aircraft by a military one is thankfully a rare event. To reduce the risk to both aircraft in the unlikely event of an interception, a series of internationally agreed signals and procedures has been devised for use in such a situation. A civilian aircraft may be intercepted if it is in or near a dangerous area, or an area sensitive for security reasons. The intercepting aircraft may lead the other away from the area, and might require it to land at an aerodrome. All international flights by a UK-registered aircraft are required to carry details of interception procedures.

If you are intercepted, there are four steps to take at once:

1) Stay calm and comply immediately with the instructions or signals of the intercepting aircraft. This is of the utmost importance for obvious reasons.

2) Notify the ATSU with which you are in contact.

3) Attempt to establish communication with the interceptor on the emergency frequency of 121.5, giving your callsign and flight details.

4) Set the distress code – 7700 Mode C – on your transponder, unless instructed otherwise by an ATSU.

This particular 'interception' was in fact a pre-arranged photo opportunity that took place in UK airspace. However, 'real' interceptions of civilian aircraft are by no means unknown – especially in Eastern Europe

The intercepting aircraft will probably first give instructions by visual signals:

INTERCEPTING AIRCRAFT	MEANING	INTERCEPTED AIRCRAFT	MEANING
Takes up position ahead and to the left and rocks wings. After acknowledgement turns slowly on to desired heading.	You have been intercepted. Follow me.	Rocks wings and follows.	Understood will comply.

Remember – comply with this instruction **immediately.** You can ask questions later.

Note: Conditions may make it necessary for the intercepting aircraft to take up position to the right and to turn to the right.

By night both aircraft flash their navigation lights at irregular intervals, in addition to the above signals.

If the intercepted aircraft is too slow for the intercepting aircraft, the intercepting aircraft will fly a race-track pattern and rock its wings each time it passes the intercepted aircraft.

The intercepting aircraft may give further instructions:

INTERCEPTING AIRCRAFT	MEANING	INTERCEPTED AIRCRAFT	MEANING
An abrupt breakaway climbing turn through more than 90° without crossing ahead of the aircraft.	You may proceed.	Rocks wings.	Understood will comply.

Rules of the Air

The intercepting aircraft may lead you to an aerodrome for landing, where it will signal as follows:

INTERCEPTING AIRCRAFT	MEANING	INTERCEPTED AIRCRAFT	MEANING
Circles aerodrome, lowering landing gear and overflying runway in direction of landing.	Land at this aerodrome.	Lowers landing gear, overflies runway and proceeds to land.	Understood will comply.

At night the intercepting aircraft will also show steady navigation lights. The intercepted aircraft should do the same and show a steady landing light if possible.

The intercepted aircraft can also display one of three signals:

INTERCEPTED AIRCRAFT	MEANING	INTERCEPTING AIRCRAFT	MEANING
Irregular flashing of all available lights.	In distress.	Makes an abrupt breakaway climbing turn.	Understood.
Regular switching on and off of all available lights.	Cannot comply.	Makes an abrupt breakaway climbing turn.	Understood.
Raises landing gear whilst overflying runway between 1000 and 2000ft above the aerodrome. Continues to circle aerodrome. Also flashes landing light or all available lights by night.	The aerodrome you have designated is inadquate.	Raises landing gear and signals intercepted aircraft to follow it. OR Makes an abrupt breakaway climbing turn.	Understood follow me. Understood you may proceed.

Note: The CAA advises against using hand signals because they could be misinterpreted!

When attempting to establish contact by radio the following phrases should be used (remembering that the pilot of the intercepting aircraft may not speak your language, nor you his).

Phrases used by the intercepting aircraft:

PHRASE	PRONUNCIATION	MEANING
Callsign	KOL SA-IN	What is your callsign?
Follow	FOL LO	Follow me
Descend	DEE SEND	Descend for landing
You Land	YOU LAAND	Land at this aerodrome
Proceed	PRO SEED	You may proceed

If any of the instructions given by the interceptor (either by signals or radio) conflict with those from the ATSU, obey the intercepting aircraft whilst requesting clarification.

Phrases used by the intercepted aircraft:

PHRASE	PRONUNCIATION	MEANING
Callsign	KOL SA-IN	My callsign is…
Wilco	VILL-KO	Understood, will comply
Can not	KANN NOTT	Unable to comply
Repeat	REE PEET	Repeat your instruction
Am lost	AM LOSST	Position unknown
Mayday	MAYDAY	I am in distress
Hijack	HI-JACK	I have been hijacked
Land (place name)	LAAND (place name)	I request to land at (place name)
Descend	DEE SEND	I require descent

▶Revision

10 You see another powered aircraft to your left on a converging course, what should be your initial action?

11 To what types of aircraft do airships give way?

12 You are planning to overtake another power aircraft in flight. To what side should you pass, and at what point does an overtaking situation exist?

13 Whilst in flight you see another aircraft ahead, which appears to stay at a constant spot on your windscreen. Is there any risk of collision?

14 What is the standard circuit direction?

15 Two aircraft are converging on approach to the same runway. Assuming that there is no ATC in operation, and neither aircraft has an emergency, which has right of way to land?

16 You are approaching a landing area where one aircraft has just landed. To which side of that aircraft should you land?

17 On the ground, does an aircraft taxying have priority over an aircraft being towed?

18 Who has the ultimate responsibility for avoiding collisions?

19 You are being overtaken on the ground by another aircraft. On what side of your aircraft do you expect to see the overtaking aircraft?

20 What is the minimum height for performing aerobatics over a congested area?

21 You are following a motorway. Which side of the aircraft should it be on?

22 A qualified pilot is planning to carryout a simulated instrument approach with a student pilot as safety pilot. Is this legal?

23 In the UK, can an aircraft legally fly below 500ft except when taking-off and landing?

24 What is the minimum height for flight over a congested area?

25 Can practice approaches be flown at an unlicensed aerodrome in the UK?

26 Is an aircraft flying on a Special VFR clearance in the UK exempt from the land-clear requirement in relation to a congested area?

27 A pilot has ATC permission to operate on a Special VFR clearance. Who is responsible for observing the low flying regulations?

28 To fly VFR you must be in VMC. What does VMC stand for and what is it defined as?

29 What RT words can be used to indicate an urgency situation regarding the aircraft itself, or something or somebody in sight of the aircraft?

30 What is the transponder code to indicate a distress situation?

31 What is the meaning of this marking in the signals square?

32 What is the meaning of this marking in the signals square?

33 What colour is used by the identification beacon of a military aerodrome?

34 What colour lights mark the stop end of a runway?

35 What is the (approximate) direction of runway 31R, and what colour will the runway designator be marked in?

36 What is the definition of EDA?

37 What is the name for the length of runway available for the landing run of an aircraft?

38 A runway surface shows a change of colour due to moisture. How can this runway be described?

39 What is the meaning of the following light signal to an aircraft in flight?

RED PYROTECHNIC
LIGHT OR RED FLARE

40 What is the meaning of the following light signal to an aircraft on the ground?

RED FLASHES

41 What light signal could you use to indicate that you are compelled to land?

42 How is a runway holding point marked?

43 How is the boundary of the airfield, or an area unfit for the movement of aircraft, marked?

44 What does the following marshalling signal mean?

45 What does the following marshalling signal mean?

46 How would you indicate to a marshaller that the brakes are released?

47 What is the definition of the manoeuvring area?

48 What does PPR stand for?

49 What is the lower vertical limit of an ATZ?

50 What is the upper vertical limit of an ATZ with a runway longer than 1850m?

51 Is a military ATZ active when the ATC unit is closed?

52 You are flying a piston-engined aircraft, and it is being refuelled from a tanker with black fuel signs. Are you happy about this?

53 Whilst on a flight you are intercepted by a military aircraft. Who should you attempt to contact by radio and on what frequency?

Answers at LAW183-184

Division of Airspace and Air Traffic Services

▶ **Division of Airspace**

▶ **Airspace Classifications**

▶ **Air Traffic Services**

▶ **Air Traffic Service Units**

▶ **Visual Meteorological Conditions (VMC) and Instrument Meteorological Conditions (IMC)**

▶ **IFR Flight**

▶ **Special VFR**

▶ **Airspace Summary**

▶ **Revision**

▶ Division of Airspace

Airspace is divided into a number of regions, and these regions are themselves subdivided in various 'classes'. Airspace above a certain level (FL245 in the case of the UK) is known generically as the *Upper Information Region* (UIR). All airspace below the UIR (that is, below FL245 in the case of the UK) is known as the *Flight Information Region* (FIR). Both FIRs and UIRs are divided geographically e.g. the London FIR and UIR, the Scottish FIR and UIR, the Paris FIR and so on. As most private pilots do all their flying below FL245 (i.e. in an FIR) this is the airspace we will consider from here on. FL stands for Flight Level, a vertical distance in hundreds of feet using the standard altimeter pressure setting of 1013mb/hPa.

Below FL245 airspace is divided into Flight Information Regions (FIRs)

Division of Airspace and Air Traffic Services

What follows is unavoidably rather heavy going; it's a case of grinning and bearing it. There are seven different classifications of airspace, known as Class A, B, C, D, E, F and G. Not surprisingly, different restrictions and criteria apply to each class. Broadly speaking, these airspace classifications fall into one of two categories:

controlled airspace – Classes A, B, C, D and E;

and

uncontrolled airspace – Classes F and G.

These two categories give a good basic indication of how the various classes of airspace operate. Controlled airspace is subject to various restrictions in respect of what type of flights may enter, how you obtain permission to enter and compliance with ATC instructions. Uncontrolled airspace is subject to none of these restrictions. Depending on whatever other rules may apply, the main point to grasp is that in uncontrolled airspace you can pretty much fly where you like – without needing anyone's permission or having to contact any Air Traffic Control (ATC) unit.

▶ Airspace Classifications

Class A This is the most restrictive class of airspace. There are set rules for what types of flight can use this airspace, and flights within class A airspace are subject to ATC control.

Class B Slightly less restrictive than class A. In the UK, class B airspace only exists above FL245 and is therefore of little interest to most PPLs.

Class C At present no class C airspace is allocated in the UK.

Class D Any flight wishing to enter this class of airspace must obtain ATC clearance to do so; be able to communicate with ATC by radio; and obey ATC instructions.

Class E Certain flights may enter this airspace without requesting permission or communicating with an ATC unit, although even in these cases pilots are encouraged to contact ATC and comply with their instructions.

Class F This is advisory airspace within which an ATC service is available (but not mandatory) to all types of flight.

Class G This is totally uncontrolled airspace, also sometimes also known as the *open FIR*.

Aeronautical charts show the various types and classes of airspace. A section of airspace with specified dimensions will normally be given a name and type, and the chart will indicate what type of airspace classification applies to the named area, zone or route.

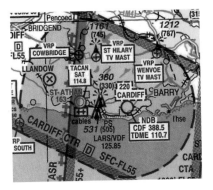

Control Zone (CTR)

Extends from ground level to a specified altitude or flight level (FL). Usually surrounds a major international airport. A CTR may be Class A or D airspace.

A Control Zone, in this case class D airspace, extending from the surface to Flight Level 55

ICAO Recommendation: A Control Zone should extend at least 5nm from the centre of the airfield in the directions from which approaches may be made.

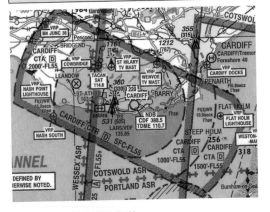

Control Area (CTA)

Extends upwards from a specified altitude or flight level to an upper limit expressed as an altitude or flight level. Can be Class A, D or E.

Around the Control Zone at Cardiff there is a class D control area. To the west of Cardiff this CTA extends from 2000ft AMSL to FL55 (FL is a vertical distance in hundreds of feet, so FL55 is essentially 5500ft)

Terminal Control Area (TMA)

A TMA is a CTA established where several routes merge in the vicinity of one or more major airfields. TMAs are usually Class A airspace, although some exist as Class D or E airspace.

This section of TMA above Manchester is class A and extends from 3500ft AMSL to FL245 (signified by the '+' symbol)

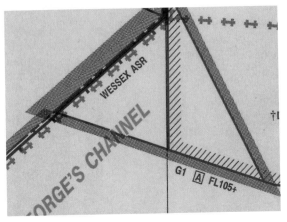

Airway

A CTA in the form of a corridor 10nm wide and extending from a specified altitude or flight level to an upper limit expressed as a flight level. In the UK, all airways are Class A airspace.

A section of airway designation 'G1' or 'Golf One'. It extends from a base at FL105 up to FL245. All airways in the UK are Class A airspace.

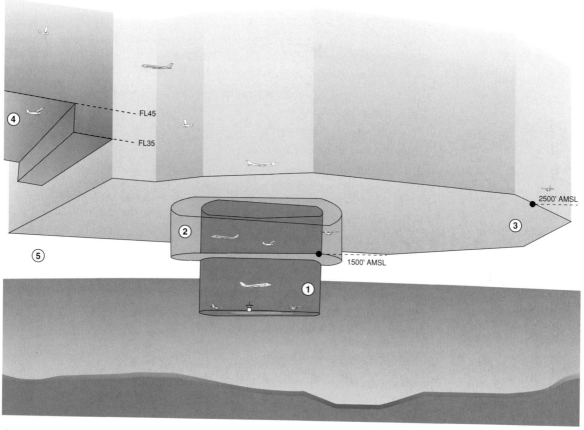

Advisory Route (ADR)

An advisory route is a corridor with the same width as an airway (i.e. 5nm either side of the centreline), although only the centreline is shown on aeronautical charts. Advisory routes are Class F airspace.

An advisory route (designator G4D) which is class F airspace and extends from FL145 to FL235

A typical arrangement of controlled airspace around a major airport:

1) A control zone (CTR) surrounds the airport, reaching from the surface to an altitude of 2500ft AMSL, protecting aircraft in the take-off and landing phase

2) A control area (CTA) is located around the control zone, starting at an altitude of 1500ft and extending up to the base of the TMA, protecting aircraft during the climb-out and initial approach to land

3) The TMA starting at an altitude of 2500ft covers a large area to protect aircraft climbing to and descending from the airways

4) Airways extend from the TMA, stepping up (base FL35, then FL45) as they leave the TMA

5) Outside these areas of controlled airspace is 'open FIR' Class G airspace – allowing the (mostly) uncontrolled movement of aircraft, but without the ATC protection prefered by commercial flights

▶ Air Traffic Services

ICAO definition: The objectives of the Air Traffic Services are set out in ICAO annex 11, and are to:

— Prevent collisions between aircraft

— Prevent collisions between aircraft on the manoeuvring area and obstructions on that area

— Expedite and maintain an orderly flow of air traffic

— Provide advice and information of the safe and efficient conduct of flights

— Notify organisations of aircraft in need of search and rescue aid, and assist such organisations

The four main types of Air Traffic Service available in the UK are:

— *Air Traffic Control Service*. This type of service provides for preventing the collision of aircraft and expediting and maintaining an orderly flow of air traffic.

— *Air Traffic Advisory Service*. This provides the same character of service as above for aircraft flying outside controlled airspace, although by the nature of uncontrolled airspace the service is more of an advisory nature.

— *Flight Information Service*. This service supplies information useful to the safe and efficient conduct of a flight.

— *Alerting Service*. This is the most basic air traffic service and is always available when an aircraft's flight details are known to an Air Traffic Service Unit (ATSU). The ATSU will alert the appropriate services if they know an aircraft to be in trouble, or if it is overdue or missing. By establishing communication with an ATSU, a pilot should be automatically assured of an alerting service at the very least.

ICAO recommendation: An alerting service will be provided to:

1   All aircraft receiving an ATC service

2   As far as practical, all aircraft having filed a flight plan or known to the ATS

3   Any aircraft known or believed to be subject to unlawful interference

In practice, sometimes an ATSU may provide an alerting service only to a pilot if controller workload does not permit a Flight Information Service (FIS) to be offered. However, ICAO annex 11 states that aircraft within a Flight Information Region (FIR) will be provided with a flight information service and alerting service.

▶ Air Traffic Service Units

There are three types of Air Traffic Service Unit in the UK. The type of ATSU a pilot is in communication with is indicated by the unit's callsign (found in the AIP and used during radio communications).

Type of ATSU	Callsign	Description
– Air Traffic Control Unit	*Tower* *Radar* *Approach* *Ground* *Director* *Control*	This is a unit manned by licensed air traffic controllers and able to provide a wide range of services. The callsign will also describe the area of responsibility. **Only** an Air Traffic Control Unit may use one of these callsigns. An ATCU may issue instructions or advice to pilots.
–Aerodrome Flight Information Service	*Information*	This unit is manned by an 'Flight Information Service Officer' who can offer a flight information service for an aerodrome including details of any known traffic. An AFIS can issue information and advice to pilots.
– Aerodrome Air/Ground Communications Service	*Radio*	This unit provides a link between the aircraft and the aerodrome authority, including an alerting service. An A/G service may only offer information, with the aim of assisting pilots.

▶Visual Meteorological Conditions (VMC) and Instrument Meteorological Conditions (IMC)

As we have already seen, any flight must conform to one of two flight rules. These are known as **visual flight rules** (VFR flight) or **instrument flight rules** (IFR flight). Whether a flight is VFR or IFR will make a vital difference in how it must be conducted, what rules apply to it and what sort of Air Traffic Service it will receive.

Most private pilots are primarily concerned with VFR flight. A VFR flight proceeds on the basis that the weather conditions allow you to see where you are going, and navigate by reference to ground features. Particularly outside controlled airspace, VFR flight gives you an awful lot of freedom over where you fly, who you communicate with (or not) and the nature of aircraft equipment and pilot ratings required. On the other hand you are solely responsible for separation from other aircraft (the 'see and avoid principle') as well as navigation, terrain clearance and so on.

For many pilots, VFR flying is what "real" flying is all about. You can in principle fly from an uncontrolled private airstrip, in an aircraft with no radio, and go more or less where the mood takes you. Provided you stay out of controlled airspace, you can fly at any legal level – without the need to seek anyone's approval and without being under any form of air traffic control.

You can only fly VFR if you are flying in **Visual Meteorological Conditions** (VMC). What constitutes VMC varies depending on the aircraft's level and the class of airspace in which it is flying.

It is necessary to detail the VMC minima for each class of airspace – although you may find the accompanying chart much easier going. Note: Flight visibility is the visibility forward from the cockpit of an aircraft in flight.

Class A   VFR flight is **not permitted** in Class A airspace.

Class B   At and above FL100; 8km flight visibility and clear of cloud

Below FL100; 5km flight visibility and clear of cloud.

Note: at present, Class B airspace is only allocated in the UK to airspace above FL245.

Class C   Subject to the same VFR minima as Class D airspace; see below.

Class D   At and above FL100; 8km flight visibility, 1500m horizontally and 1000ft vertically from cloud

Below FL100; 5km flight visibility, 1500m horizontally and 1000ft vertically from cloud

or, when flying at and below 3000ft amsl:

* for an aircraft (except a helicopter) flying at 140 knots indicated airspeed (IAS) or less:

5km flight visibility, clear of cloud and in sight of the surface

* for a helicopter:

clear of cloud and in sight of the surface.

Class E   As for Class D airspace.

Class F   As per Class G.

Class G   At and above FL100; 8km flight visibility, 1500m horizontally and 1000ft vertically from cloud.

Below FL100; 5km flight visibility, 1500m horizontally and 1000ftvertically from cloud.

or, when flying at and below 3000ft amsl:

for an aircraft (not a helicopter) flying faster than 140 knots (IAS):

5km flight visibility, clear of cloud and in sight of the surface.

– for an aircraft (except a helicopter) flying at 140 knots IAS or less:

1500m flight visibility, clear of cloud and in sight of the surface.

– for a helicopter flying at a speed which is reasonable in regard to the visibility:

clear of cloud and insight of the surface.

*These are specific exemptions to allow some general-aviation operations (e.g. circuits, zone entry and exit, etc.) which otherwise might be very restricted in Class D airspace.

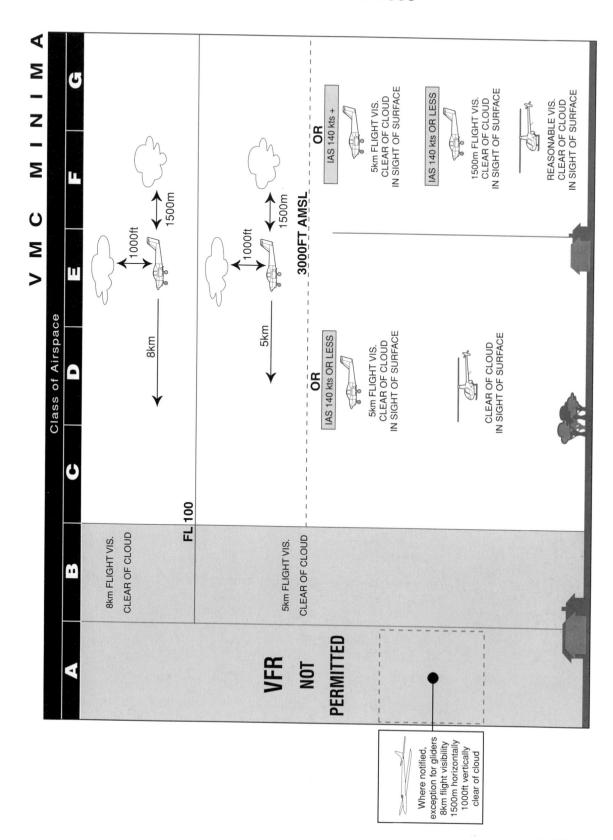

LAW61

Speed limitation: For Classes C (when flying VFR), D, E, F & G (when flying VFR or IFR) airspace, there is a speed limitation below FL100 of 250 knots indicated airspeed. Military aircraft and some other flights are exempt from this limitation.

Although overall VFR flight is not permitted in Class A airspace, certain sections of airway are 'notified' to allow gliders to cross in VMC. In this case the specified VMC minima are:

8km flight visibility, 1500m horizontally and 1000ft vertically from cloud.

Remember that 'Flight visibility' is the visibility forward from the cockpit of an aircraft in flight.

Additionally, although a powered aircraft cannot operate VFR in an airway, a pilot can cross the base of an airway in VMC without needing to talk to ATC if the base is defined as a flight level. The pilot must fly at right angles (90°) to the airway centre line.

These exceptions aside, flight in airways is the privilege of those who can comply with Class A entry requirements – i.e. filing of a flight plan, compliance with IFR, minimum aircraft equipment, pilot to hold a valid Instrument Rating, etc.

An aircraft cannot fly VFR within Class B, C or D airspace during the notified hours of ATC operation until the pilot has obtained an air-traffic control clearance to do so. Whilst within the airspace, the pilot must listen out on the appropriate radio frequency and comply with any instructions given by the ATC unit.

In Class E, F & G airspace, contact with an ATC unit is non-mandatory for a VFR flight (with some exceptions such as active ATZs). If a pilot does contact an ATSU he is assumed to be following ATC instructions unless he specifically states otherwise.

The pilot is responsible for determining whether conditions are VMC or IMC based on 'Flight Visibility', as defined above. The one exception to this is when a pilot is planning to take-off from, or land at, an airfield within class B, C or D airspace, in which case the visibility as passed by ATC is substituted for flight visibility. Remaining in VMC conditions is also the responsibility of the pilot. The obvious implication is that if ATC offers you a clearance that will not allow you to maintain VMC, VFR flight is not possible *and it is up to you to say so* – and request a different clearance if necessary.

The whole business of VMC minima is not the simplest to comprehend, so you may want to re-read and digest the foregoing before proceeding further. However, one very simple fact that you should appreciate already is that:

to fly VFR you must be in VMC.

▶IFR Flight

If conditions are not VMC, then they are IMC. Instrument Meteorological Conditions (IMC) are conditions expressed in terms of visibility, distance from cloud and ceiling, *less than* a specified minima and in IMC **Instrument Flight Rules** apply. As you might expect, an IFR flight is far more rigidly controlled than a VFR flight. A suitably qualified pilot can opt to fly IFR in *any* weather conditions, but **must** fly IFR if VMC cannot be maintained. Minimum levels of aircraft equipment and pilot ratings may apply, and a full flight plan will have to be filed for IFR flight within certain types of airspace. Additionally there are two principal rules relating to IFR flight:

Division of Airspace and Air Traffic Services

– the 'minimum height' rule; and

– the 'quadrantal and semi-circular' rule.

The 'minimum height' rule states that subject to Rule 5 (the low flying rules), an aircraft must fly at least 1000ft above the highest fixed obstacle within 5nm of the aircraft except:

– on a route notified for this rule.

– if authorised by a competent authority.

– as necessary for take-off and landing.

– when flying at 3000ft above mean sea level or below, when clear of cloud and in sight of the surface.

The 'quadrantal and semi-circular rule' stipulates that when flying IFR above the transition altitude (outside controlled airspace), the pilot must select a cruising flight level based on the quadrantal rule (below FL245) or the semi-circular rule (above FL245). The cruising flight levels are based on the standard pressure setting of 1013mb. Note that the appropriate flight level is based on magnetic track, not heading.

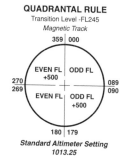

The Quadrantal Rule (Transition altitude to FL 245)

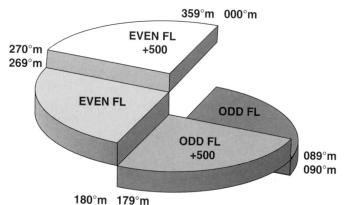

Even when not operating IFR, pilots are highly recommended to use the quadrantal or semi-circular rule when flying above 3000ft in uncontrolled airspace.

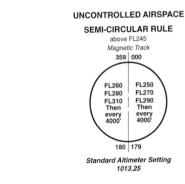

UNCONTROLLED AIRSPACE

SEMI-CIRCULAR RULE

above FL245

Magnetic Track

359 | 000

FL260 | FL250
FL280 | FL270
FL310 | FL290
Then | Then
every | every
4000' | 4000'

180 | 179

Standard Altimeter Setting
1013.25

The Semi – Circular Rule
(above FL245)

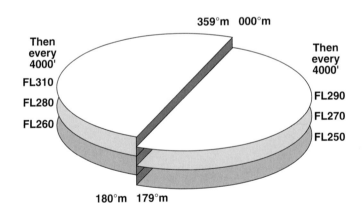

359°m   000°m

Then every 4000'

FL310

FL280

FL260

Then every 4000'

FL290

FL270

FL250

180°m   179°m

▶ Special VFR

If you are following the story so far, you may have noticed a major anomaly. VFR flight is not permitted within Class A airspace, yet the London Control Zone is Class A airspace. So how can a flight which cannot comply with all the IFRs get into and out of an airfield within a Class A control zone? Equally, if the weather is IMC, can an aircraft fly into or out of an aerodrome located in Class D airspace without complying with all the IFRs? The answer to these questions lies in a provision called 'Special VFR' (SVFR).

The concept of SVFR exists so that the pilot can make a flight without complying with full IFR requirements. Specifically, SVFR flights may enter a control zone which is Class A airspace, or enter another control zone when weather conditions are less than VMC.

You can request a SVFR clearance when airborne by passing your flight details over the RT (in essence an abbreviated flight plan) and giving an ETA for a specific entry point to the CTR. Such request should be made 5-10 minutes in advance. Permission for SVFR flight is only granted by ATC when traffic conditions permit. Whilst operating on an SVFR clearance, the pilot *must* comply with ATC instructions. ATC will provide separation between Special VFR flights and IFR traffic.

When flying under an SVFR clearance, you are absolved from the section of Rule 5 (low flying) requiring an aircraft to remain at least 1500ft above the highest fixed object within 600m when over a congested area. However, you must still observe all the other provisions of Rule 5, for instance the land-clear requirement. So you cannot accept a Special VFR clearance which will cause you to breach the other provisions of Rule 5 – even if such a clearance is offered by ATC. As you might expect, terrain clearance remains the responsibility of the pilot. Additionally a Special VFR clearance does not absolve you from avoiding an active ATZ: you may need to obtain specific permission to enter it. This is not normally necessary when the ATZ in question lies wholly within controlled airspace.

At all times the aircraft must remain clear of cloud and in sight of the surface. If the pilot holds a PPL without an IMC rating (*q.v.*), a minimum flight visibility of 10km must be maintained except in the case of certain routes specifically exempted from this rule.

At airfields within a Control Zone, ATC will not issue a Special VFR clearance for a fixed-wing aircraft to depart SVFR if the visibility is 1800m or less or if the cloud ceiling is less than 600ft – specific details are found in the AIP. Cloud ceiling is defined as the height at which more than half the sky is obscured by cloud.

▶Airspace Summary

There is no doubt that understanding the different classifications of airspace, and how to conduct a flight in each type, is not simple matter. However, it is important to establish the foundation of your knowledge in this subject as you will have to be readily able to apply a practical understanding of airspace, flight rules, meteorological conditions and air traffic services for almost every flight you undertake. ICAO annex 11 classifies airspace as follows:

Class A
IFR flight only

All flights subject to ATC service and separated from each other

Class B
IFR & VFR flight

All flights subject to ATC service and separated from each other

Class C
IFR & VFR flight

All flights subject to ATC service

IFR flights separated from all other IFR flights and receive traffic information about VFR flights

VFR flights separated from IFR flights and receive traffic information about other VFR flights

Class D
IFR & VFR flight

All flights subject to ATC service

IFR flights separated from all other IFR flights and receive traffic information about VFR flights

VFR flights receive traffic information about other VFR flights

Class E
IFR & VFR flight

IFR flights subject to ATC service separated from all other IFR flights

All flights receive traffic information as far as is practical

Class F
IFR & VFR flight

Participating IFR flights receive an air traffic advisory service

All flights receive flight information service if requested

Class G
IFR & VFR flight

All flights receive flight information service if requested

▶Revision

54 What type of airspace is Class F airspace?

55 Which airspace classifications make up controlled airspace?

56 Controlled airspace that extends from the surface, and according to ICAO should extend at least 5nm from the centre of the airfield in the directions from which approaches may be made, is a what?

57 What does TMA stand for and how is it defined?

58 What class of airspace is an airway in the UK?

59 Describe two of the objectives of the Air Traffic Services as set out in ICAO annex 11.

60 To whom is an alerting service provided?

61 According to ICAO annex 11, what type(s) of ATS are provided to an aircraft within a Flight Information Region (FIR)?

62 The callsign *tower* indicates what type of ATSU?

63 What type of ATS is indicated by the radio callsign *information*?

64 Can an ATSU with the callsign *radio* give air traffic clearances?

65 What is the minimum flight visibility to remain VMC for an aeroplane (not a helicopter) operating in Class G airspace, at 2500ft AMSL, if it has an IAS of 90 knots?

66 Must a VFR flight obtain permission to operate in Class E airspace?

67 Can a flight operate VFR in IMC weather conditions?

68 What is the definition of flight visibility?

69 You are flying IFR outside controlled airspace on a magnetic track of 175° below FL245. What are the correct flight-level options?

70 Is it mandatory to fly the correct quadrantal when operating above the transition altitude?

71 ATC gives you a Special VFR clearance which you realise will take you very close to a mountain. Do you sit tight and assume they know what they are doing?

72 You are flying on a Special VFR flight on a route that will take you through an ATZ. Can you assume that the ATC unit will have arranged a clearance through the ATZ?

73 What type of airspace is best described by the following:

IFR & VFR flight permitted

All flights subject to ATC service

IFR flights separated from all other IFR flights and receive traffic information about VFR flights

VFR flights receive traffic information about other VFR flights

74 In what type of airspace do participating IFR flights receive an air traffic advisory service?

Answers at LAW184-185

Rules of the Air and Air Traffic Services

▶ Flight Plans

▶ Altimeter Pressure Settings

▶ Transition Level

▶ Altimeter Setting Procedures

▶ Wake Turbulence

▶ Air Reports (AIREP)

▶ Area Control Service

▶ Approach Control Service

▶ Aerodrome Control Service

▶ Flight Information Service and Alerting Service

▶ Revision

Air Law

▶ Flight Plans

ICAO document 4444 (Rules of the Air and Air Traffic Services) makes provision for the format of the flight plan form. A flight plan is a message prepared by the pilot to give details of his flight to the Air Traffic Service. A flight plan should not be confused with the simple 'booking-out' procedure normally done before a VFR flight. It also has nothing to do with the form on which a pilot calculates headings, times, ETAs, radio frequencies and so on for a flight.

*The standard form used
for filing a full flight plan*

Rules of the Air and Air Traffic Services

There are two types of flight plan:

1 a 'Full Flight Plan' filed on a standard flight plan form (CA48).

2 an abbreviated flight plan, passed over the radio or by telephone to obtain clearance for a portion of a flight.

Within the UK, a flight plan **must be** filed in the following instances:

– for a flight in class A airspace.

– for an IFR flight in controlled airspace (Classes A to E).

– for a VFR flight in Classes B, C, and D airspace*.

– when wishing to use an air traffic advisory service in advisory airspace.

– for a flight which will cross an international FIR boundary.

– for a flight where the destination is more than 40km from the departure aerodrome and the aircraft is more than 5700kg MTWA (Maximum Total Weight Authorised).

* this may be an abbreviated flight plan passed over the radio. One should assume that in all other instances, a full flight plan must be filed.

A pilot is **advised** to file a flight plan for a flight:

– over the sea; more than 10 miles from the coast; or over a sparsely populated area where SAR operations could be difficult.

A flight plan **may** be filed for **any** flight.

A full flight plan for a VFR flight in the UK must normally be filed with the ATS unit at the departure airfield at least 60 minutes before start/taxi clearance will be requested. A full flight plan for an IFR flight which will not use controlled or advisory airspace controlled by London, Manchester or Scottish Control can be filed with 30 minutes notice. Otherwise 60 minutes notice is again required. An airborne flight plan can be filed with an FIR controller on the notified Flight Information Service frequency, giving at least 10 minutes notice of the intention to enter controlled airspace. Once a full flight plan has been filed, the departure ATSU must be informed of any cancellation, change to flight plan details or a delay of more than 30 minutes.

> ICAO recommendation: If a flight plan has been submitted, and a departure delay of more than 30 minutes then occurs, a new flight plan should be submitted and the old one cancelled.

A pilot who lands at an aerodrome other than the destination aerodrome specified in the flight plan *must* inform the specified destination within 30 minutes of the ETA there. This is most important. A flight plan is normally 'closed' by the ATSU at the destination airfield when the aircraft arrives; in other words, the ATS knows your flight has arrived safely. If your flight does not arrive within 30 minutes of the flight-plan ETA, the arrival ATSU will start action to find you if you have landed elsewhere. If your flight cannot be located, SAR operations will ultimately be started. This is, of course, one of the prime reasons for filing a flight plan. Somebody (in this case the ATSU at your destination) is expecting your arrival and will notice if you go missing.

Land areas within the UK
regarded as being difficult
from the Search and
Rescue point of view

When a full flight plan is filed with a UK ATSU, the details are passed on to a 'Parent ATSU'. This will normally be the flight briefing unit at one of the larger airports: at present there are nine parent ATSUs in the UK, at airports such as London Heathrow, Manchester, Glasgow, etc. If there is no ATSU at the departure aerodrome, or if the ATSU is unable to communicate the flight plan to a parent ATSU, it is the pilot's responsibility to ensure the flight plan is filed directly with the latter. This can be done by telephone or fax; the relevant numbers are listed in the UK AIP, in AICs and in flight guides such as the UK VFR Flight Guide.

Having filed a full flight plan, the aerodrome ATSU will inform the relevant parent ATSU of the time of your departure. This time is used to 'activate' the flight plan and is the basis of calculating the ETA at your destination. If the aerodrome does not have an ATSU, you should nominate a 'responsible person' to telephone the parent ATSU once the flight is airborne and pass the airborne time. If this is not possible you should contact an FIR controller and request them to pass on the airborne time.

When arriving at an aerodrome without an ATSU, the concept of the 'responsible person' arises again. In this case, he or she is informed of the flight by the pilot before departure, and is required to notify the parent ATSU if the aircraft fails to arrive within 30 minutes of its ETA at the destination. There is no strict definition of who can be a 'responsible person'. However, given the importance of their role, you will want to select someone with whom you can (literally) trust your life. In an extreme case, if you cannot find a 'responsible person' at the destination, you can contact the parent ATSU prior to departure and ask them to act in the capacity of a 'responsible person'. In this instance you *must* contact this ATSU within 30 minutes of landing at the destination. If the ATSU does not hear from you, it will automatically initiate alerting action.

▶ Altimeter Pressure Settings

Airspace boundaries, traffic separation and terrain clearance all involve a clear understanding of vertical distances – and in particular the various altimeter settings and setting procedures.

You should appreciate from the outset that the altimeter in a light aircraft is *not* some kind of magic device which faithfully measures the exact level of the aircraft above the surface. The ordinary pressure altimeter is basically a barometer, which indicates the vertical distance of an aircraft above some defined datum by measuring the atmospheric pressure. In the lower levels of the atmosphere, pressure decreases in a more or less linear way at about one *millibar* per 30ft increase in height (note: the millibar is also known as the *hectopascal*). In essence, the altimeter measures atmospheric pressure and presents the information in terms of a level in relation to the pressure datum set on the altimeter sub-scale. When you think you're flying at a constant height or altitude, you're actually flying at a constant pressure level.

High to Low...
'Down you
Go'

LOW PRESSURE   **HIGH PRESSURE**

1800ft INDICATED

*Flying from high pressure
to low pressure, the
aircraft will actually
descend if following a
constant pressure level*

1800ft INDICATED

960
mb

960
mb

QNH 990   QNH 1020

This is all very well, but imagine an aircraft flying from an area of high pressure to an area of low pressure. We'll assume that the aircraft is flying at 1800ft, and the sea-level pressure in the high-pressure area is 1020 millibars (mb). Remembering that the rate of change of pressure with height amounts to about one millibar per 30ft, we could say that the aircraft is flying at a 'pressure level' of 960mb. So what happens as we fly towards an area of lower pressure? The implication is that the sea-level pressure will be lower, so the 960mb pressure level must by definition be closer to the surface even though the aircraft is still flying at an indicated 1800ft. Suppose the pressure at sea level in the area of low pressure is 990mb – that is 30mb lower than the value set on the altimeter sub-scale at the start of the flight. The aircraft would be (30mb x 30ft) = 900ft closer to the surface than indicated on the altimeter. Obviously this is not conducive to restful flying.

Something similar happens if the aircraft flies from an area where the temperature is high to one where it is lower. Colder air is more dense, and so the same pressure level is lower in cold air than in warm air.

In summary – *High to Low, Down you Go!*

The obvious solution to this problem is to update the altimeter pressure setting regularly. The question is – what pressure setting?

Pressure settings in the UK are given in millibars (mb) although the ICAO-recognised pressure unit is the hectopascal (hPa). Fortunately the millibar and hectopascal are equal (1mb = 1hPa) so this is only a change in terminology. Be aware, however, that some countries use different units of pressure: the USA, for example, use inches of mercury as a pressure unit. This most certainly *does* require conversion to millibars/hectopascals.

Pressure settings can be given in the following terms:

– QFE

This is the atmospheric pressure at aerodrome level. When QFE is set on the altimeter sub-scale, the altimeter reads *height* above aerodrome level (AAL). The QFE datum will be the aerodrome elevation (the highest point on the landing area) or runway threshold elevation, when this is significantly different from the aerodrome elevation. Aerodrome or runway elevation is measured from Mean Sea Level (MSL).

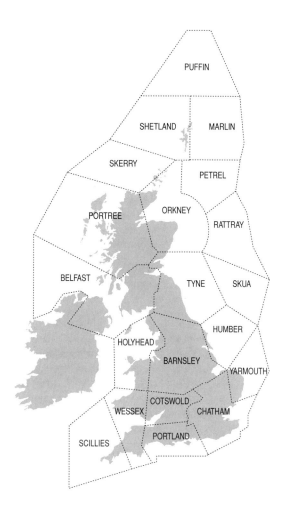

The Altimeter Setting Regions of the UK

− QNH

This is the actual atmospheric pressure reformulated to that at mean sea level in accordance with International Standard Atmosphere (ISA) conditions. When QNH is set on the altimeter sub-scale, the altimeter reads *altitude* above mean sea level (AMSL). This is the setting used for terrain clearance when flying en-route, since terrain and obstructions are marked on aeronautical charts as *altitudes* AMSL. A QNH may be given as an **aerodrome QNH**, which is valid in the immediate vicinity of the issuing aerodrome, or a **regional QNH** which is valid within a specified *Altimeter Setting Region* (ASR). For each ASR the lowest forecast pressure likely to occur in the next hour can be obtained from a meteorological office or an air traffic control unit. The regional QNH is amended on the hour, if necessary, and you can obtain the forecast regional QNH for the next hour if you feel the need to.

The regional QNH must be re-set on the hour if it has changed, and straight-away when entering a new ASR.

− STANDARD SETTING − 1013.2mb/hPa

This pressure setting is derived from the ISA and used regardless of the actual pressure setting when the aircraft is flying at *flight levels*. With 1013 set on the sub-scale, the altimeter reads flight levels if the last two zeros of the altimeter reading are taken away, i.e. 9000ft = FL90, 32500ft = FL325 etc.

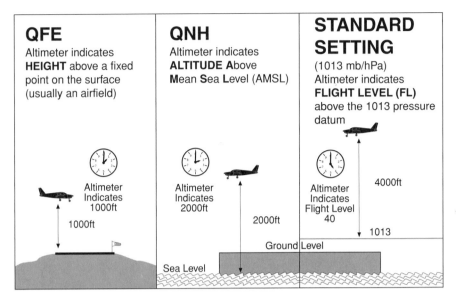

To summarise:

QFE	Altimeter reads *height*, a vertical distance above a specified datum.
QNH	Altimeter reads *altitude*, a vertical distance above mean sea level.
STANDARD SETTING – 1013	Altimeter reads *flight level,* a vertical distance above the 1013mb/hPa pressure level.

▶Transition Level

The *transition altitude* is the altitude above which the altimeter can be set to Standard Setting (1013) to read Flight Levels. In the UK, the standard transition altitude outside controlled airspace is 3000ft. The controlled airspace around certain aerodromes may have different transition altitudes, which are listed in the AIP. Flight levels are set every 500ft e.g.FL35, FL40, FL45, etc. The *transition level* is the lowest available flight level above the transition altitude. The layer between the transition altitude and the transition level is called the *transition layer*.

At first, you might imagine that if the transition altitude is 3000ft, the transition level is always FL35. In fact, it is not, because whilst the standard pressure setting to fly flight levels is always 1013mb, the actual pressure changes all the time.

Imagine a day when the QNH is lower than the standard setting, say 991mb,and assume that the aircraft we are flying has two altimeters. As we reach the transition altitude of 3000ft, one altimeter is reset from 991mb to the standard setting of 1013mb/hPa. If we level the aircraft off for a moment, that altimeter now reads 3660ft.The difference of 660ft between the two altimeters is the difference in millibars multiplied by the average feet per millibar figure already discussed, i.e. (22mb x 30) = 660ft. This is despite the fact that the aircraft is still at 3000ft on the QNH. If the desired flight level is FL35, the aircraft is above this and would need to descend below the transition altitude to reach FL35. But this is not permitted, because flight levels always start *above* the transition altitude. Therefore FL35 is not available today. The first available flight level will be FL40, and the transition layer is 340ft thick.

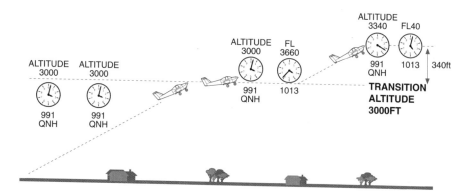

On this day with a QNH of 991mb, when the aircraft reaches the transition altitude (3000ft), it is at FL36. Therefore the lowest available flight level is FL 40

Throwing in a final variable at this stage, the flight level the pilot requires depends on the aircraft's magnetic track; for reasons already discussed in relation to VFR and IFR flight and the quadrantal/semi-circular rule.

When flying at a flight level, the actual separation from the terrain below can only be practically checked by setting the QNH on the second altimeter, if there is one. The moral is that when the QNH is below 1013mb, the minimum available flight level must be selected with great care. Also, don't assume that the transition altitude is always 3000ft. It usually is, but certain aerodromes inside controlled airspace and a few military airfields have non-standard transition levels. Details are given in the AIP.

If you're feeling a little confused by now, it might be best to work through a practical example. An aircraft will be cruising outside controlled airspace on a magnetic track of 075°, the minimum safe altitude is 3000ft and the regional pressure setting is 1006mb. Based on the magnetic track, the correct quadrantal will be an 'odd' flight level, e.g. FL030, FL050, FL070 etc. The regional pressure setting is 7mb less than the standard pressure setting (i.e. 1013-1006), which at 30ft per millibar represents 210ft. Thus, when cruising at FL30 (that is, 3000ft on the altimeter with 1013mb set), the aircraft is actually at an altitude of 2790ft (3000ft minus 210ft), which would be below the minimum safety altitude. Thus, to remain above the minimum safe altitude and comply with the quadrantal rule, the lowest available flight level would be the next highest odd FL, which is FL050 (at which FL the actual altitude is 4790ft).

▶Altimeter Setting Procedures

Before flight, the altimeter is checked whilst the aircraft is on the apron. The apron elevation for major airfields is published in the AIP and should be displayed in the flight clearance office. By setting aerodrome QNH, the pilot can check the altimeter reading against the known apron elevation (i.e. altitude).

The recommended altimeter setting procedures are summarised below.

Take-off and climb. When taking-off outside controlled airspace, any desired setting can be used. However, when flying under IFR (see later) vertical distance must be expressed as a flight level once the aircraft has climbed through the transition altitude. When taking-off beneath a TMA or CTA, aerodrome QNH should

TERMINAL CONTROL AREA ✓   ＼ CONTROL AREA.

be used when flying below the transition altitude – although aerodrome QFE may be used when flying within the circuit. When taking-off inside controlled airspace, at least one altimeter must be set to aerodrome QNH. Below the transition altitude, vertical distance is expressed as altitude based on the aerodrome QNH until cleared to climb to a Flight Level (unless ATC requests a further altitude report).

En-route. Outside controlled airspace, at or below the transition altitude, you may use any desired setting. When flying under a TMA or CTA, the QNH of an aerodrome beneath that area should be used. If flying at or below transition altitude on an advisory route, the regional QNH should be used. If flying IFR above the transition altitude, 1013 *must* be set on an altimeter, and the appropriate quadrantal/semi-circular rule adhered to. Pilots flying VFR are strongly advised to do the same wherever possible. The regional QNH should be used to check terrain clearance. When flying within a Military Aerodrome Traffic Zone (MATZ), aircraft are normally required to fly on QFE.

Inside controlled airspace, at and above the transition altitude, 1013 should be set on an altimeter and vertical distance reported as a flight level. Regional QNH is used for terrain clearance. If below the transition altitude, the aircraft will be passed the appropriate QNH.

Approach and landing. When an aircraft descends from a flight level to an altitude, the appropriate aerodrome QNH will be passed. This is to be used once the aircraft has vacated the flight level, unless further flight-level reports are requested by ATC. After the last flight-level report, the aircraft will use QNH until established on final approach, when QFE (or any other desired setting) can be used. Aircraft landing at aerodromes under a TMA or CTA should use aerodrome QNH when flying below the transition altitude, but aerodrome QFE may be used when within the circuit.

In the UK it is common practice to land using the QFE pressure setting. However, at other airfields throughout Europe (and at USAF aerodromes in the UK) QNH is commonly used for landing. The RAF went through a phase of using QNH for landing in the early 1990s but has now reverted to QFE; it seems this will remain the norm for the foreseeable future.

You **must** be quite clear as to which pressure setting you are using, and in the case of landing on QNH you **must** know the airfield elevation. The airfield elevation is the altitude of the highest point of the landing area (in other words the altitude –AMSL – of the highest part of the landing area).

If the threshold of an instrument runway is seven feet or more below the aerodrome elevation, a separate threshold QFE will be passed to the pilot by ATC. If landing on QNH the threshold elevation will be given.

Missed approach. During a missed approach the pilot can continue to use the altimeter setting used on final approach. However, in communication with ATC vertical position will be referred to as altitude based on aerodrome QNH, unless ATC instructs otherwise.

▶ Wake Turbulence

It is increasingly common for light aircraft to operate around larger aircraft such as airliners, and this has increased the importance of a working knowledge of wake turbulence. Wake turbulence is the atmospheric disturbance caused by movement of an aircraft through the air. Wake turbulence is usually described in terms of wing-tip vortices, which are generated as a consequence of the production of lift by the wings. A vortex can be visualised as a tube of whirling air, with radial velocities of up to 300ft/s. In the early days of wake turbulence research it was thought that the greatest risk to an aircraft in encountering a vortex was that of structural failure. In fact, it is now generally accepted that the biggest risk is a loss of control, essentially because a vortex can roll an aircraft faster than full opposite aileron can counteract.

Wake turbulence was only recognised as a major hazard when jet airliners a) became commonplace and b) increased in size. Research into wake turbulence is far from complete, and it is very difficult to talk in absolute terms. However, operating experience has allowed the aviation authorities to build up knowledge about the potential dangers of wake turbulence and the best way to avoid an encounter.

Vortices are generated from any wing (including the rotor blades of a helicopter) which is producing lift. Indeed, it is now thought that some wake turbulence begins as soon as an aircraft begins its take-off run, although the point at which these vortices become dangerous is not yet clear. What is certain is that vortices are strongest from a heavy aircraft flying at low speed – e.g. when it rotates for take-off and just as it touches down on landing. Unfortunately, vortices are normally invisible, so the pilot of a following aircraft has to concentrate on knowing how vortices usually behave and the conditions most likely to prolong their life.

As the vortices leave an aircraft's wing tips they tend to sink at a rate of between 250-500ft/min; the larger the aircraft, the faster the vortices sink. Eventually they level off at about 1000ft below the aircraft, if the ground does not intervene first. The two wing-tip vortices generally stay parallel, although if they reach the ground they then tend to move outwards from each other at a speed of about 5 knots. There is some evidence that on occasions a vortex can bounce after reaching the ground, possibly back up to 200ft or so. Vortices are drifted by the wind, and persist longest in light wind conditions; in actual fact, the vast majority of reported wake-turbulence encounters take place when winds are light. Most authorities agree that vortices generally last about 90 seconds, although in ideal conditions they may have a life of up to three minutes or more.

The strength of the wake vortex generated by an aircraft is directly proportional to its size and weight, and inversely proportional to its speed; the heavier and slower the aircraft, the stronger its wake turbulence. As far as a following aircraft is concerned, the golden rule is simple. The smaller and lighter it is, the more prone it is to control problems on encountering wake turbulence – especially if it has a short wingspan. Although wake turbulence is generated by an aircraft whenever it is airborne, the vast majority of serious wake-turbulence encounters occur in the approach and landing phase, with a lesser number occurring during take-off and departure. As heavy and light aircraft increasingly mix at airports world-wide, a knowledge of wake turbulence becomes all the more important. It isn't just small aircraft which suffer either: even airliners have had problems after encountering the wake turbulence of other airliners.

The number-one rule regarding wake turbulence is to avoid the areas where it might exist

In the take-off phase, the pilot of an aircraft following a larger aircraft should specifically note the latter's rotation point and climb-out path. He should then aim specifically to avoid the rotation point, and avoid flying below or downwind of the leading aircraft's climb-out path. On the longer runways from which large aircraft operate, it should not be difficult to get airborne before the leading aircraft's rotation point and – when at a safe height – turn to stay upwind of its climb path. Modern airliners have fairly spectacular rates of climb just after take-off, and it's highly unlikely that you'll be able to out-climb one unless you're flying something distinctly unusual. Bear in mind that even if you're not using the same runway as a departing larger aircraft, its wake turbulence could still affect you – either if you use a crossing runway, or if the prevailing wind drifts the vortices into your path. *Always remember that wake turbulence is at its most dangerous in light wind conditions.*

On departure aim to get airborne before the leading aircraft's rotation point, and stay away and upwind of its flight path

It is on approach that wake turbulence presents the greatest hazard. Bear in mind that the golden rule when following a larger aircraft is to avoid getting below or downwind of its flight path. An American study of wake-turbulence incidents and accidents showed that in all but one case the following aircraft were below the leading aircraft's flight path. Light-aircraft pilots tend to think that larger aircraft always fly relatively shallow instrument-type approaches of about 3°, which is a good deal shallower than the angle at which light aircraft tend to approach. However, airliners can follow a surprisingly steep glideslope, especially if flying visually (the previously mentioned five incidents/accidents all happened during visual approaches). Remember also that the wake turbulence will be at its strongest just as the aircraft touches down. As the pilot of a following aircraft, you should judge the leading aircraft's approach path and manoeuvre to stay above and upwind of it. Aim to land beyond the leading aircraft's touchdown point; assuming sufficient runway is available. Again, wake turbulence may affect you even if you are landing on a different runway from that of the leading aircraft.

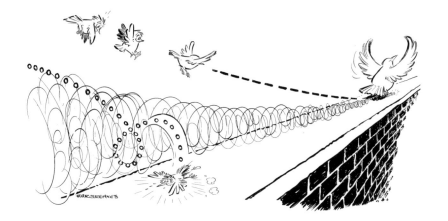

On approach, stay above the leading aircraft's flight path. Aim to touch down well beyond its touch-down point

Crossing the leading aircraft's approach path, or a light wind drifting vortices into your flight path, can easily lead to an unpleasant encounter with wake turbulence.

Wake turbulence can be a hazard when using a different runway from a larger aircraft, even if it's not taking off or landing

Remember also that wake turbulence can be a hazard if you are landing behind a departing aircraft. If you are landing on the same runway or a crossing runway, aim to touch down **before** the leading aircraft's rotation point. Be aware of the possible drift of vortices if you are using a parallel or adjacent runway. It is also worth knowing that in addition to the wake vortices, a large aircraft leaves an area of sinking air behind it. The area between the vortices may contain downdrafts of around 1400ft/min.

The general advice, then, is to avoid at all costs getting behind and below a larger aircraft. A summary of wake turbulence and avoidance techniques is given in the Flying Training section (Book 1) of the PPL Course. There is always a current AIC on the subject, which all pilots should read, and new findings are also published from time-to-time. Reading up on anything to do with wake turbulence is obviously time well spent, because an encounter with it can ruin an otherwise pleasant flight.

Having looked at the behaviour of wake turbulence, and avoidance techniques, it's necessary to consider the official spacing minima. An aircraft is allocated a **wake turbulence category** based on its maximum take-off weight, although occasionally an aircraft may be re-classified if operating experience shows this to be necessary. Categories are allocated by ICAO, and these are also those used when completing a flight-plan form.

However, the UK has also added an extra category, used solely for spacing minima:

Category	ICAO & Flight Plan Form	UK
Heavy (H)	136,000kg and above	136,000kg and above
Medium (M)	7,001-135,999kg	40,001-135,999kg
Small *	—	17,001-40,000kg
Light (L)	7,000kg or less	17,000kg or less

* UK only.

Helicopters the size of an S-61N and bigger are treated in the UK as being in the Small category.

Wake Turbulence Minima – Departures

– Following aircraft departing from the same point on the runway:

Leading Aircraft	Following Aircraft	Separation Minima
Category	Category	
Heavy	Medium/Small/Light	2 Minutes
Medium/Small	Light	2 Minutes

– Following aircraft departing from an intermediate point on the runway:

Leading Aircraft	Following Aircraft	Separation Minima
Category	Category	
Heavy	Medium/Small/Light	3 minutes
Medium/Small	Light	3 minutes

NOTE: Minimum time separation is from when the leading aircraft becomes airborne, to when the following aircraft becomes airborne.

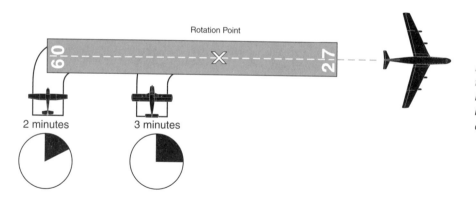

Recommended wake-turbulence minima for a light aircraft departing behind a Heavy, Medium or Small category aircraft

Medium Aircraft Leading

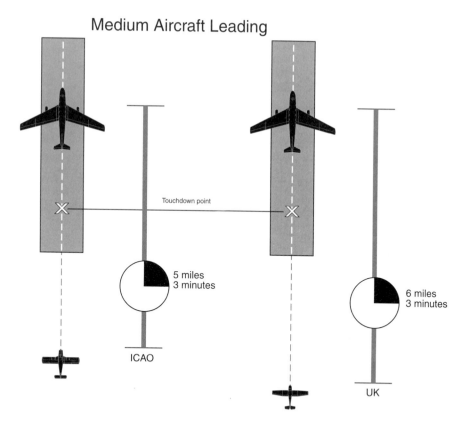

Recommended weight turbulence minima for a light aircraft approaching immedately behind a Medium category aircraft

Wake Turbulence Minima – Final Approach

(these minima also apply when an aircraft is directly behind another, or crossing behind at the same altitude or less than 1000ft below the leading aircraft.)

Leading Aircraft	Following Aircraft	Separation Minima			
Category	Category	ICAO		UK	
		nm	min	nm	min
Heavy	Heavy	4	4	2	
Heavy	Medium	5	2	5	3
Heavy	Small			6	3
Heavy	Light	6	3	8	4
Medium	Heavy	3			
Medium	Medium	3		3	2
Medium	Small			4	2
Medium	Light	5	3	6	3
Small	Heavy				
Small	Medium			3	2
Small	Small			3	2
Small	Light			4	2
Light	Heavy	3			
Light	Medium	3			
Light	Small				
Light	Light	3			

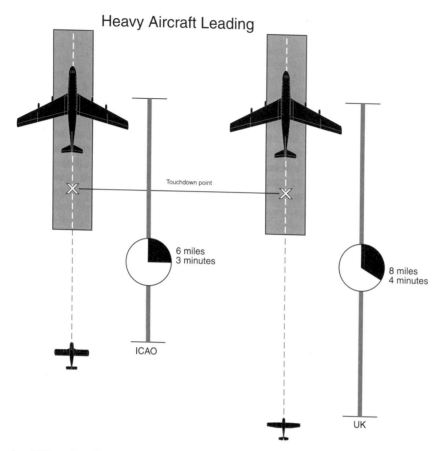

Heavy Aircraft Leading

Touchdown point

6 miles
3 minutes

ICAO

8 miles
4 minutes

UK

*Recommended wake
turbulence minima for a
Light category aircraft
approaching behind a
Heavy category aircraft*

An ATC unit will advise the pilot of a following aircraft of the relevant wake-turbulence spacing minima where necessary. This advice is only a minimum; you can increase spacing if you wish to. Aircraft in the 'heavy' category should use the prefix "Heavy" on their first contact with an ATC unit, which is a prompt for following pilots to beware of wake turbulence. By observing the recommended wake-turbulence spacing minima, and using the avoidance techniques outlined, you should be able to operate amongst larger aircraft with confidence.

Here is a summary of wake-turbulence avoidance information:

– The larger and heavier the leading aircraft, and the slower it is flying, the stronger will be the wake vortex generated. The smaller and lighter the following aircraft, the more prone it is to control problems on encountering wake turbulence. The worst case is something like a PA-38 Tomahawk or Cessna 152 following a 747 or A340.

– Except in exceptional conditions, wake turbulence is invisible.

– Wake turbulence is at its most dangerous in light wind conditions.

– Avoid getting below or downwind of the flight path of a larger aircraft ahead. On departure, aim to get airborne before its rotation point. On approach, aim to land beyond its touch-down point.

– Observe the relevant wake-turbulence minima. Increase spacing if you think it is necessary.

– If you do have a wake-turbulence encounter, tell somebody; the CAA has forms for reporting such encounter and it is well worth filling these out. Much of our knowledge of wake turbulence is based on such reports.

– Don't forget that helicopters also generate wake turbulence, and that there's considerable evidence to suggest that it's *much stronger* than that created by a fixed-wing aircraft of the same weight. It is worth giving a wide berth to **any** airborne helicopter, whether it's in full flight or just hover-taxying.

▶ Air Reports (AIREP)

In general, the concept of an air report belongs to a bygone era when aircraft might travel hundreds of miles without an exact navigational fix, when ATC radar cover was limited or non-existent and aircraft were largely separated based on their radioed position reports. When it is required an Air Report (AIREP) takes the following format:

Aircraft Identification

Position

Time

Flight Level or Altitude

Next Position and ETA

If the commander of an aircraft encounters hazardous conditions in flight, he must inform the appropriate ATC unit as quickly as possible. Such a report is known as a special air report, and typically might be given by a pilot encountering situations such as:

Severe Icing

Severe Turbulence

A SIGMET

(**sig**nificant en-route **met**eorological hazard) e.g. a thunderstorm or severe mountain wave. These are described in more detail in the meteorology section of book 3.

You may be interested to know that volcanic activity also merits a special air report!

▶ Area Control Service

First, a couple of essential definitions:

> ICAO definitions:
> Area Control Service – an Air Traffic Control service for controlled flights in control areas
> Control Areas – controlled airspace extending upwards from a specified limit above the earth (within the UK these are airways, CTAs and TMAs)
> Controlled Flight – a flight which is subject to an air traffic control clearance
> Air Traffic Control Clearance – an authorisation for an aircraft to proceed under conditions specified by an air traffic control unit

It is important to establish that only an Air Traffic Control service can issue clearances to an aircraft in flight, and the pilot is expected to follow this clearance. Occasionally this can pose a problem if, for example, obeying an ATC clearance might lead a VFR flight into IMC. If a pilot in command receives an air traffic control clearance that is not suitable he may request, and if practicable obtain, an amended clearance. Thus, if a pilot flying VFR is given ATC instructions that would take the aircraft into IMC, he should maintain the existing level and heading and request revised instructions in order to remain in VMC.

An Area Control Service will provide vertical and horizontal separation between controlled flights as follows:

Between all flights in class A and B airspace

Between IFR flights, and between VFR flights and IFR flights in class C airspace

Between IFR flights in class D and E airspace

Between IFR flights and special VFR (SVFR) flights

Between SVFR flights if prescribed by the appropriate ATS authority

So, in Class D airspace an IFR flight will be separated from other IFR flights, but not from a VFR flight; and no separation is provided between VFR flights. This only emphasises that VFR flight is all about being able to navigate and avoid other aircraft by outside visual reference. The minimum horizontal separation distances are complex, involving times, distances and/or angles, and are the preserve of Air Traffic Controller. More simply an Area Control Service will look to provide a minimum of 1000ft vertical separation at lower levels. If a flight is cleared to maintain its own separation from other traffic it is essential for that flight to remain in VMC, and for the duration of that clearance the commander of the flight is responsible for not operating so close to other flights as to create a collision hazard. Such a clearance is normally only granted for a specific portion of a flight. If a pilot that is qualified to fly in IMC that remaining VMC is not possible, ATC should be informed before entering IMC, and the flight must then proceed in accordance with any alternative instructions given.

Where an Area Control Service does not have to provide traffic separation between certain flights, it will normally give essential traffic information about flights which might conflict to enable them to avoid each other. This essential traffic information will normally include the type, direction and level of the other traffic.

If there is a communications failure between an Area Control Service and an aircraft, the ATC unit will first attempt to give the aircraft instructions to see if it is still receiving calls, even if it cannot transmit. If it seems that a total communications failure has occurred and the aircraft is in VMC, ATC will try to maintain separation from other traffic based on the following assumptions:

The flight will remain in VMC

It will land at the nearest suitable aerodrome

After landing it will report its arrival to the ATC unit by the fastest means

The rules regarding action in the event of a communications failure with a flight operating in IMC are more complex, but as such flight is largely outside the basic privileges of a JAR PPL we can leave them for now.

If an Area Control Service becomes aware that a flight has been intercepted (as already described), it should attempt to contact the intercepted aircraft, and also contact the unit in contact with the intercepting aircraft, with the aim of relaying messages as necessary and ensuring the safety of the intercepted aircraft.

▶ Approach Control Service

ICAO definitions:

Approach Control Service – an air traffic control service for arriving and departing controlled flights.

Approach sequence – the order in which two or more aircraft are cleared to approach to land at an aerodrome.

Minimum Fuel – a situation where an aircraft's fuel has reached the state where little or no delay can be accepted. Note: in the UK this term has no meaning as far as ATC are concerned, and if necessary pilots are recommended to make an Urgency or Distress call as appropriate.

Radar approach – an approach where the final approach phase is conducted under the direction of a radar controller

Radar contact – the situation when the radar position of a particular aircraft is seen and identified on a radar display

Radar identification – the situation when the radar position of a particular aircraft on a radar display is positively identified by an air traffic controller

Radar vectoring – the provision of navigational guidance to aircraft, in the form of specific headings, based on the use of radar

ICAO doc 4444 provides for an Approach Control Service to reduce the normal separation minima in the vicinity of aerodromes if:

- adequate separation can be provided by the aerodrome controller when each aircraft is continuously visible to this controller;

- each aircraft is continuously visible to the pilots-in-command of the other aircraft and the pilots can maintain their own separation;

- the pilot-in-command of a following aircraft has the leading aircraft in sight and can maintain separation.

When a flight first contacts an Approach Control Service prior to arrival, it can expect to be given the following information:

The runway in use

Current meteorological information

Runway surface conditions – if it may be wet or hazardous

Any change in the status of approach and landing aids.

In practice, meteorological information is not normally given to a VFR arrival. At most larger airfields there is a recorded broadcast of the above information, known as ATIS (Automatic Terminal Information Service). On first contact with an Approach Control Service the flight confirms that is has received this information.

▶ Aerodrome Control Service

> ICAO definitions:
>
> Aerodrome Control Service – an air traffic control service for aerodrome traffic.
>
> Aerodrome Control Tower – a unit to provide air traffic control service to aerodrome traffic.
>
> Aerodrome Traffic – all traffic on the manoeuvring area of an aerodrome and all aircraft flying in the vicinity of an aerodrome.
>
> Aerodrome Traffic Circuit – the specified path to be flown by aircraft operating in the vicinity of an aerodrome.

Aerodrome control towers issue information and clearances to achieve a safe, orderly and expeditious flow of air traffic on and in the vicinity of an aerodrome, with the aim of preventing collisions between:

- aircraft flying in the aerodrome traffic pattern;
- aircraft operating on the manoeuvring area;
- aircraft landing and taking-off;
- aircraft and vehicles on the manoeuvring area;
- aircraft and obstructions on the manoeuvring area.

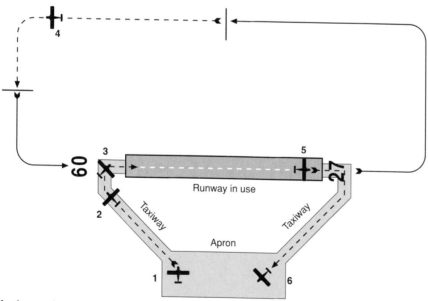

As far as the aerodrome control service is concerned, the key points of traffic flow on the aerodrome and in the traffic circuit are:

1 Initial call from a departing flight
2 Point of departing traffic to be held if there is conflicting traffic. This is also usually the point used for power and pre-take off checks
3 Take-off clearance issued here if not at position 2
4 Landing clearance issued
5 Clearance to taxi to parking area given
6 Parking information given if necessary.

When an aircraft requests taxying permission, the following information is normally given:

- – the runway in use;
- – the surface wind direction and speed;
- – the QNH altimeter setting

As with information given to arriving aircraft, at a larger airfield there may be an ATIS broadcast, in which case the flight can monitor this information and then confirm receipt of the ATIS information when requesting taxying instructions.

Prior to take-off an aircraft is advised of:

- – any significant changes in surface wind or visibility;
- – any significant weather conditions in the take-off and climb-out area.

Before entering the traffic circuit an aircraft must be provided with the following information:

- – the runway in use
- – the surface wind direction and speed
- – the QNH altimeter setting, and the QFE if appropriate.

Information on essential local traffic will also be given to help the pilot-in-command of an aircraft to avoid collisions. Essential local traffic includes any aircraft, vehicle or personnel on or near the manoeuvring area, or traffic operating in the vicinity of the aerodrome, which may be a hazard to the aircraft concerned.

▶ Flight Information Service and Alerting Service

> ICAO definitions:
>
> Alerting service – a service provided to notify appropriate organisations regarding aircraft in need of search and rescue aid, and assist such organisations as required
>
> Flight Information Service – a service provided for the purpose of giving advice and information useful for the safe and efficient conduct of flights
>
> Traffic Avoidance Advice – advice provided by an ATSU specifying manoeuvres to assist a pilot to avoid a collision
>
> Traffic Information – information issued by an ATSU to alert a pilot to other known or observed air traffic which may be in the proximity of the flight or its intended route, and to help the pilot to avoid a collision

From the above it should be clear that a Flight Information Service (FIS) primarily offers advice and information, as opposed to clearances and instructions. A typical example is the service offer on a designated FIS frequency within a Flight Information Region. On this frequency you may be able to obtain general information, such as altimeter settings, and also traffic information. However, the unit providing the FIS may have a huge area of responsibility, and no access to radar information. Therefore, you can only be given traffic information about other flights whose details have been notified to that unit, and if the unit becomes overloaded, they may not be able to offer any service at all.

In certain circumstances, i.e. IFR flights operating in advisory airspace or on advisory routes (class F airspace), an air traffic advisory service may be provided. Such a service is provided where it is not possible to provide an air traffic control service, but an FIS on its own is not adequate. An air traffic advisory service does not issue clearances, but rather it can offer advice and suggestions when a course of action is proposed to a pilot. It follows that it is for the pilot to decide whether or not to comply with the advice or suggestion received, and inform the ATSU of his decision without delay.

Whenever a flight has established satisfactory two-way communication with an ATSU, it can be assumed that it is receiving at least an alerting service. In some cases, there may be designated areas or routes for which a flight plan must be filed and, additionally, radio reports made every 20 to 40 minutes to indicate that the flight is proceeding according to plan. Although this procedure is not normally used for civilian flying in the UK, military aircraft may make such reports using their callsign and the phrase "Operations normal". Even where this procedure is not in use, if no report of any kind has been received from an aircraft within a reasonable period of time, the ATSU last in contact with the flight will start requesting other units to assist in trying to locate the aircraft, and ultimately contact the relevant rescue co-ordination centre. The point is that if an aircraft merely 'disappears' from a frequency, the ATSU have no immediate way of knowing if it has merely changed frequency or if something more serious has occurred, but in the absence of evidence to the contrary it must assume the worst. It follows that changing frequency without informing the ATSU can involve it in a lot of work trying to trace the flight – none of which will make the pilot overly popular with the ATSU concerned! Besides, it's not polite to leave without saying goodbye, and pilot and controllers are (usually) at pains to be polite to each other.

▶Revision

75 After you have filed a full flight plan, your departure is delayed by 45 minutes. What should you do?

76 At the end of the flight above, you have to divert to an alternate aerodrome. Do you have to inform anybody?

77 There are no facilities to file a full flight plan at your airfield of departure; with whom can you file it?

78 When QNH is set on an altimeter, what is the resulting vertical distance called and from what datum is it measured?

79 What is the name of the altitude above which the altimeter can be set to Standard Setting (1013) to read Flight Levels?

80 An aircraft is flying on a magnetic track of 075°, the QNH is 1010. What is the lowest available Flight Level to fly in accordance with the quadrantal rule?

81 When taking-off from an airfield within controlled airspace, what pressure setting must be used on at least one altimeter?

82 What altimeter pressure setting should be used when flying beneath a TMA or CTA?

83 What altimeter pressure setting is normally used when flying through a MATZ?

84 If an aircraft has begun a descent from a Flight Level to an altitude, and if no further Flight Level reports are required, what altimeter setting should be used?

85 A 'light' wake turbulence category aircraft is departing from an intermediate point on the runway following a 'full length' departure by a 'Heavy' aircraft. What is the minimum separation required for wake turbulence reasons?

86 You encounter a thunderstorm whilst in flight and consider it a hazard to other pilots (they always are). How should you report this meteorological hazard?

87 What is the definition of an Area Control Service?

88 An Air Traffic Control service gives you a clearance with which you cannot comply. What should you do?

89 What is the name of an air traffic control service for arriving and departing controlled flights?

90 What is the definition of 'Radar contact'?

91 Under what circumstances can an Approach Control Service reduce the normal separation minima in the vicinity of aerodromes?

92 What is the name given to an air traffic control service for aerodrome traffic?

93 What information is normally given when an aircraft requests taxying permission?

94 How is an alerting service defined?

95 What type of ATS service should be offered to IFR flights operating in advisory airspace or on advisory routes?

Answers at LAW185-186

Aircraft Registration

▶ Aircraft Registration

▶ Revision

Air Law

▶ Aircraft Registration

> ICAO definitions:
>
> Aeroplane – a power-driven heavier-than-air aircraft, deriving its lift principally from aerodynamic reaction against fixed surfaces (e.g. a wing). Therefore a helicopter is not an aeroplane because its 'wings', i.e. rotors, are not fixed.
>
> Aircraft – any machine that can derive support from the reactions of the air, other than the reaction of the air against the earth's surface. This rules out machines such as hovercraft and the like which can only 'fly' very close to the surface in what is known as 'ground effect' or 'air cushion'.
>
> State of registry – the state on whose register an aircraft is entered.

All aircraft must be registered by a state of registry, normally the country in which the aircraft is built or a country to which it is later exported. ICAO has allocated a nationality (or common) mark to each state, which is normally in the form of letter(s) and/or number(s) that precede the registration mark. In the case of the UK the nationality (or common) mark is the letter G, which is followed by the registration mark which for UK-registered aircraft is four letters. This makes a total registration of five letters, for example G-BEWR. In the Republic of Ireland the nationality mark is EI, which is followed by three letters, e.g. EI-BOE.

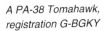

*A PA-38 Tomahawk,
registration G-BGKY*

*A Spectrum microlight
registration G-MWTD*

Registrations are normally allocated sequentially, i.e. G-BUGD, G-BUGE, etc.; although the letter Q is not used in aircraft registrations. Microlight aircraft have separate registration sequences, although they retain the normal nationality mark. Microlight registrations commence G-M...

A few years ago somebody made the discovery that one could register almost anything for a nominal fee as long as it displayed its registration – hence toy balloons and similar items soon acquired a registration and a listing in the national register. It is said that the CAA's reluctant tolerance of this practice finally expired when it was pointed out that someone was registering manhole covers...

Aircraft Registration

ICAO annex 7 deals with the registration of aircraft, and its standards are largely followed within the UK by the CAA. Heavier-than-air aircraft must carry their registration on the lower wing surface, at least 50cm high, and on each side of the fuselage or vertical tail in characters at least 30cm high.

The CAA will usually allow an aircraft to be given a new registration, and may allow an out-of-sequence registration (e.g. G-WIZZ) for a fee, although there are certain letter sequences it will not register. You can no doubt work these out for yourself if the mood takes you. Sometimes an aircraft may be granted an exemption from displaying its registration, for instance in the case of a historic military aircraft which the owner wishes to display in military markings. In these circumstances the aircraft owner requires permission from either the UK Ministry of Defence (MoD) or the appropriate foreign government to carry the markings, and such permission often specifies certain countries over which the aircraft cannot be flown.

This Spitfire T.IX has a civilian registration (G-LFIX), but is permitted to display military markings

When the aircraft is registered, a **Certificate Of Registration** is supplied which forms part of the aircraft documentation. The C of R will show the aircraft's registration, the aircraft type, the airframe serial number and the name and address of the registered owner(s). ICAO annex 7 states that the C of R must be carried in the aircraft at all times, although in UK law (promulgated through the Air Navigation Order) there is no such stipulation, except in specified circumstances which are covered later. Annex 7 also states that an aircraft must carry a fireproof metal identification plate showing at least the nationality and registration mark of the aircraft. The annex states that this plate must be secured in a prominent position near the main entrance, although in practice the identification plate on most light aircraft is often well-hidden on the rear fuselage somewhere under the horizontal tail.

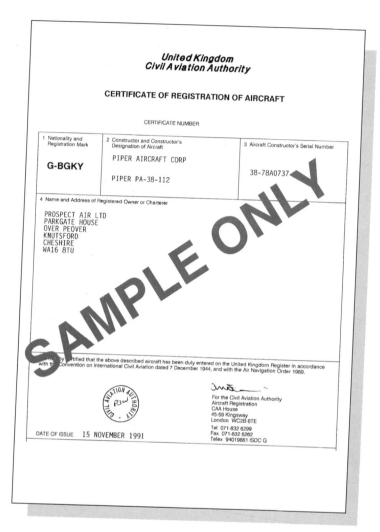

*The Certificate of
Registration for PA-38
Tomahawk G-BGKY*

There are various duties placed upon the registered owner of an aircraft on the UK register, such as a duty to inform the CAA of any change of ownership. The former owner must notify the CAA of the change immediately; the new owner must inform the CAA within 28 days of the change. A registered owner must also inform the CAA of a change of address.

The CAA maintains a UK Register of Civil Aircraft which is available for public inspection. Using the register, anyone can check the details of an aircraft – the aircraft type, the name and address of the registered owner(s), etc – either in person, by telephone or via the CAA website. It is also possible (for a fee) to check the CAA register of mortgages and charges attached to an aircraft.

Aircraft Registration

When an application is made to register an aircraft in the UK, it is described in terms of the **Classification Of Aircraft:**

AIRCRAFT

POWER-DRIVEN

NON-POWER-DRIVEN

LIGHTER THAN AIR

POWER-DRIVEN	NON-POWER-DRIVEN
AIRSHIP	FREE BALLOON
	CAPTIVE BALLOON

HEAVIER THAN AIR

An aircraft will be described in relation to the 'Classification of Aircraft'

POWER-DRIVEN	NON-POWER-DRIVEN
AEROPLANE* (landplane)	GLIDER**
AEROPLANE (seaplane)	KITE
AEROPLANE (amphibian)	
AEROPLANE (self-launching motor glider)	
POWERED LIFT (tilt rotor)	
ROTORCRAFT (helicopter)	
ROTORCRAFT (gyroplane)	

* Including microlights and powered parachutes

** Including hang gliders

This classification broadly follows the ICAO table, except that a power driven heavier than air aircraft is also known as a 'Flying Machine', a term used frequently in the UK rules of the air.

▶Revision

96 What is the name given to a state on whose register an aircraft is entered?

97 What is the minimum height for registration marks on the side of an aircraft?

98 What details are shown on a Certificate of Registration?

99 Under ICAO recommendations, when must the C of R be carried in an aircraft?

100 Other than the C of R, what other identification item should an aircraft carry?

101 Under the UK classification of aircraft, what name is given to a power driven heavier than air aircraft?

Answers at LAW186

Airworthiness of Aircraft

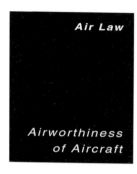

▶ Airworthiness of Aircraft

▶ Certificate of Maintenance Review

▶ Certificate of Release to Service

▶ Weight Schedule

▶ Technical Log

▶ Aircraft, Engine and Propeller Logbooks

▶ Noise Certificate

▶ Aircraft Limits and Information

▶ Insurance Requirements

▶ Revision

Air Law

▶ Airworthiness of Aircraft

Article 33 of the Convention on International Civil Aviation establishes the principle of internationally recognised standards of airworthiness. For aircraft to operate internationally there must be a basic confidence between states that other states aircraft have been designed, manufactured and maintained to a minimum standard and essentially are not in dangerous or inadequate in any respect. ICAO annex 8 provides for states to certify that an aircraft meets the appropriate airworthiness standards by issuing it with a **Certificate of Airworthiness**. If the Certificate of Airworthiness of an aircraft is endorsed as not meeting full international standards, in order to fly over the territory of a state other than the state of registry, the permission of the state whose territory is to be overflown must be obtained.

Within the UK, a C of A will be issued in a certain category, which indicates the purpose for which the aircraft can be used:

Transport Category (Passengers)	– any purpose.
Transport Category (Cargo)	– any purpose except the public transport of passengers.
Aerial Work Category	– any purpose except public transport.
Private Category	– any purpose except public transport or aerial work.
Special Category	–any purpose (except public transport) specified on the C of A, but usually excluding the carriage of passengers.

The Certificate of Airworthiness for G-BGKY

Note that the C of A states that the aircraft is certified in the Transport Category (Passenger) and bears an expiry date

United Kingdom
Civil Aviation Authority

CERTIFICATE OF AIRWORTHINESS

Certificate No:

Nationality and Registration Marks	Constructor and Constructor's Designation of Aircraft	Aircraft Serial Number
G-BGKY	PIPER AIRCRAFT CORP PIPER PA-38-112	38-78A0737

TRANSPORT CATEGORY (PASSENGER)

This Certificate of Airworthiness is issued pursuant to the Convention on International Civil Aviation dated 7 December 1944, and to the Civil Aviation Act 1982, and the Orders and Regulations made thereunder, in respect of the above-mentioned aircraft which is considered to be airworthy when maintained and operated in accordance with the foregoing and the pertinent operating limitations. The CAA Approved Flight Manual forms part of this Certificate.

Condition(s): This Aircraft must be maintained to the CAA Approved Maintenance Schedule.

Date: 27 June 1991

for the Civil Aviation Authority

This Certificate is valid for the period(s) shown below

Official Stamp and Date

From:	To:	
27 June 1991	26 June 1994	C.A.A.
1st July 1994	30 June 1997	C.A.A.
From:	To:	

airworthy when maintained and operated in accordance with the foregoing and the pertinent operating limitations. The CAA Approved Flight Manual forms part of this Certificate.

Condition(s): This Aircraft must be maintained to the CAA Approved Maintenance Schedule.

The C of A will describe the aircraft and show the period of validity (usually three years for aircraft below 2730kg MTWA). There are some exceptions in the UK to the requirement to hold a valid C of A (e.g. gliders, balloons on private flights, kites, test flying) but these are few and far between, and the CAA are very serious about enforcing this issue. In the UK certain aircraft may be granted a **Permit to Fly** as an alternative to a C of A. A Permit to Fly generally applies to homebuilt and kitbuilt aircraft, experimental aircraft or an aircraft which might not be suitable for a C of A (e.g. a vintage ex-military aircraft). Permits to Fly for homebuilt and kit-type aircraft in the UK, are handled by the Popular Flying Association (PFA). The PFA inspectors monitor the construction and design of such aircraft and make renewal inspections. A Permit to Fly is valid for one year only and usually contains specific conditions regarding the operation of the aircraft (e.g. private flights only, daytime flight in VMC only, no flight over built-up areas, etc.) Aircraft which have a Permit to Fly must carry a placard in the cockpit stating: "This aircraft is not certified to an international standard". Essentially, a Permit to Fly allows the operation of an aircraft which by nature of its age, rarity, design, construction or intended use does not justify the time and expense involved in obtaining a C of A.

Certain aircraft (such as this homebuilt Evans VP-1) may be operated under a Permit To Fly, in this case arrangement through the Popular Flying Association

For a C of A to remain valid or be revalidated, the state of registry must establish a system of periodic inspection to determine that the required standards of airworthiness are being maintained. In the UK a C of A may be invalidated if an aircraft is repaired or modified in some way which is not approved by the CAA. This includes the provision that any equipment (including radio equipment) fitted to an aircraft with a C of A must also meet minimum airworthiness standards. To ensure that these requirements are being met there are various aircraft documents to consider. The following information relates to aircraft with a UK C of A.

▶Certificate of Maintenance Review

If an aircraft has a Transport or Aerial Work Category C of A, it must be maintained in accordance with an approved maintenance schedule and a valid **Certificate of Maintenance Review** must be in force to show that the aircraft has been maintained to this approved schedule. The C of MR will show the date of issue, the date or flying hours at which the next review must take place, and the signature of the issuing licensed aircraft maintenance engineer.

A Certificate of Maintenance Review for G-BGKY

▶Certificate of Release to Service

An aircraft with a C of A is usually required to have a valid **Certificate Of Release To Service** which states that any maintenance, repair or replacement carried out to the aircraft or its equipment has been done in accordance with CAA approvals.

▶Weight Schedule

All flying machines and gliders with a C of A must have a **weight schedule**. This document is created when an aircraft's weight and centre of gravity position is established and enables the pilot to calculate an aircraft's weight and centre of gravity position (often referred to as a "weight and balance check"). A new weight schedule will be prepared after a significant repair or modification to an aircraft. In this case, the original weight schedule must be preserved until at least six months after the aircraft has been re-weighed and a new weight schedule prepared.

The weight schedule for G-BGKY

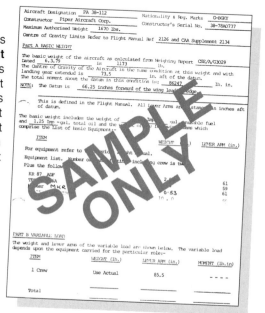

▶ Technical Log

An aircraft with a Transport or an Aerial Work category C of A will have a **Technical Log.** After each flight the aircraft commander must enter details of the flight into the aircraft's technical log. These include the time the aircraft took off and landed, and details of any defects.

▶ Aircraft, Engine and Propeller Logbooks

The aircraft operator must maintain **Aircraft, Engine and Propeller logbooks** for any aircraft registered in the UK, although a propeller logbook is only required for a variable-pitch propeller. These logbooks are used to record not just the flying time of each flight undertaken, but also repairs, modifications, maintenance etc. In common with the technical log, these logbooks must be maintained by the aircraft operator until at least two years after the aircraft, engine or propeller has been destroyed or permanently withdrawn from use.

▶ Noise Certificate

Almost all UK-registered aeroplanes (including helicopters), with the exception of certain jet Short Take-off Or Landing (STOL) types, require a **Noise Certificate**. However, foot launched powered flying machines (e.g. powered paragliders) are exempted from this requirement.

▶ Aircraft Limits and Information

As part of the airworthiness requirements, an aircraft manufacturer must determine limitations, restrictions and procedures for the safe operation of the aircraft. This information is compiled into a form of 'users' handbook', approved by the relevant

airworthiness authority and known as the Pilots Operating Handbook (POH) or the Flight Manual (FM). Each individual aircraft with a C of A will have its own individual copy of the POH/FM. The C of A will refer to the aircraft's POH/FM and state that the POH/FM forms part of the C of A. The significance of the above statement is that, *for the C of A to remain valid, all the limitations, procedures and restrictions in the POH/FM must be complied with.* If the pilot, knowingly or otherwise, operates the aircraft outside the scope of the POH/FM, the results are not only dangerous but have serious legal consequences. The C of A is

The Pilot's Operating Handbook/Flight Manual for G-BGKY

automatically invalidated, which leaves the pilot liable to legal proceedings. The aircraft's insurance and any personal insurance the pilot has are also invalidated; and any guarantee or warranty belonging to the aircraft becomes invalid. It follows that you should be *very* familiar with the POH/FM of any aircraft you intend to fly – for legal as well as safety reasons. Certain key limitations and information from the POH/FM may be displayed in the cockpit in the form of placards.

▶Insurance Requirements

You may well be rather surprised to learn that in the UK insurance for an aeroplane is not mandatory. Nevertheless, it is obviously not very sensible to fly an uninsured aeroplane. Although it is the owner/operator of an aircraft who normally arranges insurance, remember that it is always the pilot in command who is responsible for ensuring that the flight can safely and legally be undertaken. If you fly an aircraft that is not properly insured and there is an incident, you could end up with a serious problem even if you are not the owner or operator.

It is also worth bearing in mind that both the aircraft's and the pilot's insurance companies may well refuse to pay out if they can prove that a flight was in some way illegal (e.g. if the pilot exceeded his/her licence privileges, if the aircraft was being operated outside the POH/FM limits, if the documentation was not properly in order etc.). This is not merely an academic point; there are several known cases where insurance companies have refused claims in such circumstances.

A further point regarding insurance. The aircraft should have 'third-party' cover, which is insurance in respect of the damage it could potentially do to people or other property. In most instances the minimum cover is £250,000 – which sounds a lot, but in fact covers little in these litigious days. Some airfields (especially military ones) may specify a **minimum** third-party insurance cover, often up to £5,000,000, for any aircraft wishing to use their facilities. Ensuring that the required level of cover exists is the responsibility of the pilot in command, *not* the aircraft owner or operator.

Some airfields specify a minimum insurance cover, as seen in this extract from the UK VFR Flight Guide

▶Revision

102 How does a state certify that an aircraft meets the appropriate airworthiness standards?

103 If the Certificate of Airworthiness of an aircraft is endorsed as not meeting full international standards, can it make an international flight?

104 How is a C of A affected if an aircraft is repaired or modified in some way which is not approved?

105 What information is found on a Certificate of Maintenance Review?

106 An aircraft has been re-weighed on the 14th June and a new weight schedule prepared. Up until what date must the old weight schedule be preserved?

107 Other than flying time, what details should be recorded in an aircraft, engine and propeller logbook?

108 Do propeller-driven light aircraft require a Noise Certificate?

109 Where would you expect to find information about limitations, restrictions and procedures for the safe operation of an individual aircraft with a C of A?

Answers at LAW186-187

JAA Regulations

▶ JAA Regulations – General

▶ Student Pilots (Aeroplanes)

▶ Private Pilot Licence (Aeroplane) – PPL (A)

▶ Instrument Rating

▶ Type and Class Ratings (Aeroplane)

▶ Private Pilot Licence (Helicopter) – PPL (H)

▶ Private Pilot Licence – Microlights, Gyroplanes and Self Launching Motor Gliders (SLMG)

▶ Private Pilot Licence – Balloons and Airships

▶ Instructor Ratings

▶ Further Ratings

▶ Other Licensing Provisions

▶ Personal Flying Logbook

▶ Revision

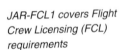
▶JAA Regulations – General

Arguably the biggest upheaval in aviation law in recent years has come from the process of harmonising of licensing procedures and standards between most European states. This has been carried out under the auspices of the Joint Aviation Authorities (JAA), and the results are known as the JAR – Joint Aviation Requirements. A number of those requirements concerning pilot training, licensing and regulation are known as Flight Crew Licensing (FCL), and the collective result goes under the term of JAR-FCL. The so-called JAR-FCL procedures are now being implemented as law in the UK and will, eventually, be implemented in other JAA states too. The aim is to have a uniform set of licensing standards and procedures across the JAA states although, as you might expect, such a major undertaking is highly unlikely to take place without some hitches. Thus it is only realistic to expect that operational experience may result in changes and modifications to these rules. There are also a number of

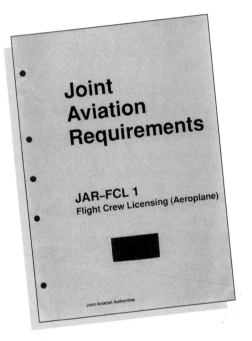

JAR-FCL1 covers Flight Crew Licensing (FCL) requirements

areas where the wording of the regulations is open to interpretation, which will presumably be based on operational experience. Therefore it is prudent to check the following against current information, such as Aeronautical Information Circulars (AICs), for any changes or new procedures. As with the situation regarding ICAO procedures and UK law, there are some discrepancies between JARs and what has actually been enacted as law in the UK. Where there are significant differences, these are discussed in what follows.

At the time of writing, the JAA full member states are:

Austria, Belgium, Denmark, Finland, France, Germany, Greece, Iceland, Ireland, Italy, Luxembourg, Monaco, The Netherlands, Norway, Switzerland, Portugal, Spain, Sweden, United Kingdom.

Licence Validity   To exercise the privileges of a licence or rating issued by a JAA member state, the licence or rating holder must maintain competency in accordance with the relevant requirements of JAR-FCL. The validity of a licence is determined by the ratings it contains and the validity of the medical certificate. A licence is issued for a maximum period of five years. It can be re-issued within a five year period after the initial grant or renewal of a rating, or when a rating is revalidated (as well as for administrative reasons). It is the licence holder's responsibility to apply for the re-issue of the licence with an application that includes all necessary documentation.

Medical Requirements   To apply for a licence, and to exercise the privileges of a JAR licence, the applicant or licence holder must hold a medical certificate appropriate to the privileges of the licence and issued in accordance with JAR-FCL3. The holder of a medical certificate must be mentally and physically fit to safely exercise the privileges of the applicable licence. Medical examinations are made by an Authorised Medical Examiner (AME), who will advise the applicant if he/she is fit, unfit, or needs to be referred to the authority for further examination. The AME will inform the applicant of any conditions that might restrict flying training or the privileges of any licence issued. JAR-FCL contains advisory information for holders of a restricted medical certificate that requires the pilot-in-command to carry a safety pilot.

Student pilots and licence holders must not act as a member of the flight crew of an aircraft registered in the UK if they know that their physical or mental condition renders them temporarily or permanently unfit to do so. The JAR-FCL provision is slight different:

JAR-FCL definition:

Student pilots and licence holders must not exercise the privileges of their licence, ratings or authorisations if they are aware of a decrease in their medical fitness which might make them unable to safely exercise those privileges. They must seek advice from the authority or an AME without delay upon becoming aware of:

– hospital or clinic admission for more than 12 hours

– surgical operation or invasive procedure

– the regular use of medication

– the need to regularly use correcting lenses.

A PPL holder is required to hold at least JAR-FCL Class 1 or Class 2 medical certificate. The standard of medical fitness required for a Class 2 medical certificate is broadly similar to the old UK class 3 medical certificate, however the periods of validity are slightly different:

Age	Medical Interval
Up to 30	Every five years
30-49	Every two years
50 and older	Annual

The holder of a medical certificate issued in accordance with JAR-FCL must inform the authority in writing of any significant personal injury involving incapacity to function as a member of a flight crew, or of becoming pregnant. In the case of an illness involving incapacity to function as a member of flight crew throughout a period of 21 days or more the authority must be informed in writing as soon as the period of 21 days has elapsed. The medical certificate will then be considered as suspended; this suspension shall cease or be lifted subject to a medical examination under arrangements made by the authority. The authority may exempt the holder from a medical examination, or impose conditions to the lifting of the suspension, as it sees fit.

Flight Time   Except where specifically stated in JAR-FCL, flight time to be credited for a licence or rating must be flown in the same category of aircraft for which the licence or rating is sought. Category of aircraft is defined as specified basic characteristics, e.g. aeroplane, helicopter, glider etc. An applicant for a licence or rating is credited in full with all solo, dual instruction or Pilot-In-Command (PIC) flight time towards the total flight time needed for the relevant licence or rating.

The graduate of a course of Airline Transport Pilot (ATP) integrated flying training may be credited with a maximum of 50 hours of student pilot-in-command (PIC) instrument time towards the PIC time required for the issue of the ATP licence and a multi-engine type or class rating.

The graduate of a course of Commercial Pilot Licence/Instrument Rating (CPL/IR) integrated flying training may be credited with a maximum of 50 hours of student pilot-in-command (PIC) instrument time towards the PIC time required for the issue of the Commercial Pilot Licence and a multi-engine type or class rating.

A pilot licence holder acting as a co-pilot can be credited with 50% of that co-pilot time towards the total flight time required for a higher grade of pilot licence. A pilot licence holder acting as a co-pilot performing the functions and duties of PIC, under the supervision of the pilot-in-command, may be credited in full with this flight time towards the total flight time required for a higher grade of pilot licence. This is provided that the method of supervision is agreed with the authority.

Licence Application   An applicant applies for licence issue to the Authority of the state under whose Authority the training and testing for the licence were carried out. Further ratings under JAR-FCL requirements can be obtained in any JAA Member State, but will be entered into the licence by the original state of licence issue as above. For administrative convenience a licence holder may transfer a licence to another JAA Member State – who now become the state of licence issue – if employment or normal residency is established in that state. Normal residency is the place where a person normally lives for at least 185 days a year for personal and occupational reasons (still following this?). If a person does not have occupational ties, personal ties showing close links to the place where he or she is living may be sufficient to prove normal residency. An applicant can only hold one JAR-FCL aeroplane licence at a time.

▶ Student Pilots (Aeroplanes)

A student pilot must meet the requirements specified by the Authority in the state in which the student intends to train. Student pilots must not fly solo unless authorised by a flight instructor, and must be at least 16 years old before first solo flight. A student pilot must hold a valid Class 1 or Class 2 medical certificate in order to fly solo, for the issue of a PPL (A) a Class 2 medical certificate is sufficient (Class 1 being required for a professional licence). In general, student pilots are highly recommended to obtain a medical certificate as early as possible in their flight training.

UK legislation places a few extra conditions for solo flight by students:

– No other person is to be carried in the aircraft.

– The aircraft must not be flown for the purposes of public transport, or aerial work; except aerial work which consists of flying instruction or flying tests.

▶ Private Pilot Licence (Aeroplane) – PPL (A)

The training for a JAR PPL (A) must be conducted at a Flying Training Organisation (FTO) or accepted registered facility in accordance with the syllabus set out in JAR-FCL. Flight instruction will include at least 25 hours dual instruction and 10 hours of supervised solo flight time. Solo flight time is flight time during which the student is the sole occupant of the aircraft. This solo flight time must include at least five hours solo cross-country flight time, with at least one cross country flight of a minimum of 150nm during which two full stop landings are made at two aerodromes different from the aerodrome of departure. An applicant for a JAR PPL (A) must have completed at least 45 hours of flight time, five hours of this may have been completed in a flight simulator.

The holder of a pilot licence or equivalent for helicopters, gliders and motorgliders, or microlights with fixed wings and moveable three axis control surfaces, may be credited with 10% of their total PIC flight time towards the JAR PPL (A), up to a maximum of 10 hours. For such applicants the dual instruction requirement is reduced to not less than 20 hours.

A JAR PPL (A) applicant must demonstrate an appropriate level of theoretical knowledge. In practice this is done by undertaking theoretical knowledge instruction and passing a series of written exams. The PPL (A) applicant must also demonstrate their ability to act as PIC appropriate to the licence by passing a flight test known as a 'Skill Test' – defined as a demonstration of skill for licence or rating issue, including such oral examination as the examiner may require. The skill test must be taken within six months of completing flight instruction.

The minimum age for an applicant for a PPL (A) is 17 years old. To apply for or exercise the privileges of a JAR PPL (A), a valid Class 1 or Class 2 medical certificate is required and the licence is valid for five years.

The basic privileges of the JAR PPL (A) as issued in the UK are set out in Schedule 8 of the Air Navigation Order (ANO). The principle privilege is to act as pilot-in-command (PIC) or co-pilot on non-revenue flights, but not for remuneration. The recency requirement is that to act as PIC whilst carrying passengers, the PPL (A) must have made three take-offs and three landings as the sole manipulator of

W E A T H E R   M I N I M A

for a JAR PPL holder WITHOUT IMC rating or Instrument Rating

Class of Airspace

A	B	C	D	E	F	G

8km FLIGHT VIS.

CLEAR OF CLOUD

FL 100

1000ft

1500m

8km

5km FLIGHT VIS.

CLEAR OF CLOUD

1000ft

1500m

5km

3000FT AMSL

VFR

NOT

PERMITTED

SVFR may be permitted in a control zone

OR

IAS 140 kts OR LESS

5km FLIGHT VIS.
CLEAR OF CLOUD
IN SIGHT OF SURFACE

OR

IAS 140 kts +

5km FLIGHT VIS.
CLEAR OF CLOUD
IN SIGHT OF SURFACE

IAS 140 kts OR LESS

3km FLIGHT VIS.
CLEAR OF CLOUD
IN SIGHT OF SURFACE

the controls, in an aeroplane of the same type or class (*q.v.*), within the preceding 90 days. The JARs as enacted in the UK also state that the holder of a JAR licence who does not have an Instrument Rating (described shortly) cannot fly in accordance with Instrument Flight Rules (IFR). In other words the pilot must fly VFR, which means that the flight must remain in Visual Meteorological Conditions (VMC). There is a further stipulation in UK law that the licence cannot fly as PIC outside controlled airspace if the flight visibility is less than 3km. However, if the licence holder has an Instrument Meteorological Conditions (IMC) rating, he may fly IFR in class D and E airspace. The IMC rating is described more fully later, but in essence a JAA member state may establish ratings for special purposes associated with the PPL (A) – for example IMC flying, glider towing etc. for use solely within that member state's airspace. To use such a rating in the airspace of another member state requires that state's prior agreement and an IMC rating is an example of one such special rating: at present it is recognised only within the UK.

Because the introduction of the JAR PPL inevitably involves a period of transition, the majority of PPL holders still have a UK PPL. The privileges and limitations of a UK PPL are subtly different to those of a JAR PPL.

The minimum age for holding a UK PPL is 17, there is no maximum age for obtaining or holding a UK PPL, nor is there a maximum period of validity. A UK PPL in itself lasts for life, but its privileges can only be exercised when the licence is valid. As with the JAR PPL fair amount of responsibility is placed on the pilot not to undertake a flight outside the licence limitations. The legal, insurance and safety penalties for ignoring this common-sense fact are extremely severe. Essentially the UK PPL enables the holder to fly by day, in visual flying conditions, carrying passengers, but *not* to fly for 'valuable consideration'. 'Valuable consideration' is mostly taken to be **public transport** or **aerial work**, although there are a few exceptions:

– Aerial work involving flying instruction, where the PPL holder has an instructor rating. In this case the aircraft must be owned or operated by a flying club, of which the student and instructor must both be members. The instructor cannot receive any remuneration for such a flight. However, microlight and self-launching motor-glider instructors can receive remuneration.

– Glider towing and parachute dropping, subject to certain conditions.

– Air racing and charitable flights, subject to certain conditions.

Cost sharing between a PPL and his passengers is permitted, provided that no more than four persons (including the pilot)are carried and that the contributions by the passengers to the direct costs of the flight do not include the pilot's share of the costs. Such a flight cannot have been advertised before hand except within a flying club. So, for example, if a pilot makes a flight lasting one hour at a cost of £60.00 with two passengers, the pilot must pay not less than 1/3 (£20.00) of the costs. There are some further specific restrictions regarding cost-sharing in a flying-club aeroplane (e.g. the passengers must be members of the flying club and over18, etc). Any pilot planning a cost-sharing flight should carefully check the Air Navigation Order (ANO) and the FTO's Pilot Order Book to ensure the flight can be carried out legally.

In the case of air racing or contests, the prize money awarded to the Pilot In Command must not exceed £500.

The ANO definitions of what constitutes public transport, aerial work and a private flight are involved and complex, but they should be checked carefully if you are in

the slightest doubt about the nature of the flight you are thinking of making. The term 'valuable consideration' is generally taken to be any consideration, promised or given, that is of more than a nominal nature. For example, if you take a friend flying and he treats you to a cup of tea and a doughnut in the flying club afterwards, it is unlikely that hordes of CAA officials will descend on you from a great height. However, if the same friend presents you after the flight with a new television from the boot of his car, that is more like a 'valuable consideration'. In the case of what the CAA calls "illegal public transport" the pilots' insurance and the aircraft insurance are almost certainly invalidated and all concerned run the risk of prosecution. The CAA takes this issue very seriously and has prosecuted a number of operators for carrying out illegal public transport.

The weather minima for a UK PPL holder are rather involved, and so they merit detailed consideration. The following assumes a UK PPL holder with no instrument flying qualification– e.g. no IMC Rating or Instrument Rating.

1　You must remain in sight of the surface at all times.

2　When flying *outside* controlled airspace (e.g. class F & G airspace) you must remain in a flight visibility of 3km or more

3　When flying *inside* controlled airspace (e.g. class A, B, C, D & E airspace):

– You may not fly IFR.

– If flying on a Special VFR flight in a control zone, flight visibility must be 10km or more. Some routes and areas have a specific exemption to allow Special VFR flight by a PPL in a flight visibility of less than10km.

The weather minima for a PPL inside controlled airspace deserves a little further explanation.

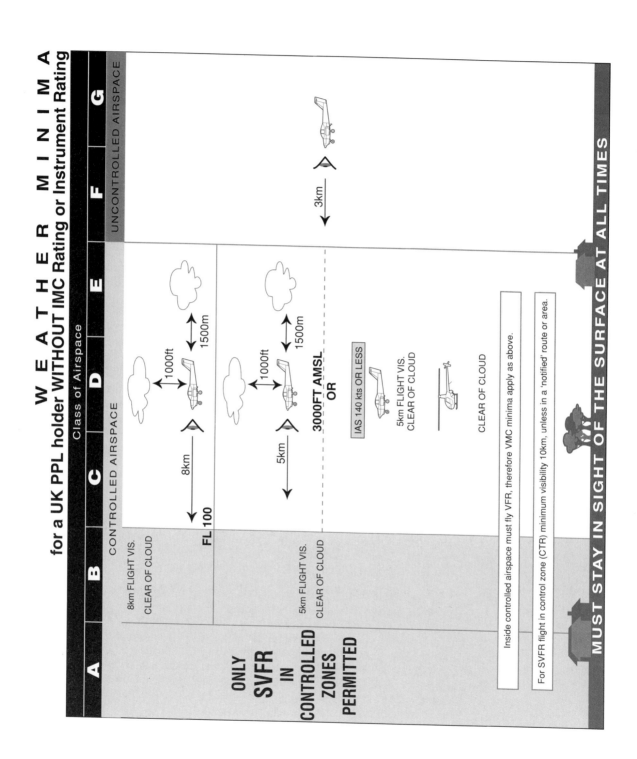

WEATHER MINIMA
for a UK PPL holder WITHOUT IMC Rating or Instrument Rating

Class of Airspace

A	B	C	D	E	F	G

CONTROLLED AIRSPACE

UNCONTROLLED AIRSPACE

ONLY SVFR IN CONTROLLED ZONES PERMITTED

8km FLIGHT VIS.
CLEAR OF CLOUD

5km FLIGHT VIS.
CLEAR OF CLOUD

FL 100

8km
1000ft
1500m

5km
1000ft
1500m

3000FT AMSL
OR

IAS 140 kts OR LESS

5km FLIGHT VIS.
CLEAR OF CLOUD

CLEAR OF CLOUD

3km

Inside controlled airspace must fly VFR, therefore VMC minima apply as above.

For SVFR flight in control zone (CTR) minimum visibility 10km, unless in a 'notified' route or area.

MUST STAY IN SIGHT OF THE SURFACE AT ALL TIMES

PPL privileges are set-out in schedule 8 of the ANO, which is the official reference for privileges relating to all licences and ratings issued by the UK CAA. Schedule 8 states that a PPL holder without an IMC Rating or Instrument rating *cannot* fly under IFR – Instrument Flight Rules – **inside controlled airspace**. Mostly, this means that you must fly VFR in controlled airspace; and to fly VFR you *must* be in VMC. What constitutes VMC in controlled has been covered in relation to 'Visual Meteorological Conditions and Instrument Meteorological Conditions', which are worth revising now. If the conditions are not VMC, then a Special VFR flight inside controlled airspace may be possible, as already covered.

The term 'flight visibility' is used above. To recap, 'flight visibility' is the visibility forward from the cockpit of an aircraft in flight. For example, if the visibility all around is a glorious 50 kilometres, but there is a cloud 1000m directly ahead of the aircraft, then the flight visibility is 1000m.

Flight visibility is the criteria used for determining VMC and compliance with licence privileges when flying outside controlled airspace, and when 'transiting' through controlled airspace. However, if departing from, or inbound to, an airfield within controlled airspace, the pilot must use the visibility as passed by ATC (e.g. the met. visibility as reported at the airfield) as the basis for determining VMC and compliance with licence privileges.

These are the basic privileges of a UK PPL in relation to weather conditions. You should appreciate that whilst it may be *legal* to fly, for example, in a flight visibility of only 3km outside controlled airspace; that does not necessarily mean that it is *safe* to do so. Regardless of **any** rule or regulation, the ultimate responsibility for the safety of an aircraft and its occupants will always rest with the Pilot In Command (PIC). That's **you.**

You should now appreciate that outside controlled airspace the UK PPL weather minima are not the same as *VMC* minima. So, in some cases (e.g. uncontrolled airspace above 3000ft AMSL), a UK PPL holder can legally fly in IMC, provided he remains within his licence privileges and can comply with the IFRs. Conversely, in uncontrolled airspace below 3000ft AMSL and slower than 140 knots IAS, the UK PPL weather minima are more restrictive than the VMC minima.

You should also be aware that the responsibility for staying within your licence minima, or staying in VMC, or maintaining SVFR minima, *always* rests with the pilot in command – regardless of any ATC clearance. Remember, to fly **VFR** you *must* be in **VMC**. Thus you must refuse an ATC clearance or instruction that will compromise licence minima, or VMC minima (when flying VFR).

To fly as PIC at night a further course of five hours flight time at night must be completed, leading to a JAR night qualification (the former UK equivalent is known as a night rating). This course includes three hours of dual instruction (incorporating at least one hour of cross country navigation), and five solo take-offs and five solo landings. The recency requirement to exercise night privileges carrying passengers is that of the three take-offs and three landings as the sole manipulator of the controls, in an aeroplane of the same type or class, within the preceding 90 days already required to carry passengers, at least one take-off and landing must have been made at night. In the Air Navigation Order (ANO) night is defined as the period from half an hour after sunset until half an hour before sunrise (sunset and sunrise are determined at surface level). Sunrise and sunset tables are widely available for checking that the planned flight can be completed in daylight.

DATE	EGAA Belfast Aldergrove SR/SS	EGBB Birmingham SR/SS	EGPF Glasgow SR/SS	EGLL London Heathrow SR/SS	EGCC Manchester SR/SS	EGSH Norwich SR/SS	EGHD Plymouth SR/SS	EGPB Sumburgh SR/SS
Jan 1	0847/1610	0817/1604	0847/1555	0807/1604	0824/1602	0806/1551	0816/1624	0905/1512
Jan 15	0840/1628	0811/1621	0838/1615	0800/1621	0816/1620	0759/1619	0810/1649	0852/1536
Feb 1	0814/1702	0748/1653	0812/1650	0740/1651	0754/1651	0737/1640	0751/1709	0818/1619
Feb 15	0750/1728	0726/1716	0740/1723	0713/1718	0725/1721	0710/1708	0725/1720	0740/1659
Mar 1	0712/1800	0655/1742	0710/1750	0650/1740	0654/1748	0640/1734	0658/1759	0700/1735
Mar 15	0640/1828	0622/1811	0631/1822	0614/1811	0623/1815	0605/1800	0628/1823	0620/1808
Apr 1	0556/1902	0540/1840	0529/1831	0535/1836	0540/1845	0527/1830	0551/1849	0528/1850
Apr 15	0523/1928	0510/1905	0546/1857	0535/1836	0540/1845	0527/1830	0551/1849	0528/1850
May 1	0446/1958	0436/1931	0424/1922	0432/1926	0433/1939	0421/1923	0450/1937	0401/2004
May 15	0410/2041	0411/1956	0405/2024	0410/1948	0409/2004	0428/1957	0329/2036
June 1	0355/2050	0350/2019	0340/2052	0349/2010	0346/2027	0336/2009	0428/1957	0329/2036
June 15	0348/2102	0344/2030	0332/2104	0344/2020	0340/2038	0330/2020	0404/2029	0254/2114
July 1	0352/2104	0348/2032	0337/2104	0349/2021	0340/2038	0330/2020	0404/2029	0308/2110
July 15	0407/2053	0400/2022	0352/2052	0401/2011	0400/2029	0336/2020	0409/2030	0249/2127
Aug 1	0434/2025	0426/1959	0420/2025	0425/1949	0425/2004	0348/2010	0422/2021	0310/2107
Aug 15	0457/2000	0450/1930	0450/1950	0449/1923	0445/1939	0413/1947	0444/2000	0345/2034
Sept 1	0528/1920	0516/1858	0519/1914	0512/1849	0515/1900	0437/1921	0501/1936	0422/1955
Sept 15	0552/1841	0539/1826	0550/1832	0538/1814	0543/1822	0503/1844	0530/1900	0457/1910
Oct 1	0625/1803	0605/1747	0620/1757	0559/1740	0610/1743	0532/1808	0552/1828	0535/1822
Oct 15	0650/1728	0631/1711	0650/1715	0552/0626	0637/1711	0559/1730	0615/1753	0608/1710
Nov 1	0724/1651	0659/1640	0721/1639	0651/1635	0705/1638	0621/1659	0643/1723	0645/1655
Nov 15	0753/1623	0727/1615	0755/1609	0721/1611	0735/1611	0650/1620	0705/1651	0725/1610
Dec 1	0823/1603	0751/1557	0823/1550	0745/1556	0800/1555	0718/1600	0731/1630	0804/1534
Dec 15	0840/1558	0810/1553	0842/1543	0801/1553	0818/1550	0742/1544	0755/1615	0840/1509
						0800/1540	0811/1612	0902/1459

A sunrise/sunset table from the UK VFR Flight Guide

ICAO Definition:

Night – the hours between the end of evening civil twilight and the beginning of morning civil twilight. Civil twilight ends in the evening when the centre of the sun's disc is six degrees below the horizon and begins in the morning when the centre of the sun's disc is six degrees below the horizon.

Under the Air Navigation Order, to operate an aircraft radio the user must hold a suitable radio licence, normally a Flight Radiotelephony Operator's (FRTO) Licence. Simply having a PPL does not confer any right to use an aircraft radio; the FRTO licence has its own syllabus and exams.

Student pilots, and glider pilots on private flights, are exempt from this requirement.

▶Instrument Rating

Except when undergoing dual training or a skill test, a JAR licence holder must not act in any capacity as a pilot of an aeroplane under Instrument Flight Rules (IFR) unless the holder has a valid Instrument Rating. As has already been seen, for JAR licences issued by the CAA there is an exemption to this requirement for holders of an Instrument Meteorological Conditions (IMC) rating.

▶Type and Class Ratings (Aeroplane)

JAR-FCL definitions:

Rating – An entry in a licence stating special conditions, privileges or limitations pertaining to that licence.

Renewal – The action taken <u>after</u> a rating or approval has lapsed that renews the privileges of the rating or approval for a further specified period.

Re-validation – The action taken <u>within</u> the period of validity of a rating or approval that allows the holder to continue to exercise the privileges of a rating or approval for a further specified period.

Single Pilot Aeroplanes (SPA) – Aeroplanes certified for operation by one pilot.

Multi Pilot Aeroplanes (MPA) – Aeroplanes certified for operation with a minimum of at least two pilots.

Except when undergoing a skill test or receiving flight instruction, a pilot licence holder must only act as pilot of an aeroplane when he or she has a valid and appropriate class or type rating. Any limitations or conditions are endorsed on the rating. It is important for a UK PPL holder to appreciate that the following <u>does</u> apply to their licence. The JAR class and type ratings have replaced the former aircraft rating 'groups' and the currency requirements apply equally to JAR PPLs and UK PPLs – no matter how long they have had their licence.

Most single pilot aeroplanes are covered by one of the following *class ratings*:

Description	Designation
Single-engine piston aeroplanes (land)	– SE piston (land)
Single-engine piston aeroplanes (sea)	– SE piston (sea)
Touring motor gliders	– TMG
Multi-engine piston aeroplanes (land)	– ME piston (land)
Multi-engine piston aeroplanes (sea)	– ME piston (sea)
Each manufacturer of single-engine turbo-prop aeroplanes (land)	
Each manufacturer of single-engine turbo-prop aeroplanes (sea)	

A class rating allows the pilot to fly aeroplanes within that class. However, additional 'differences' training and knowledge may be required in respect of variants of aeroplane within a class. Within the SE piston and ME piston classes such variants are:

variable pitch propeller	(VP)
retractable undercarriage	(RU)
turbo/supercharged engines	(T)
cabin pressurisation	(P)

At the time of writing there is a proposal to extend variants to include tailwheel aircraft which do, after all, have handling characteristics all of their own.

Notwithstanding the requirement for 'differences' training, you should realise that even aircraft within the same class can have very different flying characteristics and specifications. Accepting that this is part of the challenge and fun of flying, it is

A single pilot, SE piston (land) aeroplane, with variable pitch propellor (VP) and retractable undercarriage (RU)

strongly recommended that you should always seek proper instruction before flying a new aircraft type. Even if the new type does not have any 'variants' as described above, it may have some other feature or handling characteristic which is new to you. A study of accidents in America showed that around half of all accidents to home-built aircraft were due to the pilot's lack of knowledge of the aircraft handling characteristics. Nearly a sixth of accidents occurred during the first flight on the type!

More complex aeroplanes, such as multi-pilot aeroplanes; single-engine jet (turbojet) aeroplanes; multi-engine turboprop or jet aeroplanes or aeroplanes with particular handling characteristics will require the pilot to have an individual *type rating*. This last clause means that some aeroplane types that are within a class rating, require a separate type rating e.g. the Piper Malibu.

In general, to be issued with a class or type rating the applicant must complete theoretical knowledge instruction and demonstrate a level of knowledge appropriate to the safe operation of the applicable aeroplane type; undertake flight instruction and successfully complete a skill test.

The periods of validity of class and type ratings are as below:

- Type ratings and multi-engine class ratings:
  One year

- Single-pilot, single-engine class ratings (including touring motor gliders):
  Two years

Revalidation of type and class ratings may involve a *proficiency check*. A proficiency check is defined as a demonstration of skill to revalidate or renew ratings, including such oral examination as the examiner may require.

The revalidation requirements for different type and class ratings are as below:

- Type ratings and multi-engine class ratings:
  Pass a proficiency check within the three months immediately preceding the expiry of the rating;

And

During the period of validity of the rating undertake at least ten route sectors as pilot of the relevant class or type of aeroplane, or one route sector with an examiner. A route sector is defined as a flight including take-off, departure, cruise of at least 15 minutes, arrival, approach and landing.

■ Single-engine piston (land) and all touring motor glider class ratings:

Pass a proficiency check within the three months immediately preceding the expiry of the rating;

Or

Within 12 months preceding rating expiry complete 12 hours of flight time, including six hours PIC time and 12 take-offs and landings. Also complete a training flight of at least one hour with a flight instructor within the 12 months preceding the expiry of the rating. This training flight may be replaced by any other proficiency check or skill test for a class or type rating.

■ Single-engine piston (sea):

Revalidation requirements are at the discretion of the authority.

Now is a good time to re-stress to existing UK PPL holders that the above does apply to their licence, as do the 90 day 'currency' requirements already described.

If a pilot fails any test for a particular rating, that pilot may not fly in the capacity for which the test would have qualified him.

▶ Private Pilot Licence (Helicopter) – PPL (H)

From the 1st January 2000 helicopter licences will be revalidated in accordance with JAR-FCL2 – helicopters. Under JAR-FCL2 a helicopter type rating is valid for one year. In essence, the revalidation requirements consist of :

– proficiency check in the relevant type of helicopter within the three months immediately preceding the expiry date and the rating;

And

– at least two hours (including the proficiency check) as pilot of the relevant helicopter type within the validity period of the rating.

With the exception of those single engine piston types within the common group listed in JAR-FCL2, all helicopter types are exclusive and each must be separately revalidated. For the 'common group' helicopters, a proficiency check is required for only one of the types listed, if within the validity period the pilot has achieved at least five hours on each of the other types listed in the group (although only two hours are required on the type used for the proficiency check). You should note that Robinson helicopters are considered as exclusive types by the JAA while Federal Aviation Administration (FAA) Special Federal Aviation Requirement No 73 remains in force.

From the 1st July 2000, to carry passengers a helicopter pilot is subject to the '90 day' rule. In other words he cannot fly as PIC of a helicopter carrying passengers unless within the preceding 90 days he has made at least three solo circuits as sole manipulator of the controls, each circuit to include take-offs and landings by day, in the same type of helicopter. To fly passengers at night, the pilot will have to have made three solo circuits as sole manipulator of the controls, each circuit to include take-offs and landings by night, in the same type of helicopter

Note: Schedule 8 of the Air Navigation Order (which deals with flight crew licensing and qualifications) defines solo flight as a flight on which the pilot of the aircraft is not accompanied by a person holding a pilot's licence granted or rendered valid under the Order.

▶ Private Pilot Licence – Microlights, Gyroplanes and Self Launching Motor Gliders (SLMG)

JAR-FCL provisions are not expected to come into force for these types in the foreseeable future, therefore they will continue to be revalidated under the existing system of **Certificates of Test** (C of T) and **Certificates of Experience** (C of E) stamped and signed in the pilot's logbook. A Certificate of Test (C of T) for these aircraft is valid for 13 months from the date of the a test (usually the test for the grant of the appropriate licence). The Certificate of Experience for these aircraft certifies that the holder has flown at least five hours in the preceding 13 months, and it is valid for a further 13 months. If this experience requirement is not met, you will have to carry out a flight test or further training; the amount of this will depend on how long ago the experience requirement lapsed.

Microlight aeroplanes are presently defined in the ANO as aeroplanes with a maximum total weight authorised (MTWA) not exceeding 390kg, a wing loading at MTWA not exceeding 25kg per square metre, a maximum fuel capacity not exceeding 50 litres and designed to carry not more than two people. In the near future it is likely that many aeroplanes in the 390-450kg weight category will be redefined as microlights. Until the required legislation is put into force, an exemption has been drafted which introduces a temporary definition of a Small Light Aeroplane. A pilot licensed to fly a microlight can exercise the same privileges in a Small Light Aeroplane. A Small Light Aeroplane is defined as an aeroplane (other than a microlight) designed to carry not more than two persons, with a maximum total weight authorised not exceeding 450kg (or 300kg for a single seat

aircraft), a wing loading at MTWA not exceeding 25kg per square metre or a stall airspeed at MTWA not exceeding 65 kilometers per hour.

▶ Private Pilot Licence – Balloons and Airships

JAR-FCL has also yet to reach licensing procedures for balloons and airships. A balloon PPL continues to be valid provided the pilot has made at least five flights of a free balloon as PIC in the preceding 13 months. These flights must each be of not less than five minutes duration, there is no requirement for a C of T or C of E. A pilot can act as PIC without fulfilling this recency requirement if he acts in accordance with instructions from an authorised person and carries nobody other than that person.

▶ Instructor Ratings

No one can carry out flight instruction required for the issue of a pilot licence or rating unless his or her pilot licence contains an instructor rating. As an alternative to an instructor rating, an authority may grant a specific authorisation for someone to carry out flight instruction on a new aeroplane being introduced; a vintage aeroplane or aeroplane of special manufacture for which nobody has an instructor rating; or where training is conducted outside the JAA member states. Apart from this specific exemption you should appreciate that even if your best friend is a Concorde captain with 30,000 hours on a hundred types, that person cannot teach you to fly unless he or she has a valid instructor rating.

Additionally, within the UK flying training for the issue of a licence can only take place from a licensed or military airfield and a training flight is not allowed to land or take-off at an unlicensed airfield. Having said that, at the time of writing microlight and Small Light Aeroplane training flights are exempt from this requirement.

▶ Further Ratings

The PPL acts as a basic licence to which various ratings can be added. To give an idea of the scope of these ratings, the basic privileges of some are listed below. Bear in mind that each of these ratings has its own currency and validation requirements.

IMC Rating (Aeroplanes). This is a UK-only rating, which allows the holder to fly as PIC without being subject to the weather minima for the relevant PPL as previously listed, except that the holder must not:

– Fly on a Special VFR flight in a control zone in a flight visibility of less than 3km.

– Take-off or land if the flight visibility is less than 1800m.

Instrument Rating (Aeroplanes). The holder is entitled to fly as PIC without being subject to the weather minima previously listed, and can command an IFR flight in controlled airspace.

Instrument Rating (Helicopters). As for Instrument Rating (Aeroplanes).

Night Rating (Aeroplanes) or Night Qualification. Entitles the holder to act as PIC at night.

Night Rating (Helicopters) or Night Qualification. As for Night Rating (Aeroplanes).

Flying Instructor Rating. Entitles the holder to give instruction in flying.

▶ Other Licensing Provisions

A licence granted by the CAA is not valid until the holder has signed it in ink. Therefore, at the end of your PPL course, even when you have completed all the requirements for the grant of a PPL and the paperwork has gone to the CAA, you cannot fly as a PPL until you have received your licence from the CAA and signed it.

▶ Personal Flying Logbook

A licensed pilot, or someone flying to obtain or renew a licence, must keep a personal flying logbook. In this logbook the holder must record:

– his/her name and address

– licences held

For each flight made as a member of the flight crew, or for the purpose of obtaining or renewing a licence, the following details must be recorded:

– the date, departure point, destination point and flight time

– aircraft type and registration

– capacity in which the holder acted during the flight

– details of any special conditions and training exercises

– particulars of any test or examination undertaken during flight

– details of flight simulator tests

Entries in a logbook must be made in ink or indelible pencil and a logbook must not be intentionally damaged, altered or mutilated. A personal flying logbook must be kept until at least two years after the last entry in it (although practically all pilots aim to keep even their oldest logbooks for life) because up to that time it must be produced within a reasonable time if requested by an authorised person.

Your personal flying logbook will become the only complete record of your flying experience. You should take great care of it and even consider keeping a duplicate copy. If you have to send your logbook away or leave it in someone else's possession, it is sensible to take a photocopy of the most recent pages so that you have a back-up record of your total flying hours.

You should guard your logbook carefully. It is usually the only complete record of your flying experience

▶Revision

110 What is the period of validity of a JAR licence?

111 JAR-FCL3 relates to what aspect of Flight Crew licensing?

112 If you hold a JAR licence and have a medical issued in accordance with JAR-FCL, how should you act if you become aware of the need to regularly use correcting lenses?

113 What is the validity of a JAR-FCL Class 2 medical if you are 37 years old?

114 For how long must you be too ill to fly before you have to inform the authority and consider your medical certificate suspended?

115 As an applicant for a licence or rating, what flight time is credited in full towards the total flight time needed for the relevant licence or rating?

116 Under JAR how is 'normal residency' defined?

117 What is the minimum age for solo flight by a student pilot?

118 Can a student pilot who is the owner of an aeroplane fly it solo on his own authorisation?

119 What is the minimum supervised solo flight time before completing training for a JAR PPL (A)?

120 If you are a licensed microlight pilot with 250 hours PIC experience, how much time can you be credited with towards the JAR PPL (A)?

121 To carry passengers a JAR PPL holder must have made a certain number of take-offs and landings as sole manipulator of the controls. These must have been made within how many days before a flight carrying passengers?

122 What is the minimum flight visibility outside controlled airspace for flight by a PPL holder with no instrument qualification?

123 You plan a passenger-carrying flight to a particular airfield, with an ETA of 16:45. Official sunset for that airfield is 16:07. If you do not hold a night rating or night qualification, can you legally complete the flight?

124 What is the ICAO definition of night?

125 What is the period of validity of a type rating or multi-engine class rating?

126 Which of the following is NOT a requirement to revalidate a single-pilot, single-engine class ratings:

– Pass a proficiency check four months before the expiry of the rating

– Within 12 months preceding rating expiry complete 12 hours of flight time, including six hours PIC time and 12 take-offs and landings

– Complete a training flight of at least one hour with a flight instructor within the 12 months preceding the expiry of the rating

127 In general, is the IMC rating recognised outside the UK?

128 The last entry in your personal flying logbook in dated 7th March 2000. Up until what date must you retain it?

Answers at LAW187

Operational Procedures

Operation of Aircraft

Operational
Procedures

Operation of
Aircraft

▶ Operation of Aircraft

ICAO annex six part II contains standards and recommended practices for international general aviation. Although the ICAO definition of General Aviation (GA) is given shortly, it is commonly thought of as civil aircraft operations involving aeroplanes below airliner size, the 'cross-over' point being somewhere around the business jet size of aircraft. It is recognised that General Aviation operations may involve crews that are less experienced, and with a greater freedom of operation, than those in commercial air transport operations. The equipment these crews use may also be designed or maintained to a less rigorous standard than that for commercial air transport operations.

ICAO definitions:

Aerial Work – An aircraft operation such as agriculture, construction, photography, surveying, observation and patrol, search and rescue, advertisement etc.

Alternate Aerodrome – An aerodrome to which an aircraft may proceed when it becomes impossible or inadvisable to proceed to or land at the aerodrome of intended landing.

Commercial Air Transport Operation – An aircraft operation involving the transport of passengers, cargo or mail for remuneration or hire.

Dangerous Goods – Articles or substances capable of posing a significant risk of health, safety or property when transported by air.

Flight Crew Member – A licensed crew member charged with duties essential to the operation of an aircraft during flight time.

Flight Time – The time from the moment an aircraft first moves under its own power for the purpose of taking-off until it comes to rest at the end of the flight.

General Aviation Operation – An aircraft operation other than a Commercial Air Transport Operation or Aerial Work.

Pilot-In-Command – The pilot responsible for the operation and safety of the aircraft during Flight Time.

ICAO annex six part II places great emphasis on the pre-flight actions required of the pilot-in-command, and his responsibilities during the flight. In UK legislation the Air Navigation Order (ANO) contains various 'articles' which relate directly to the operation of aircraft and follow the ICAO standards and recommendations. In many cases the articles of the ANO merely enshrine in law the sort of common sense and sound practice that all good pilots seek to apply to their flying anyway.

▶ Pre-flight Actions

The ultimate responsibility for the safe conduct of the flight lies with the *pilot in command* (PIC). It is the PIC's responsibility to be satisfied before flight that the flight can be safely carried out, taking into account:

– The latest Aeronautical Information Service and meteorological information.

– Whether the required aircraft equipment (including radio) is fitted and serviceable.

– Whether the aircraft is fit for flight and all relevant aircraft documentation is in order.

Responsibility for the proper completion of the pre-flight actions ALWAYS lies with the Pilot In Command

– That any load carried is safe in terms of weight, distribution and security.

– That sufficient fuel, oil, coolant and ballast (if appropriate) is carried with a reasonable safety margin.

– That the aircraft performance will permit a safe take-off, climb to a safe cruising altitude and a safe landing at the intended destination.

– That all the required pre-flight checks have been carried out.

It is worth reiterating that the sole responsibility for the correct completion of these actions lies with the PIC. Even if the PIC delegates one or more of the pre-flight items to somebody else, it is still the PIC who remains responsible for any failure to perform a pre-flight item properly. Put another way, if something important is missed, the consequences could hurt you a lot more than it will hurt anyone else. In this respect there is little or no difference between the PIC of a Cessna 150 and the PIC of a Boeing 747.

▶Flight Preparation and In-Flight Procedures

■ Passenger Briefing

No matter how big or small the aircraft, the PIC has a duty to ensure that all passengers are properly briefed before flight. The PIC must ensure that all passengers have been made aware of the location and use of the emergency exits, safety equipment and harnesses, together with their actions in the event of an emergency. As a minimum you should ensure that your passengers will be able to:

● open the doors or exits unaided and operate any folding seatbacks;

● fasten and release their seat belts or safety harnesses unaided;

● locate the fire extinguisher and first-aid kit;

● use any emergency equipment carried (life-jackets, life rafts, etc.).

The Pilot In Command is responsible for ensuring that all passengers are properly briefed before flight

In addition, it makes sense to brief novice passengers on items such as the use of the intercom and mention times when the pilot should not be distracted. You might want to show them where the sick bags are, and you certainly need to know the location of these items. Passengers should be reminded not to touch any of the controls or switches without your permission, and to tell you right away if they move something accidentally.

Operational Procedures

■ Pilots to Remain at the Controls

At least one pilot must remain at the controls at all times. A pilot at the controls must wear the safety belt or harness fitted.

■ Operation of the Radio in an Aircraft

Anyone operating an aircraft radio must hold the appropriate radiotelephony licence or '...be permitted to do so'. Additionally the radio equipment must be licensed and operated under the conditions of that licence.

■ Towing Gliders

An aircraft may only tow a glider if its Certificate of Airworthiness (C of A) permits it to do so. The combination of aircraft, towrope and glider must not exceed 150m in length and signals must be agreed between the pilot of the aircraft and the glider. The aircraft commander must be satisfied that the aircraft/glider combination will be capable of making a safe take-off and reaching a safe operating altitude.

An aircraft must be expressly permitted to tow gliders. Signals must be agreed between the aircraft pilot and the glider pilot

■ Towing, Picking Up and Raising Persons and Articles

An aircraft must not tow, pick up or raise any object, person or animal unless its C of A expressly permits it to do so.

An aircraft may only pick up tow ropes, banners, etc. at aerodromes.

An aircraft must not tow any article (except a glider) at night, or in a flight visibility of less than one nautical mile.

The combination of aircraft, tow rope and article must not exceed 150m in length.

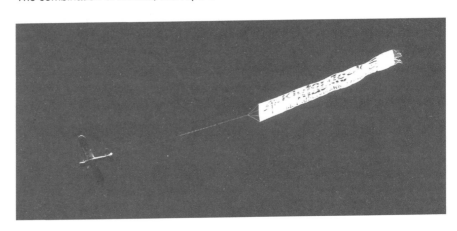

Specific rules also apply to banner towing. Remember that, in accordance with the rules of the air, aircraft towing a glider or object have precedence over powered heavier-than-air aircraft

A helicopter must not fly over a built-up area with an object, person or animal suspended beneath it.

For the purposes of this rule the picking up or raising of a person, animal or article is permitted in an emergency or to save life (e.g. a helicopter carrying out a rescue operation).

■ Dropping of Articles and Animals

Articles and animals (whether or not attached to a parachute) must not be dropped from an aircraft so as to endanger persons or property. Articles and persons may be dropped in certain circumstances, such as; doing so in accordance with dispensations from the CAA (for tasks such as crop spraying), the emergency jettisoning of fuel, dropping of ballast, and the dropping of tow ropes and banners at an aerodrome.

■ Dropping of People

Except in an emergency or for the purpose of saving life, no-one must drop (or be lowered or project) from an aircraft without the written permission of the CAA, and even then not in a manner that will endanger people or property. An aircraft used for parachuting must have a C of A with a provision for parachuting and the aircraft must be operated in accordance with the parachuting manual.

■ Carriage of Weapons and Munitions of War

Munitions of war (weapons, ammunitions, explosives, tear-gas canisters, etc.) must only be carried with the written permission of the CAA and in accordance with its instructions.

Any munitions, weapon of war or sporting weapon must be carried in a part of the aircraft not accessible to passengers, and firearms must be unloaded.

■ Carriage of Dangerous Goods

Certain goods have been classified as 'dangerous'. Where these are permitted to be carried by air, special conditions may apply and CAA advice may need to be sought.

Some items are obviously dangerous and are not to be allowed on to an aircraft; for example acids and other corrosive liquids, thinners, poisons, weedkillers and insecticides, gas containers, lighter fuels, explosives, radioactive materials, mercury barometers, wet-cell batteries, compressed gas canisters, fireworks, etc. Other items may be less obviously dangerous at first sight, such as paints.

However, probably the greatest danger is posed by items which might be brought onto an aircraft in the pilot's and passenger's baggage, or those which might appear to be harmless in normal circumstances. The CAA gives detailed advice regarding dangerous goods in the case of airline operations, and the same advice applies to smaller aircraft. If anything, the possible consequences of carrying dangerous goods are more serious in a light aircraft, and it is important to pay close attention to what is being carried in an aircraft you are flying.

For instance, if you are intending to make a night-stop, be aware of the following items:

● Hair sprays, after-shaves, etc. should be limited to containers of 500ml/500gr, with no more than four such containers per person.

● Gas-powered hair curlers (one per person) are acceptable, provided the safety cover is fitted. Separate refills should not be carried.

Operational Procedures

● Safety matches or a lighter are acceptable if carried on the person, lighter refills are not acceptable.

● Mace or CS-gas devices are not permitted.

If you are intending to camp, or stay self-catering:

● Camping gas containers, non-safety matches, flammable liquids and fire lighters are all prohibited.

● The carriage of securely boxed sporting cartridges is allowed; up to 5kg per person.

● Oxidisers (such as those used in kitchen cleaners) should not be carried.

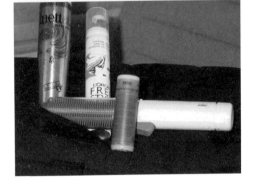

Some examples of dangerous goods:

LEFT> Paints, thinners etc.

RIGHT> Batteries, camping gas cylinders

BOTTOM> Hairsprays and hair curlers

If you are scuba-diving:

● Compressed gas canisters (e.g. compressed air cylinders) must not be carried unless they are empty. Heat-producing articles (such as underwater torches or diving lamps) are usually acceptable provided the pilot is aware of them.

The list is not exhaustive, and there are other items that are not dangerous goods but which might cause problems. In principle, these include almost any items containing steel, which can badly affect the aircraft's compass – golf clubs are notorious for inducing spectacular navigational errors. Equally, the use of electronic devices such as 'Walkman' personal stereos, electronic games, radios, portable computers and so on may affect some aircraft equipment– especially in a small aeroplane, where such devices are relatively close to the cockpit instruments and avionics. The use of mobile

Note how this light aircraft compass is deflected by more than 90° by the magnet within an ordinary radio. Headsets can have the same effect if placed near the compass

telephones is **specifically prohibited** in an aircraft. Apart from widespread disruption to the cellular system and possible disconnection of a large number of other users, mobile phones can cause major problems to the aircraft's avionics. Even in 'standby' mode when no calls are being made or received, *all* cellular telephones transmit periodic short bursts of data. This can cause erratic behaviour of avionics, usually at precisely the wrong moment. Whenever any type of mobile phone is carried in an aircraft, it **must** be switched **off** at all times.

■ Method of Carriage of Persons

In flight, no-one must be carried in any part of an aircraft not designed to accommodate people. A person is exempted from this article if, for reasons of safety, they have to gain access to cargo or stores designed to be accessible in flight. The aircraft's Pilots Operating Handbook/Flight Manual (POH/FM) will also state the maximum number of people that may be carried in the aircraft.

■ Endangering the Safety of an Aircraft

A person must not act in a manner likely to endanger an aircraft or any person in it, e.g. by vandalising an aircraft or blocking a runway.

■ Endangering the Safety of any Person or Property

A person must not cause or allow an aircraft to endanger any person or property. 'Buzzing' people or buildings would be one example of an infringement of this article – which applies equally to a deliberate action or endangerment caused by negligence.

■ Drunkenness in Aircraft

A person must not board an aircraft when drunk, or be drunk in an aircraft.

A person must not act as a crew member when under the influence of drink or a drug to such an extent as to impair their capacity.

You will note that this rule does not state a specific blood-alcohol concentration that amounts to being 'over the limit' (although this may change in the near future). In this respect it is different from the law on drinking and driving. The most widely quoted guidance is that at least eight hours should elapse between the consumption of **any** alcohol and flying. This is commonly expressed as **"8 hours bottle to throttle"**. In certain circumstances, of course, an interval of eight hours may not belong enough, and a bit of personal integrity and discipline may be called for. *Flying with even a minor hangover is emphatically **not** recommended.* The subject of alcohol is covered more fully in the 'Human Factors' section of the PPL course.

It should also be borne in mind that carrying passengers who are under the influence brings its own risks. All airlines will refuse boarding to a passenger if they think he or she is so intoxicated as to be a danger to those on the aeroplane. In a small aircraft, where such a person could quite easily have access to the cockpit, pilot(s) and flight controls, the possible consequences are nothing short of disastrous. Think very carefully indeed before getting airborne if one or more of your passengers has been drinking.

The subject of drug abuse is less well-researched in this respect. It is pretty clear that any person who could be considered a drug addict, or is using illegal drugs, is by definition not fit to fly an aeroplane. The subject of drug usage is considered in the 'Human Factors' section of the PPL course.

■ Smoking in Aircraft

Any notices displayed prohibiting smoking in an aircraft must be obeyed. This is particularly important because the materials contained in many aircraft interiors can give off highly toxic fumes if they burn.

■ Authority of the Aircraft Commander

Every person on an aircraft must obey all lawful commands of the aircraft commander that are given for the purpose of securing the safety of the aircraft and those aboard, and for the purpose of the safety, efficiency, or regularity of air navigation.

■ Acting in a Disruptive Manner

In response to the trend towards so-called 'air rage' incidents, under the ANO it is now a specific offence by a person in an aircraft to:

- Use threatening, abusive or insulting words towards the crew
- Behave in a threatening, abusive, insulting or disorderly manner towards the crew
- Intentionally interfere with the performance of the duties of the crew.

Whilst most of us might think that this has little to do with passengers in light aircraft, at least one such incident in a General Aviation (GA) aircraft has already come to court!

■ Exhibitions of Flying

When organising a flying exhibition or flying display, the organiser and participating pilots must ensure that the necessary permissions and authorisations are obtained from the CAA. Pilots in particular must hold a pilot display authorisation.

LEFT> Even a small display or fly-in can attract a surprisingly large number of visitors. Around 3000 people attended this relatively small-scale event

RIGHT> Organisers and participating pilots will require CAA authorisations for even a small air display

▶Instruments and Equipment

ICAO annex six sets out recommended minimum equipment for aircraft. Now is a good time to reiterate that these ICAO recommendations do not have the force of law in a state unless that state has put them through the law-making process. For the purpose of passing the air law and operations procedures examination you need to know the ICAO recommendations, as well as the law of the state of registry which may be different.

ICAO recommend that all aircraft on all flights carry:

An accessible first aid kit

A portable fire extinguisher

A seat for each person over an age determined by the state of registry

A seat belt for each seat

A flight manual, current and suitable charts, interception procedures

Spare electrical fuses to replace those accessible in flight.

Aircraft on a VFR flight should be equipped with:

A magnetic compass

An accurate timepiece

A sensitive pressure altimeter

An airspeed indicator

Any additional instrument prescribed by the relevant authority

All single-engine aircraft should carry accessible life jackets if flying more than 50nm from land suitable for an emergency landing, plus accessible liferaft(s) and flares if flying more than 100nm from land suitable for an emergency landing.

In terms of radio communications equipment of VFR flight, the ICAO recommendation is that a controlled flight (a flight subject to an ATC clearance) must carry a radio capable of providing two-way communication with the appropriate units, unless exempted by the appropriate authority. In accordance with this, schedule five of the UK ANO states that private (i.e. non-public transport flights), operating VFR or Special VFR in controlled airspace and below FL100 are only required to have a two-way communications radio to maintain communication with the appropriate radio station. Even this requirement may be waived if the appropriate ATC units permits it in relation to a particular flight. At and above FL100 an aircraft must also carry a transponder. ICAO recommend that if an aircraft is navigating under VFR, by visual reference to landmarks at least every 60nm (110km), no radio navigation equipment need be carried.

Before flight in a UK-registered aircraft, the aircraft commander must be reasonably satisfied that the aircraft is properly equipped for the planned flight. Schedules 4 and 5 of the ANO set out scales of Aircraft Equipment and Radio Equipment required for UK-registered aircraft – which vary according to the aircraft's weight, type of flight, C of A category and other circumstances. The scales of equipment required are complex and it is not practical to summarise them, although the required equipment is far less than you might imagine. However, it is worth noting that for flight above FL100 an unpressurised aircraft should have some means of supplying oxygen to the flight crew, and an aircraft (other than a glider) must carry a transponder.

Operational Procedures

Radio equipment fitted in an aircraft registered in the UK must be of a type approved by the CAA. An aircraft fitted with radio equipment will require a **Radio Licence,** which is essentially permission to operate a radio unit. This licence is validated by an annual payment, upon which a fresh certificate is issued. This annual disbursement does not make the radio work any better but, like the taxman, the Radiocommunications Agency is energetic in chasing those who have not made the required payment. In addition to the radio licence, a **Certificate of Approval of Radio Installation** must be in force. The purpose of this certificate is self-explanatory and it must be renewed after any change in the aircraft's radio equipment.

A Radio Licence for
G-BGKY
Note the date for renewal

Aircraft Radio Licence

Validation Document

Date for Renewal: 30-NOV-94

This licence (the "Licence") granted under section 1 ... The Wireless Telegraphy Act 1949. on 12-OCT-88 (the "Date of Issue") by ... of State for Trade and Industry ("The Secretary of State") to the Licensee ("Licensee") (whose ... possession includes all persons from time to time owning any share in the aircraft ... named in column 5 below ("the Licensee") authorises the establish ... ation described ... clause 1 subject to the provisions contained in the Aircraft ... Licence Clause Booklet.

SAMPLE ONLY

1	Aircraft Reg		
2	Call		G - BG...
3	Aircraft Make		PA38 ... HAWK
4	Tier Code (See Attached Form)		
5	Licensee Name		PROSPECT AIR LTD
6	Licensee Address		PAREGATE HOUSE OVER PEOVER KNUTSFORD CHESHIRE

Date for Renewal: 30-NOV-94

The Certificate of
Approval of Aircraft Radio
Installation for G-BGKY

United Kingdom Civil Aviation Authority

Certificate of Approval of Aircraft Radio Installation

Ref: 9/23/G-BGKY

Registration Marks G-BGKY   Date   14th July 1989

Type   PIPER PA-38-112

NOTE: (i) This Certificate supersedes Certificate dated
       (ii) This Certicate must be passed to subsequent Operators   28th July 1988
       (iii) The Operator must be in possession of a current Department of Trade Aircraft Licence, which is validated by this Certificate. Any modification to the Radio Installation will necessitate the re-issue of this Certificate.

ISSUE   REPLACEMENT

The above named aircraft's radio apparatus, details of which are listed below, and its installation is approved as complying with all relevant requirements of British Civil Airworthiness Requirements.

VHF COMMUNICATION
DME   118 to 137 Mhz
ATC TRANSPONDER   960 to 1215 Mhz
                             1090 Mhz

The Airborne Radio Apparatus installed on the aircraft is approved to transmit within the frequency bands listed above. The equipment that comprises the radio station is recorded by the Civil Aviation Authority and conforms to the performance and operational classifications of CAP 208.

Any modification to the Radio Installation will necessitate the re-issue of this Certificate.

►Maintenance

ICAO states that it is the owner or lessee of an aircraft who is responsible for ensuring that an aircraft is properly maintained in airworthy condition as prescribed by the state of registry, that maintenance personnel certify the appropriate records and that a maintenance release is completed as appropriate. Nevertheless, it is still the responsibility of the pilot-in-command to satisfy him/herself before flight that the aircraft is fit to fly.

ICAO also recommend that maintenance records are kept for the aircraft detailing the mass (weight) and location of the centre of gravity when empty, the installation and removal of equipment, maintenance carried out and compliance with airworthiness directives (ADs). Records should also be kept for major components recording the total time in service, date of last overhaul, time in service since last inspection and date of last inspection. The documentation used for this type of recording has already been described in some detail in respect of the airworthiness of aircraft.

If a UK-registered aircraft has a Private or Special category C of A, and its maximum total weight does not exceed 2730kg, certain minor repairs and replacements can be made by a licensed pilot who is the owner or operator of the aircraft. The permitted repairs or replacements are detailed in the Air Navigation (General) Regulations; however in brief they allow:

'Prescribed repairs' which a pilot may carry out are listed in the Air Navigation (General) Regulations

– Replacement of undercarriage tyres, skids or skid shoes.

– Replacement of elastic shock absorbers on the undercarriage.

– Replacement of defective safety wiring or split pins, **except** those in engine, transmission, rotor or flight control systems.

– Patch repairs to fabric covering not needing rib stitching and not involving the removal of control surfaces or structural parts.

– Repairs to the interior upholstery and furnishing of an aircraft not involving the operation of any system nor the structure of the aircraft.

– Repairs (other than welding) to non-structural fairings, cover plates and cowlings.

– Replacement of side windows.

– Replacement of belts and harnesses.

– Replacement of seats and seat parts.

– Replacement of bulbs, reflectors, lenses or lights.

– Replacement of a cowling which does not involve the removal of propellers/rotors or the disconnecting of engine or flight controls.

– Replacement of unserviceable spark plugs.

– Replacement of batteries.

– Replacement of wings, tail surfaces or controls designed to be attached immediately before flight and removed after flight.

– Replacement of main rotor blades designed to be removed and not requiring special tools.

– Replacement of generator and fan belts designed to be removed and not requiring special tools.

– Replacement of a VHF communication radio which is not combined with a navigation radio.

In addition to prescribed repairs and replacements, and in accordance with the same restrictions, a pilot can carry out a check 1 on an aeroplane (*not* a rotorcraft) maintained to a certain schedule.

Of course, the fact that you might be legally entitled to replace a safety belt – for example – does not count for much unless you are capable of doing the job properly and have the necessary equipment and information. That is a decision only you can make, although the CAA is on record as advising that pilots who carry out their own maintenance should consider co-operating with an approved maintenance organisation. This seems like sound advice.

Details of any pilot maintenance are recorded in the aircraft's logbooks.

▶ Flight Crew

ICAO recommends that the Pilot-In-Command should ensure that the licences of any flight crew member are properly issued and validated, and that they have maintained competence. On a more practical note it is also recommended that the number and composition of flight crew should be not less than that specified in the POH/FM or similar document. The Air Navigation Order states that an aircraft must not fly unless it has the required number of crew and the crew have the appropriate licences. For most single-engine light aircraft, the specified minimum number of crew is one pilot (known under JAR as a 'single-pilot' aeroplane). Light aircraft have been known to get airborne without a pilot (or anybody else) on board, but such flights were strictly illegal according to the letter of the law and tended not to last long anyway.

▶Lights to be Displayed by Aircraft

By Night

The basic PPL does not allow a pilot to fly at night unless he has undertaken specific training to obtain a night rating or night qualification. However, even a PPL holder without a night rating should know the rules concerning the display of lights by aircraft.

To avoid collisions at night, the pilot must be able to interpret the aircraft lights. The three *navigation lights*, which can be steady or flashing, are:

Green	starboard (right-hand side) showing through 110°
Red	port (left-hand side) showing through 110°
White	rear showing through 140°

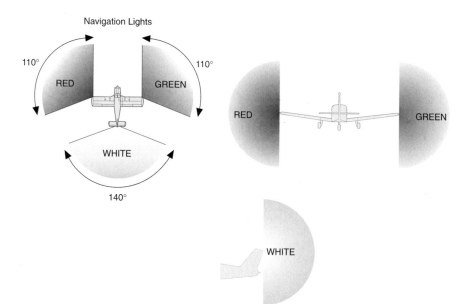

The standard navigation lights

These basic 'navigation lights' are provided for in ICAO annex 6 part II. UK-registered aircraft are also subject to further rules regarding lights.

In addition to the navigation lights, a flying machine may also display:

Anti-collision lights	flashing red lights showing in all directions, or flashing white lights (e.g. wing-tip 'strobes')*
Landing lights	generally in the approach and landing phase, although military aircraft and helicopters operating at low level may have landing lights on at all times for bird deterrence and collision avoidance.
Tail lights	illuminating the tail section of the aircraft – often seen on airliners.

* in the case of rotorcraft, 'anti-collision light' means a flashing red light only.

Should the lights which a flying machine is required to show fail at night, the aircraft should land as soon as safely possible unless an ATC unit authorises the flight to continue. Most aircraft with a maximum total weight authorised (MTWA) of 5700kg or less are not legally required to show any lights at night other than the three basic navigation lights.

Other than flying machines, other aircraft in flight show different displays of lights:

Gliders: as above **or** a steady red light showing in all directions.

Free Balloons: a steady red light showing in all directions, suspended between 5 and 10 metres under the basket.

Airships: In addition to the standard navigation lights, an airship in flight must display a white nose-light showing through 110° either side of straight ahead, and must also display an anti-collision light.

With this knowledge of the basic navigation lights, the pilot can assess the risk of collision and take the appropriate avoiding action.

In the case of two powered aircraft, the following rules apply:

Red and green lights visible	the other aircraft is head-on.
White light visible	the other aircraft is tail-on.
Red light to the left visible	'red on red' – the other aircraft should pass down your left-hand side.
Green light to the right visible	'green on green' –the other aircraft should pass down your right-hand side.

Should you see a red light to the right (red on green) or green light to the left (green on red) there is a possibility of collision. Remember, if the bearing of the light stays constant to you, **constant bearing means constant danger.**

By Day

A UK-registered aircraft fitted with an anti-collision light must display this light in flight, or a red anti-collision light (if fitted) when stationary on the aerodrome apron with the engine(s) running. Should an anti-collision light fail by day, the aircraft may continue flying by day so long as the light is repaired at the earliest practical opportunity. Note that this rule is not as strict as the rule concerning the failure of navigation lights at night.

In the case of flashing lights, a commander can turn them off if they are a distraction to the crew, or might dazzle an outside observer. This is particularly relevant when an aircraft is fitted with high-intensity white 'strobe' lights. Pilots often switch these off when flying through cloud or rain, and when taxying close to other aircraft or ground personnel.

▶ Revision

129 What is the definition of a Flight Crew member?

130 Who is responsible for checking that aircraft documentation is in order before flight?

131 Who is responsible for briefing passengers on an aircraft before flight?

132 When must a pilot wear the safety harness or seat belt fitted to a seat?

133 Can a PPL holder flying solo legally operate an aircraft radio if he/she does not have a radiotelephony licence?

134 Can matches be taken on to an aircraft?

135 Can a mobile telephone be used in an aircraft in flight?

136 Where can you find information regarding the maximum number of people to be carried in an aircraft?

137 Which of the following items are not amongst those ICAO recommend to be carried on all flights:
A portable fire extinguisher, spare electrical fuses, a Heading Indicator (HI), a flight manual?

138 If you are flying a single-engine aircraft more than 100nm from land suitable for an emergency landing, what items do ICAO recommend be carried in the aircraft?

139 What minimum radio communications and navigation equipment is required for a VFR flight in Class D airspace?

140 At night you see a green light steady ahead and to your left. Is there a danger of collision, and who has right of way?

141 At night you see a white light dead ahead, with a red light to the right of it and a green light to the left. If these lights all belong to the same aeroplane, what is it, and how is it heading relative to you?

Answers at LAW187-188

Search and Rescue

▶ Search and Rescue Organisation

▶ Alerting Phases

▶ Procedures for the Pilot in Command

▶ Search and Rescue Signals

▶ Revision

Operational Procedures

▶Search and Rescue Organisation

Each state that 'contracts' to ICAO is responsible for establishing search and rescue services in their territory, and making them available on a 24 hour a day basis. Each state delineates search and rescue regions for which they will be responsible, and as far as possible these search and rescue regions coincide with the relevant Flight Information Regions (FIRs). Each search and rescue region has a designated Rescue Co-ordination Centre (RCC). If an aircraft is known or thought to be in trouble, it is the RCC who will be informed and who will co-ordinate the search and rescue effort.

ICAO definitions:

Alert phase – A situation where apprehension exists regarding the safety of an aircraft and its occupants.

Distress phase – A situation where there is reasonable certainty that an aircraft and its occupants are threatened by grave and imminent danger or require immediate assistance.

Ditching – The forced landing of an aircraft on water.

Emergency phase – A generic term covering an uncertainty, alert or distress phase.

Rescue Co-ordination Centre – A unit responsible for promoting the efficient organisation of a search and rescue service and co-ordinating search and rescue operations within a search and rescue region.

Search and Rescue Region – An area of defined dimensions within which a search and rescue service is provided.

Uncertainty phase – A situation where uncertainty exists regarding the safety of an aircraft and its occupants.

▶Alerting Phases

The first sign of a situation that might lead to a search and rescue operation is often the uncertainty phase, usually meaning that an aircraft has gone missing or is seriously overdue. Each year, a number of pilots needlessly create such a situation through simple carelessness, such as failing to inform an ATSU that they are changing frequency, failing to 'close' a flight plan when they arrive at their destination, or making an unscheduled diversion or stop without informing their original destination. Clearly a lot of time and expense can be saved by avoiding needlessly setting off an uncertainty phase, not least because search and rescue resources might be needlessly deployed when they could be used elsewhere for a real emergency.

During the uncertainty phase the Rescue Co-ordination Centre (RCC) will co-operate with ATSUs and other appropriate organisations, evaluating incoming reports and trying to determine if a real emergency does exist. If this phase does not locate the flight in question, or if there is some evidence of a problem, an alert phase may be instigated, at which point the RCC will notify the appropriate search and rescue units and initiate any necessary action. The 'highest' state of alert – the distress phase – will come into play if there is a reasonable certainty that a flight is in grave and imminent danger or requires immediate assistance. This might well be triggered by a distress (Mayday) call or reports from other aircraft or observers.

Then the RCC will implement an action plan to locate the aircraft concerned. They will notify anybody who needs to know (such as nearby ATSUs, the aircraft operator, the relevant state of registry and accident investigation authorities) and request any nearby aircraft and vessels to listen-out on the emergency frequencies, assist the aircraft if possible and inform the RCC of any developments.

▶ Procedures for the Pilot in Command

Any pilot who intercepts a distress message should record the details, inform the appropriate ATSU and – at his discretion – proceed to the position given in the distress message.

If a pilot sees another aircraft or surface vehicle in distress he shall, unless unable to assist or if it is unreasonable or unpractical to do so;

- Keep the craft in distress in sight
- Determine the position if not already known
- Report to an ATSU details such as the type and identification of the craft in distress, its position and the number and situation of any survivors spotted
- Act as instructed by the ATSU or RCC.

A pilot who is first on the scene of an accident should take charge of on-scene activities of other arriving aircraft until the first search and rescue aircraft arrives. It is particularly important to keep the distress craft and its occupants in sight during this time as, especially in the case of a ditching, it can be very difficult for another pilot to spot people in the water, even when the aircraft is in the correct location. To direct surface craft to the site of the emergency may require knowledge of search and rescue signals. This knowledge is equally important for the pilot of a downed aircraft.

▶ Search and Rescue Signals

The GEN section of the UK AIP contains details of the organisation of the search and rescue services in the UK, together with advice to pilots concerning SAR signals.

If an aircraft has force-landed in an inhospitable area (or the sea) it is obviously important to attract the attention of the SAR services.

If the aircraft has ditched in the water, the survivors can use the following methods to attract attention:

– Fire distress flares.

– Signal with an object with some bright reflective surface, such as a mirror.

– Flash a torch or light.

– Blow whistles (these are normally attached to life jackets).

– If possible fly the international distress signal of a kite (or similar) with a ball (or similar) above or below it.

– Use fluorescent markers to leave a trail in the sea.

If the aircraft has force-landed in an inhospitable land area, the following additional measures can aid location:

– Make the aircraft as conspicuous as possible.

– Keep a continuously burning fire; three fires in a triangle make a particularly good signal. Have to hand material to create smoke (e.g. green branches and leaves, oil or rubber from the aircraft, etc.) if an aircraft or surface unit is seen.

– Use distress flares, reflecting surfaces or lights, blow whistles as available. If the aircraft radio is usable, attempt to establish contact on 121.5 MHz.

– Additionally, the following ground signals should be laid out. The symbols should be at least 2.5m (8ft) long and should be made to contrast from the background they are laid on. They could be formed from material from the aircraft, pieces of wood, stones, or by trampling or staining the surface with oil, etc. If the surface is snow the symbols should be dragged, shovelled or trampled into the snow.

Search And Rescue ground signals, and their meanings

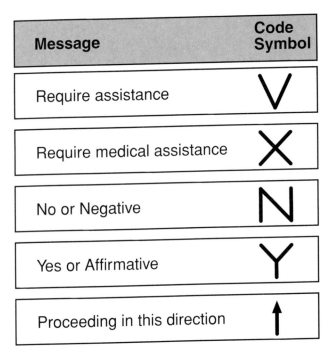

Message	Code Symbol
Require assistance	V
Require medical assistance	X
No or Negative	N
Yes or Affirmative	Y
Proceeding in this direction	↑

For obvious reasons, survivors should conserve flares, lights or fluorescent markers until they can see that an aircraft or surface unit is in the vicinity.

Another invaluable device for locating survivors is an 'Emergency Locator Transmitter' (ELT), often referred to by military or ex-military pilots as a PLB or 'Personal Locator Beacon'. The ELT or PLB is an emergency radio which, when activated, transmits a special signal on one or more of the international distress frequencies (usually 121.5MHz and one or more others such as 243 and/or 406MHz). A sensitive satellite system known as 'COSPAS/SARSAT' detects and locates the signal, with an accuracy of between 10 and 20km. The location information is passed to a ground station in not more than 90 minutes from the activation of the ELT; in the more populated parts of the world it is usually much faster. As a matter of interest, the emergency signal from an ELT or PLB sounds like a rasping "whoop-whoop" repeated every second or two. If you hear this on 121.5MHz, an ELT/PLB in the vicinity has been activated and you should report the fact to someone.

Search and Rescue

Civilian pilots are not usually involved in SAR operations, and in fact are well advised to keep clear if they are not involved. However, should you spot someone on the surface in distress, you can direct surface craft towards their location by:

– circling the surface craft at least once.

– crossing ahead of the surface craft at low level, in the direction they should follow, whilst either rocking the wings; opening and closing the throttle; or changing the propeller pitch.

Where SAR operations are in progress, the search aircraft will be monitoring 121.5 MHz. Additionally there may be communications on one of the 'scene of search' frequencies. For civilian operations this latter is usually 123.1MHz, with130.425 MHz also used as a 'unicom' frequency for use at major emergency incidents.

▶ Revision

142 What does the abbreviation 'RCC' stand for?

143 What is the definition of an uncertainty phase?

144 During an uncertainty phase which organisation co-operates with ATSUs and other appropriate organisations, evaluating incoming reports and trying to determine if a real emergency does exist?

145 If a Pilot-In-Command intercepts a distress message, what should he do?

146 If SAR operations are in progress, on what VHF frequency would you expect to be able to contact a search aircraft?

147 What is the SAR ground signal by survivors to indicate that medical attention is required?

Answers at LAW188

Accident and Incident Investigation

▶ **Definitions**

▶ **National Procedures**

▶ **Airprox Reporting**

▶ **Revision**

Operational Procedures

▶ Definitions

The investigation of accidents and incidents is one of those areas where the vast majority of nations appear able to be generally able to set aside national differences and politics and co-operate in discovering the causes of accidents and sharing information to prevent accidents.

The ICAO definition of an accident, and the ANO definition of a reportable accident, are practically identical as one of three possible instances occurring between the time when any person boards the aircraft with the intention of flight and when all persons have left the aircraft after flight:

> 1.) A person is killed or seriously injured while in, on, or in direct contact with, the aircraft. Also included is death or serious injury caused by jet blast or by parts that have become detached from the aircraft. Natural causes, or self-inflicted injuries, are excluded.

> 2.) The aircraft incurs damage or structural failure affecting its structural strength, performance or flight characteristics and will require major repair or replacement. Exceptions are engine failures or damage limited to the engine or cowlings; damage limited to propellers, wingtips, antenna, tyres, brakes, fairings; and small holes or dents in the aircraft skin.

> 3.) The aircraft is missing or completely inaccessible.

Other definitions worth noting are:

ICAO definition:

Incident – An occurrence, other than an accident, associated with the operation of an aircraft which affects or could affect the safety of operation.

Serious Incident – An incident involving circumstances indicating that an accident nearly occurred.

Serious Injury – An injury sustained by a person in an accident and which:

> Requires hospitalisation for more than 48 hours, commencing within seven days of the date of injury;

> Results in a bone fracture (except simple fractures of fingers, toes or nose);

> Involves lacerations causing severe haemorrhage, nerve, muscle or tendon damage;

> Involves injury to any internal organ;

> Involves 2nd or 3rd degree burns, or any burns affecting more than 5% of the body surface; or

> Involves verified exposure to infectious substances or harmful radiation.

▶ National Procedures

If a 'reportable' accident occurs to a UK-registered aircraft, the Department of Transport Air Accident Investigation Branch (AAIB) must be informed by the quickest means available. Where the accident occurs in or over the UK, the local Police Authority must also be informed. Notification of a reportable accident is the duty of the aircraft commander, or the aircraft operator if the commander is unable to do so. It is worth noting that in the event of a reportable accident, the aircraft must not be moved from the accident site until the AAIB has given its permission.

Additionally, a 'serious incident' must be reported to the AAIB. Examples of such an incident include:

– An 'airprox' (near collision).

– Flight into terrain only marginally avoided.

– A landing or take-off on a closed runway.

– A landing or take-off incident such as undershooting or overrunning the runway, or running off the side.

– Structural failure or engine failure not classified as an accident.

– In-flight flight crew incapacitation.

– Fuel level requiring the pilot to declare an emergency.

– System failures, weather hazards or flight outside the approved limitations or another occurrence that could have caused difficulty in controlling the aircraft.

A reportable accident or serious incident is investigated by the AAIB (which is independent of the CAA) and summaries of their investigations are reported in a monthly AAIB bulletin. Summaries of AAIB reports –which do *not* identify individual operators and pilots – are published in the quarterly Flight Safety Bulletin, which also contains various articles related to flight safety. Most pilots read these publications avidly, not out of ghoulish curiosity but on the basis that all pilots can learn from the experiences (and sometimes mistakes) of others.

If an incident occurs which is not covered by the above criteria, it might be worth making an 'Occurrence Report'. This is sent to the CAA, either on the standard Occurrence Reporting Form or just by letter. There may well be a safety message from the incident which could be passed on to other pilots.

AAIB monthly bulletin

Finally, if there is a birth or death in a UK-registered aircraft, or if someone is missing as a result of an accident or incident to a UK-registered aircraft, the details must be notified to the CAA as soon as possible. The only exception is when a death occurs in the UK as a result of an aircraft accident, in which case it is presumably a reportable accident in any case. In case you are interested, there are an average of two births on board UK-registered aircraft each year. Most of these occur during air-ambulance flights in the Scottish Highlands and Islands. It's not exactly standard practice for an aircraft to land with more passengers than it took off with...

▶ Airprox Reporting

If you consider that your UK-registered aircraft has been endangered by the proximity of another aircraft, an Airprox (Aircraft Proximity) Report should be made – by radio if possible – straight away. If this is not possible a telephone report should be made to the ATSU after landing. In any case, a report must be confirmed within seven days on a CAA form provided for this purpose. The primary purpose of reporting an airprox is so that it can be investigated by the United Kingdom AIRPROX Board (UKAB). Their conclusions do not have any legal significance and the anonymity of individuals and companies involved is preserved throughout. However, the findings of the UKAB are of great help in safety education and preventing further airprox incidents.

▶ Revision

148 Which of the following is <u>not</u> a reportable accident:

Someone is seriously injured by an aircraft's jet blast; a propeller bent on landing; an engineer seriously injured whilst an aircraft is manoeuvred by tractor in a maintenance hanger.

149 Who is responsible for reporting an accident, and to whom is it reported in the UK?

150 To whom must a 'serious incident' be reported in the UK?

151 How should an Airprox be reported?

Answers at LAW188

Noise Abatement

▶ General Procedures

▶ Take-off, Approach and Landing

▶ Revision

▶ General Procedures

There is an increasing environmental awareness about the effect of noise. This means that all pilots must seek to operate every flight in a considerate way, taking into account the sensitivities of those they fly over. Simply complying with the low-flying rules will go a long way towards keeping noise nuisance to a minimum, and common sense dictates that orbiting one spot at low-level for any period of time will quickly become tiresome for any non-aviation enthusiast on the ground. Likewise, certain manoeuvres – such as stalling and aerobatics – can be particularly wearisome with the frequent changes in engine note. It makes sense not to practice any such manoeuvres in the same location for more than a few minutes, even though you may be operating at a safe height. Remember that 4,000ft above the ground is still only around two thirds of a mile – and aircraft noise can carry much further than that especially over open countryside.

Even on an airfield, noise is a consideration. Engine run-ups at eight o'clock on a Sunday morning are unlikely to be popular with the airfield's neighbours, and some airfields restrict circuit training during certain hours – especially at weekends.

▶ Take-off, Approach and Landing

Nose abatement procedure first came into being for commercial air transport operations, and usually involve specific routings to avoid noise sensitive areas, and a reduction in engine power at a safe stage of the departure. Most General Aviation (GA) aircraft do not have much latitude for reducing power significantly during the climb, but routings designed specifically to avoid noise sensitive areas are becoming more common even at the smallest airfields. Pilots can help to keep noise as much within the airfield boundary as possible by starting take-offs at the beginning of the runway and using the recommended climb speeds, so as to be at a reasonable height by the time they leave the airfield. If there is a specific routing to be followed on departure, it will normally be promulgated in the airfield's entry in the AIP, as well as in commercial flight guides such as the UK VFR Flight Guide. It is part of the pre-flight responsibility of the Pilot-In-Command to be aware of such routings.

Noise abatement procedures normally involving altering the standard circuit pattern to avoid specific towns or villages.

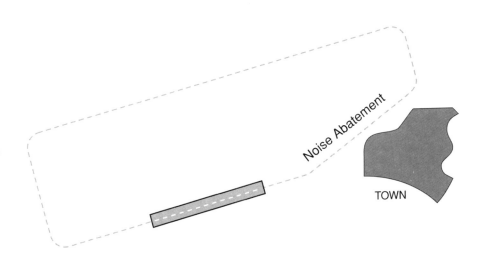

Noise Abatement

Noise abatement procedures for arriving aircraft normally consist of specific routings to avoiding certain areas (e.g. a village or town) and possibly a slightly non-standard circuit pattern. Once again such routings or procedures will normally be promulgated in the airfield's entry in the AIP, as well as in commercial flight guides such as the UK VFR Flight Guide and knowing about these is the responsibility of the Pilot-In-Command. Likewise it is important to know the correct circuit height, as this may also be determined in order to reduce noise. A low, high-power final approach from miles away is one of the surest ways to generate noise complaints, as well as being generally poor airmanship. It is usually safer and more considerate to make a steeper, low-power approach which should present no problems in a light aircraft.

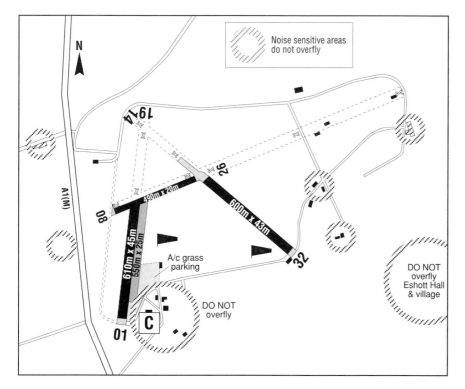

An extract from the UK VFR Flight Guide showing noise-sensitive areas around an airfield

The final point to make about noise abatement procedures is that in any emergency, you should over-ride the procedure if at all necessary and take whatever alternative course of action the situation dictates. This may sound like no more than simple common sense, but experience has shown that often, having decided on a particular course of action (e.g. a left turn at 500ft after take-off), a pilot can be reluctant to decide on an alternative procedure even if circumstances change dramatically.

▶**Revision**

152 Where would you expect a noise abatement routing to be promlugated?

Answers at LAW188

Contravention of Regulations

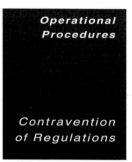

▶ **Offences and Penalties**

▶ **Revision**

Operational Procedures

▶Offences and Penalties

The matter of how to treat those who commit offences in relation to aviation law is dealt with in the UK by the CAA who have a prosecutions section. They are keen to point-out that they are not seeking to prosecute pilots who simply make a mistake or get caught-out by circumstances, but rather looking to protect the public from the actions of pilots who are deliberately or negligently reckless. Until recently a common situation leading to prosecution was alleged low-flying. The CAA are now showing a greater interest in aircraft that run-out of fuel, prompted no doubt by the number of engine failures and subsequent forced landings every year attributable to lack of fuel. Contravention of a requirement contained in the Air Navigation Order is a criminal offence, and thus being found guilty of such contravention can lead to a criminal record. Although fines are mostly the order of the day if found guilty of an offence under the ANO, there has been at least one case of an individual going to prison for forging entries in aircraft logbooks. It is an offence to forge or alter documentation, lend documentation to another person or procure a licence, etc. by false representation. All entries in a logbook must be made with "...ink or indelible pencil" and the logbook must not be mutilated or altered. And if you can find an indelible pencil in this day and age, you probably deserve some sort of award.

The commander of an aircraft, if requested by an authorised person (e.g. a police constable), must produce certain documents. Under UK legislation these documents are the C of A and C of R, the flight-crew licences and any other documents and records required for the flight. These documents must be produced within a reasonable time. Any person who keeps a personal flying logbook must also produce this within a reasonable time of such a request by an authorised person, within two years of the last entry in the logbook.

▶Revision

153 With what writing material must entries be made in a logbook?

154 Within what period must those documents that are required to be produced, be produced to an authorised person?

Answers at LAW188

UK Procedures

The Aeronautical Information Service

▶ The Aeronautical Information Service

▶ The Aeronautical Information Publication

▶ Aeronautical Information Circulars

▶ Facilitation

▶ The Prevention of Terrorism Act

▶ Meteorology

▶ Revision

UK Procedures

▶ The Aeronautical Information Service

The Aeronautical Information Service (AIS) exists to distribute aeronautical information to pilots and is part of an organisation known as 'National Air Traffic Services' (NATS). The headquarters of the AIS is at London Heathrow airport, and AIS documents can be found at aerodrome units or FBUs (Flight Briefing Units) at many aerodromes. Details are given in the AIP.

▶ The Aeronautical Information Publication

In accordance with ICAO Annex 15, the UK publishes operational aeronautical information in a document called the 'Aeronautical Information Publication' (AIP) which is also sometimes known as the *Air Pilot.* All ICAO countries have an AIP, and the information within it is set out in a standard form. Once you know your way around the UK AIP, you will be able to use almost any country's AIP.

The three sections of the AIP are:

GEN – General

Air Traffic services and procedures, the Aeronautical Information Service, customs and immigration procedures, meteorology, sunrise and sunset tables, search and rescue organisation and procedures.

ENR – En Route

Radio-navigation aids, airspace classifications, obstacles, airspace hazards, VFR & IFR, VMC minima, interception procedures, flight plans.

AD – Aerodromes

Use of aerodromes, aerodrome details including runways and facilities, contact details, radio frequencies, obstructions etc.

The AIP is supported by a system of amendments and supplements:

– AIRAC (Regulated System for Air Information) Amendments

Published monthly, giving four weeks notice of changes which will occur on a particular date. AIRAC amendments are usually in the form of replacement pages for the AIP.

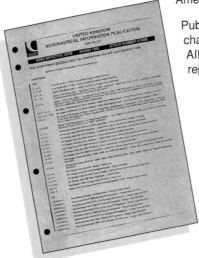

AN AIRAC amendment

The Aeronautical Information Service

– AIP Amendments (non-AIRAC)

Published as amendment pages each month and concern non-operational changes.

– AIP Supplements (Formerly known as Class II NOTAMs)

Published every two weeks; cover changes of a temporary nature.

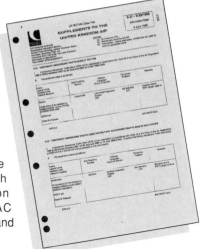

An AIP supplement

The AIP is part of what is called the Integrated Aeronautical Package, which covers the AIP, Aeronautical Information Circulars (described below), AIRAC amendments, AIP supplements, NOTAMS and Pre-flight Information Bulletins.

Any information not covered by AIP amendment or supplements will be issued as a NOTAM (Notices to Airmen) on the AFS (Aeronautical Fixed Service) to Air Traffic units etc.

Most UK general aviation pilots obtain information about NOTAMS and temporary changes from a set of bulletins called the Pre-flight Information Bulletins. These are available at most licensed airfields and FBUs, and can also be accessed from the Internet.

Check NOTAMS and pre-flight bulletins for anything that may affect your flight.

▶ Aeronautical Information Circulars

Also available to the pilot are 'Aeronautical Information Circulars' (AICs). These are issued by the AIS and deal with matters of interest to aircrew. AICs are colour-coded as below:

White	Administrative matters, examination dates, etc.
Yellow	Operational matters, e.g. ATC services.
Mauve	Amendments to UK Airspace, Airspace Restriction Charts.
Green	Availability of CAA Maps and Charts.
Pink	Matters concerning air safety.

A sample 'pink' AIC

AICs are numbered in sequence and cross-refer each other by colour and serial number. AICs are well worth reading and keeping up to date with. Most are withdrawn after a few years or are replaced by more recent material. Some AICs such as those on carburettor icing, wake turbulence, etc. are repeatedly re-issued and amended. An AIC automatically lapses five years from date of issue.

▶ Facilitation

The GEN section of the AIP sets out procedures and facilities for flights leaving and entering the UK, these procedures are still known under the old Air Pilot term of 'Facilitation'. At the time of writing, the regulations for such flights –particularly to or from other EC (European Community) countries – are changing frequently. It is in your best interests to check the up-to-date regulations when planning an international flight.

For the purposes of the facilitation procedures, the member states of the EC at the time of writing are:

Austria

Belgium

Denmark

Finland

France

Germany

Greece

Ireland

Italy

Luxembourg

Netherlands

Portugal

Spain

Sweden

United Kingdom (including the Isle of Man)

When a flight is leaving the UK for a destination in the EC, there are no customs restrictions on where the flight may depart from and it is not necessary to advise customs of the departure. When arriving from the EC, there are no customs restrictions as to where the flight may land. However, if the flight is not landing at a Customs and Excise airport, flight details and the names and nationalities of those on board must be advised to the local customs contact point a short time before departure.

Unfortunately, not all EC countries are applying the same rules to international flights, and some still require flights to route via a customs airport in their country. Here again, the position was fluid at the time of writing.

If a flight is departing for a destination outside the EC, it must leave from a designated Customs and Excise airport in order to clear customs. Customs and Excise airports are listed in the GEN section of the AIP. Once a flight has cleared customs outbound, it may not land again in the UK other than at a Customs and Excise airport (except in an emergency, of course). When arriving in the UK from anon-EC airport, the flight must land at a Customs and Excise airport to clear customs. When flying either inbound or outbound, remember to check the customs hours of attendance since these may not be the same as the airport operating hours.

Countries outside the EC include Switzerland and Norway. For the purposes of the facilitation regulations, the Channel Islands are also considered to be outside the EC, although the Isle of Man is not.

If an aircraft is forced to make a landing away from a Customs and Excise airport (if inbound to or outbound from a non-EC country) the commander must immediately report the landing to a Customs and Excise officer or a police constable. Except to preserve life and limb, no person may leave the immediate vicinity of the aircraft, nor can cargo be unloaded, without the consent of an officer.

For international flights there are specific documents to be carried, although under the ANO for a private flight within the UK (including the Channel Islands and Isle of Man) no documents are required to be carried.

For an international private flight, the following must be carried:

– C of A

– C of R

– Radio Licence

– Crew Licences

– A copy of the procedures relating to aircraft interception.

The new freedom which general-aviation aircraft have in respect of flight to and from EC countries is obviously tempered by a responsibility to help prevent abuses. Even after a flight from an EC country, customs officers still have the right to meet your flight, ask you questions and search the aircraft. HM Customs and Excise is of the opinion that light aircraft are increasingly being used for smuggling, especially where drugs are concerned. In an effort to help combat this problem, several UK general-aviation organisations (including AOPA and the PFA) have joined an 'Anti-Drugs Alliance' with Customs and Excise, to encourage pilots to be alert for the signs of light aircraft being used for drug smuggling. Pilots are not asked to get involved directly, but more to act on the principle of:

Don't just ignore it – report it

Specific things to look out for include:

– Unauthorised night flights from small and unlicensed airfields, especially if the aircraft is not displaying navigation lights.

– Unauthorised use of private or disused airstrips.

– Aircraft flying at an unusually low level, especially approaching he coastline.

– Unusual activity at normally disused sites (vehicles or small fires being used to illuminate a landing site, etc.).

– Packages being loaded or unloaded at a remote part of an airfield under suspicious circumstances.

– Extra fuel tanks fitted to aircraft, or doors re-hinged from above, for no obvious reason.

Any person who becomes suspicious as a result of observing such activities is urged not to get involved, but to take as many details as possible and pass them on. A special freephone line has been set up for this purpose: ask for '**Customs Freefone Drugs**' **on 0800 595000**. You might like to know that information leading to an arrest is eligible for a cash reward, which is one way of financing your flying! There are several recorded instances in which information from pilots has led to the successful prosecution of drug dealers.

▶ The Prevention of Terrorism Act

This Act requires aircraft flying between Great Britain and the Republic of Ireland, Northern Ireland and the Isle of Man or the Channel Islands to do so via certain designated aerodromes, where they will have to complete Special Branch procedures. A pilot or aircraft operator can apply to use a non-designated aerodrome by writing to the Chief Officer of Police in whose area the non-designated airport is situated. It was not clear at the time of writing whether the fluid political situation in Northern Ireland would have any effect on this requirement.

▶ Meteorology

The GEN section of the AIP gives details of the meteorological services available to pilots in the UK. This includes information on the dissemination of met. information, met. codes, abbreviations and so on.

At the larger aerodromes, weather forecasting and actual weather report documentation is available for you to 'self-brief' before flight. Usually this documentation includes weather charts, warnings, forecasts, actual reports and so on. In addition to these self-briefing units, pilots can also obtain weather information from a number of sources. These include:

– automated recorded messages accessed by telephone;

– charts, satellite pictures, area forecasts, aerodrome forecasts and actual reports by fax;

– on-line services via the Internet.

Always check ACTUAL as well as FORECAST weather conditions.

The Aeronautical Information Service

Full details of these services are usually found in AICs, the AIP and commercial flight guides. If, having self-briefed as far as possible, you still have a safety-related query regarding a particular forecast or report, it is possible to talk to a forecaster free of charge by telephoning a forecast office (details are found in the AIP, AICs and commercial flight guides). Because forecasters are usually very busy, they will want to know that you have already obtained the relevant information and you should specify what particular aspect of a report or forecast you wish to query.

Specialised forecasts may also be available by individual arrangement from the designated meteorological offices for gliding, ballooning, hang-gliding, microlighting, etc.

Both the Air Navigation Order and the Rules of the Air place specific responsibility on the pilot in command to obtain the latest meteorological information before flight. This, of course, is simply good airmanship; a large percentage of accidents involving light aircraft are directly related to flight in unsuitable weather conditions. The CAA and the Met Office spend tens of millions of pounds annually to provide quality met. information either at the departure aerodrome or via telephone/fax/computer services. You might think that a pilot who chooses to make no use of such an advanced and comprehensive facility is somewhat reckless, and you'd be right.

▶Revision

155 In what section of the AIP will you find information on arrival, departure and transit procedures, customs and immigration procedures?

156 What colour is an AIC relating to an air safety matter?

157 If you are flying directly from the UK to Zurich, can you depart from any airfield?

158 If flying VFR on a private flight from Southampton to Jersey, does the Prevention of Terrorism Act apply to you?

Answers at LAW189

Airspace Restrictions and Hazards

▶ Prohibited, Restricted and Danger Areas

▶ ADIZ

▶ Other Hazards to Flight

▶ Temporary Hazards

▶ Royal Flights

▶ Obstacles

▶ Gas Venting Operations

▶ Revision

*Airspace
Restrictions
and Hazards*

▶Prohibited, Restricted and Danger Areas

Controlled airspace, and the constraints it places on a flight, has already been discussed. There are also portions of airspace which are restricted for one reason or another. All significant airspace restrictions are marked on aeronautical charts, and details of airspace restrictions are to be found in the ENR section of the AIP. The location and dimensions of a prohibited, restricted or danger area is depicted on an aeronautical chart, together with its designated upper limit; e.g. 2.2 = 2200ft AMSL. Restricted, prohibited and danger areas usually start at ground level. The three main airspace restrictions are as follows:

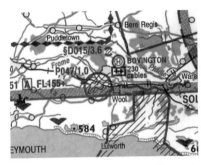

Prohibited area P047 extends from the surface to 1000ft AMSL

– Prohibited Area

An area extending from ground level to a specified altitude, within which flight is prohibited.

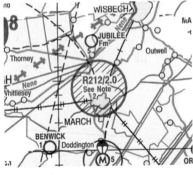

Restricted area R212 extends from the surface to 2000ft AMSL

– Restricted Area

An area extending to a specified altitude in which flight is restricted in accordance with certain conditions. These areas are shown on aeronautical charts in the same way as prohibited areas. Some restricted areas may be only restricted to certain types of aircraft (for example helicopters and microlights).

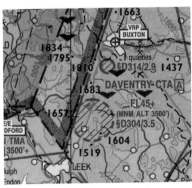

A scheduled danger area (D314) and a notified danger area (D304)

– Danger Area

An area extending to a specified altitude in which activities dangerous to aircraft take place at notified times e.g. weapons ranges, military testing and training areas, etc. On an aeronautical chart, an area marked with a **solid** red outline is a *scheduled* danger area and is active during published hours. A danger area marked with a **pecked** red outline is a *notified* danger area, inactive unless notified by NOTAM. Other hazards that may be encountered within danger areas include missile firings, tethered balloons, free-fall parachuting (day and night), aircraft towing targets, flight of pilotless target aircraft, anti-aircraft weapon firing, etc. Clearly none of these activities is compatible with safe and pleasant flight for a non-participating aircraft – which is, of course, precisely why the danger area is established in the first place.

Airspace Restrictions and Hazards

Although no single article in the ANO specifically prohibits flying in a danger area, doing so would probably contravene various articles (such as those regarding endangering an aircraft). Many military danger areas are also protected by bylaws which make trespass an offence. All this, of course, is in addition to the dangerous activity that the danger area has been established to protect you from.

Danger Area D203 extends up to 23000ft AMSL, but this top is occasionally increased to 50000ft

Some of the activities found in danger areas:

TOP> Military aircraft on exercise

BOTTOM LEFT> Freefall and static-line parachuting

BOTTOM RIGHT> Static balloons

Most danger areas have either a **Danger Area Crossing Service** (DACS) or a **Danger Area Activity Information Service** (DAAIS) radio frequency which you can contact if you wish to fly through, or near, a danger area. In the event that you are unable to contact these services, you should obviously assume the area is active and stay well clear. It's good airmanship to avoid danger areas on principle anyway.

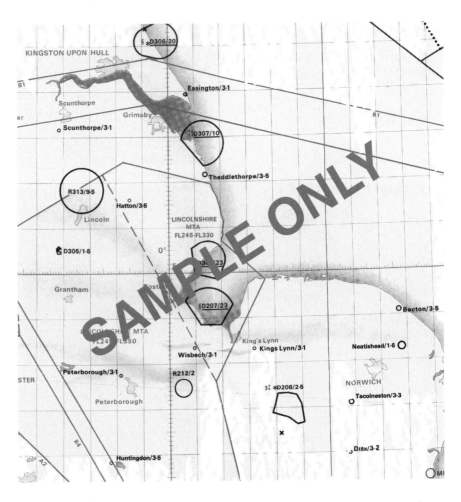

A detail from the chart of airspace restrictions, found in the AIP but also available separately

Danger areas whose upper limit does not exceed 500ft AGL (e.g. rifle ranges) are *not* shown on aeronautical topographical charts but are listed in the ENR section of the AIP. Illicit low flyers beware.

Temporary danger areas (TDAs) may be established at short notice in the event of a major incident. Details will be given by Class 1 NOTAM, which is distributed by teleprinter to places (principally ATSUs) connected to the Aeronautical Fixed Telecommunication Network (AFTN) and may also be distributed on the AIS website. A danger area of this type is usually established principally for the protection of aircraft engaged in SAR operations, and non-participating aircraft are expected to keep well clear. If a temporary danger area does not have the desired effect, a 'Temporary Restricted Area' (TRA) may be established instead. It is an offence to fly within a Temporary Restricted Area without the permission of the Emergency Controlling Authority (ECA). Sometimes an area of Temporary Restricted Airspace

A Temporary Danger Area or a Temporary Restricted Area is usually established at the scene of a major emergency, principally to protect aircraft involved in Search and Rescue operations. If you see a SAR aircraft at any time, you should give it a wide berth as it may be involved in complex and demanding manoeuvres

may be established (with details given well in advance) to cover major airshows, particular sporting events and displays by aerobatic teams such as the Red Arrows.

If an area of Temporary Restricted Airspace is set up at very short notice (e.g. in the event of a major emergency), details are sent out on the AFTN. Because very few flying schools or smaller airfields are connected to the AFTN, the CAA has set up a free service so that you can check if any Temporary Restricted Airspace will affect your flight. This service is accessed by calling a freephone number, which is **0500 354802,** and information on such events as Red Arrows transits and displays, Temporary Restricted Airspace, airspace covered by Emergency Restrictions of Flying and Royal Flights is all available for free. It's nice to get something for free in aviation, and also good airmanship to get into the habit of calling this number when you're planning a cross-country flight in the UK. If an aircraft finds itself inside a danger/restricted/prohibited area, it should take the shortest possible route to leave the area and not descend until clear of the area.

Temporary Restricted Airspace may be established for Red Arrows displays, and for major airshows (such as this one – Farnborough)

▶ ADIZ

Though not found in the UK, some countries have one or more **Air Defense** (sic) **Identification Zones** (ADIZs) which are usually at or near their borders and marked on aeronautical charts. If you are planning a flight which will route through an ADIZ, you should research the entry/transit requirements *very* carefully – many ADIZs are enforced by armed interceptor aircraft. Normally it is necessary to file a flight plan, maintain contact with a specified ATSU and follow procedures that may be specified in the AIP of the country concerned. The consequences of not following the established procedures are best not dwelt upon.

▶Other Hazards to Flight

Areas of Intense Aerial Activity (AIAA). AIAAs are marked on aeronautical charts, and are often found where several military airfields are situated close together. If you intend to fly in or close to an AIAA, you should establish radio contact on the frequency indicated. A radar service is usually available when an AIAA is active. Details of each AIAA are found in the ENR section of the AIP.

The Yeovilton Area of Intense Aerial Activity, extending from 2000 to 5000ft AMSL

Aerial Tactics Areas. These are often located offshore, and extend upwards from a Flight Level. A contact frequency is marked on the CAA charts, and full details can be found in the ENR section of the AIP.

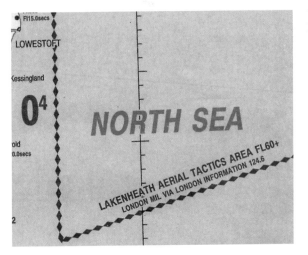

An Aerial Tactics Area, extending from FL60 to FL245

Air-to-Air Refuelling Area (AARA); **Military Training Areas** (MTA) and **Military Temporary Reserved Airspace**. These areas are located in upper airspace (i.e. above FL245) and so do not usually concern the private pilot. Details are found in the ENR section.

Airspace Restrictions and Hazards

Military Low Flying System. Although the military low-level flying system extends across the whole of the UK below 2000ftAGL, in practice military aircraft are directed to avoid controlled airspace, ATZs, built-up areas and other sensitive locations. For these and other reasons, low-level military aircraft tend to congregate in certain corridors, especially approaching danger areas and tactical training areas.

The best defence against an encounter with high-speed military aircraft is to avoid the low levels at which they tend to fly

Military aircraft are normally subject to a 'Minimum Separation Distance' of 250ft, although in three specially designated areas (located in Mid-Wales, SW Scotland and the North of Scotland) a few specially authorised and briefed flights may go as low as 100ft MSD. In practice the greatest concentration of military low flying takes place in the height band of 250-600ft MSD.

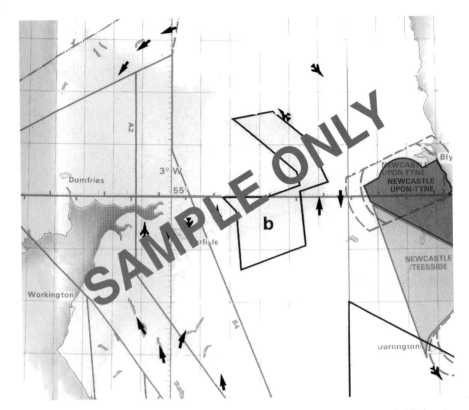

A section from a chart found in the AIP showing elements of the Military Low Flying System

Military fast-jet aircraft usually travel in this height band at around 450knots (although they may temporarily accelerate to 550 knots), are camouflaged and are being specifically flown in such a way as to avoid detection by radar and other aircraft. Therefore even a pilot maintaining a very good lookout will have difficulty seeing and avoiding such machinery. Elements of the military low-level flying system are depicted on a chart found in the ENR section of the AIP, although in practice military low flying may take place almost anywhere outside controlled airspace. All in all, civil pilots are well advised to fly above 2000ft wherever possible, and when arriving at or departing from an airfield outside controlled airspace should remain below 1000ft for as short a time as possible. Remaining within the ATZ whilst climbing or descending should in theory give protection from low-flying military aircraft although, in practice, the occasional infringement is not unknown. Military low-level flying tends to take place mostly during weekdays in daylight hours.

Low-flying military aircraft tend to fly in pairs – if you spot one, look for its companion

Airspace Restrictions and Hazards

A low-level 'Civil Aircraft Notification Procedure' (CANP) exists so that civil aircraft intending to operate at low level can advise their flight details on a freephone number. Military flights will then be advised of these details and will be able to avoid the area. The full CANP procedure is set out in the AIP and AICs.

Aircraft planning to operate at low level (such as this crop-spraying helicopter) can advise the military of their flight details using the Civil Aircraft Notification Procedure

Military Aerodrome Traffic Zone (MATZ). Most active military airfields in the UK are surrounded by a MATZ. A MATZ theoretically has a standard shape and dimensions, although in practice there are quite a few variations on the shape in particular. Additionally, where two or more military airfields are close together they may have a combined MATZ (CMATZ). The upper limit of 3000ft is measured from aerodrome level. In the case of a CMATZ the ceiling is 3000ft above the highest aerodrome.

MILITARY AERODROME TRAFFIC ZONE (MATZ)

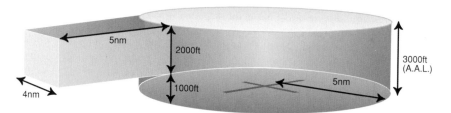

The standard dimensions of a MATZ

Civilian flights wishing to enter a MATZ are *strongly* recommended to contact the controlling ATSU and obtain some form of air traffic service – however, this is not mandatory. MATZs tend to be active on a 9-5, Monday-to-Friday basis – although you should always make a radio call to check if it is active. Remember that the ATZ at a military aerodrome is active during the notified hours (usually H24) regardless of whether or not the MATZ or ATSU is active.

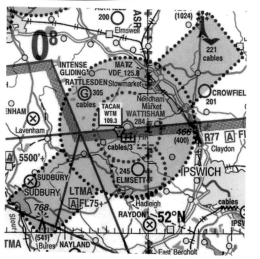

A MATZ with two 'stubs'

AN ATZ WITHIN A MATZ

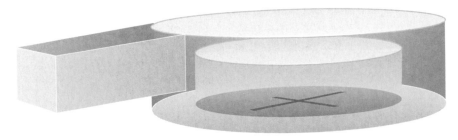

Remember that the ATZ at the vast majority of military airfields is active 24 hours a day, even when the MATZ is inactive

Small Arms Ranges. The ENR section of the AIP contains details of known small-arms ranges, which might be a hazard to aircraft flying below 500ft AGL. These ranges do not attract danger-area status and so are not marked on topographical aeronautical charts, although they are listed in the ENR section of the AIP.

Free-Fall Parachuting Sites. The ENR section of the AIP lists sites where regular free-fall parachuting from as high as FL150 takes place, and these areas are marked on the CAA charts. A parachutist in free fall can be almost impossible to spot, and free-fall parachuting may also take place at night at some sites. Parachutists tend to be dropped up-wind of their intended landing site.

LEFT> A depiction of a parachuting area on a CAA aeronautical chart

RIGHT> Parachutists are best given a wide berth, whether they are in the air or landing

Glider Launching Sites. Glider launching takes place at designated sites which are regarded as aerodromes (several aerodromes also operate both gliders and powered aircraft together). Gliders may be launched by aerotow or by ground winch, in which case the cables are often carried up to 2000ft AGL or even higher at some designated sites.

RIGHT> The glider aerodrome of Tibenham, where gliders may be winch-launched up to 3000ft. Gliders can be difficult to spot in the air and the launch cables are almost impossible to see unless you are much too close.

Hang Glider and Parascending Sites. Hanggliders/paragliders may be winch-launched, with the cables reaching 2000ft AGL or higher at notified sites. These sites are listed in the ENR section of the AIP and marked on aeronautical charts.

LEFT> Hang-glider sites are often found along cliffs, hills and ridges

RIGHT> Although hang gliders can fly 'cross-country', they tend to be launched and remain on the up-wind side of cliffs and ridges

Microlight Flying Sites. Sites of intensive microlight flying are detailed in the ENR section and are marked on CAA charts. Microlight flying may also take place at an aerodrome where other activities (such as powered flying) take place and also at sites not marked on CAA charts.

A microlight airfield at Sutton Meadows

Bird Hazards and Bird Sanctuaries. There are no defined bird migratory routes in the UK, although they maybe found in other countries. Bird sanctuaries which are marked on aeronautical charts (together with an upper limit as an altitude) and listed in the AIP, should be avoided – particularly during the stated breeding season.

The bird sanctuary at Havergate, effective up to 2000ft AMSL. These areas really are best avoided, and not just for ecological reasons. A bird strike can cause a surprisingly large amount of damage to an aeroplane – and the bird usually comes off even worse...

High Intensity Radio Transmission Areas. A HIRTA is an area where intense radio energy may interfere with (and on rare occasions actually damage) the aircraft radio equipment. HIRTAs are listed in the ENR section and marked on CAA charts if their radius exceeds 0.5nm. Their vertical limit is shown in thousands of feet AMSL. On a similar topic, Airborne Early Warning (AEW) aircraft operate in Europe. Due to possible radiation hazards, these should always be avoided by at least 1km laterally and 1000ft vertically.

The High Intensity Radio Transmission Area at Tacolneston, effective up to 3300ft AMSL

▶ Temporary Hazards

Hazards of a temporary nature (e.g. air displays, military exercises, etc.) are notified by NOTAM as 'Temporary Navigation Warnings'. Additionally, hazardous activities may take place inside the ATZ of an aerodrome not normally available to civilian aircraft, without any prior notification.

A sample preflight bulletin showing various temporary hazards

```
AB 5229
            0900-0930 1100-1130 1300-1330 1500-1530   1500ft agl  (J3984/97)
            ROWLEY REGIS: quarry blasting 5229N 00202W 1   2nm

AB 5230
            0500-2300   495ft agl   (N303/97)
            DUDLEY: Balloon 5230N 00204W ra    5

AB 5234
            1630-1800   3500ft agl   J3 93/98
            WATTON: PJE 5234N 00052E   ad 3nm

AB 5238a
            0700-1800   U           (H2103/97)
            LEICESTER:    a  s ades from one of following sites:- 5236N
            00102W  525   00111W, 5238N 00110W

AB 5251
                 5 1145-1245   FL245    (H1121/98)
            Air  TLP 98/5 East Anglia and over targets chosed fm 5247N
            00045E (West Raynham) 5221N 00046E (Honington) 5208N 00057E
            (Wattisham) 5239N 00033E (Marham) 5205N 00124E (Woodbridge)
            5208N 00126E (Bentwaters) 5243N 00128E (Neatishead) 5245N 00121E
```

▶ Royal Flights

A Royal Flight can be a civilian or military flight carrying certain members of the British Royal Family, or some reigning sovereigns or Heads of State from other countries. A Royal Flight in a fixed-wing aircraft always takes place in what is known as 'Purple Airspace'. Wherever possible the flight utilises controlled airspace and special ATC procedures apply. When a Royal Flight takes place in class C, D, E, F or G airspace, a 'Purple Airway' which is normally 10nm wide, is established. Where a class A airspace CTR does not exist at the aerodrome to be used, a 'Purple CTR' is established – normally with a radius of 10nm from the centre of the aerodrome, although it may use the same dimensions as a Class D CTR. Purple Airspace is usually notified as Class A airspace, and it exists from fifteen minutes before to thirty minutes after the arrival/departure/passage of the Royal Flight.

A Royal Flight in a helicopter will normally be allocated a Royal Low Level Corridor (RLLC). Although specific rules apply to military aircraft, civilian aircraft are only required to keep a good lookout and maintain adequate separation from the royal helicopter. Flights carrying members of the royal family and other VIPs tend to use the radio callsigns "Kittyhawk" or "Ascot".

Advance notification of Royal Flights is given by an R. NOTAM, which will give full details of the flight, including special procedures to be followed by all aircraft during the Royal Flight, the route and an ETA for various waypoints and turning points.

Airspace Restrictions and Hazards

```
--------------------------------------------------------------------
FREEPHONE     A FREEPHONE service providing abbreviated details of Royal
              Flight NOTAM, Red Arrows Temporary Restricted Areas and other
              Temporary Restrictions of Flying is available on 0500 354802.
              Information is also available on the AIS Web site
              WWW.AIS.ORG.UK. Full details of all activity is available from
              AIS Central Office Tel 020 8745 3464.

              ROYAL FLIGHTS                    SEE ROYAL FLIGHT NOTAM for Details
R 95
              Sandringham House 1000 to Peterborough Lido 1014/1140
              to Kensington Palace 1208

              --------------------------------------------------------
```

Notification of a Royal Flight on the AIS website

As Royal Flights sometimes take place at short notice, and as R NOTAMS are not as widely available as other NOTAMS, a special freephone number has been established so that you can always check on Royal Flights during your flight planning. The number is **0500 354802.** As mentioned earlier, on this number you can also obtain information regarding Temporary Restricted Airspace such as that to be used for Red Arrows displays or areas with an Emergency Restriction Of Flying.

▶ Obstacles

It is widely accepted that a flight will pass more smoothly if the aircraft does not fly into an obstruction between the departure and destination airfields. Obstacles such as buildings, works or waste heaps which exceed a height of 300ft AGL are listed in the ENR section of the AIP. Land-based obstructions in excess of 300ft AGL are marked on CAA aeronautical charts, although the charts also depict a number of lower obstructions considered to be useful landmarks to aviators. The position of the obstruction is marked together with its height AGL and altitude AMSL. Exceptionally high obstacles (1000ft or more AGL) are depicted slightly differently from lower obstacles, with rather grander symbology. You should be aware that some very tall obstructions such as radio or television transmitter masts may be supported by wires spreading out a considerable distance from the top and sides of the mast. These should be given a very wide berth indeed.

The wires that support very tall masts can be almost impossible to spot from the air, but are quite capable of downing an aircraft. Avoid all tall masts by a good margin

Obstructions exceeding a height of 492ft AGL (150m) must be lit, although certain obstacles of 150m or less in height may be lit if they present a hazard to aircraft, particularly if they are close to an aerodrome. Obstacles over 492ft in height are lit by high-intensity flashing white lights by day and night. Should the lights on an obstruction exceeding 492ft fail, a NOTAM will be issued.

The depiction of obstacles on CAA topographical charts. The exceptionally high obstacle reaches 1684ft AMSL (1265ft above ground level) and is lighted. The other obstacle reaches 844ft AMSL (350ft above ground level)

Where an obstacle is annotated as a 'Flarestack', the burning-off of high-pressure gas can give a flare up to 600ft high –which may not be visible in bright sunlight. Again, give these a wide berth.

UK Procedures

Permanent offshore obstructions (oil and gas rigs, etc.) are listed in the ENR section and shown on CAA aeronautical charts regardless of their height. The vast majority are lit.

▶ Gas Venting Operations

A Gas Venting Station with a hazard altitude of 3500ft AMSL (in other words, do not fly over this site below 3500ft altitude)

At sites marked on CAA aeronautical charts and listed in the ENR section, severe turbulence may be experienced during gas venting. The chart depiction of a Gas Venting Station (GVS) will include an advisory minimum altitude for over-flight, although there's a lot to be said for going round it instead.

▶ Revision

159 What type of airspace restriction is R311/2.2 and what are its vertical limits?

160 On an aeronautical chart a danger area is marked with a pecked boundary. When is it active?

161 You are unable to contact a specified DACS for a danger area. Can you assume the danger area is inactive?

162 In what section of the AIP can you find information regarding prohibited, restricted and danger areas?

163 You realise that you are flying within a danger area – what should you do?

164 What is the extent of the UK Military Low Flying System?

165 What is the standard upper limit of a MATZ?

166 Are there any danger areas not shown on the CAA 1:500 000 aeronautical charts?

167 What is the minimum height of a land-based obstacle for it to be marked on a CAA aeronautical chart?

168 Obstructions that exceed XXX must be lit (what is the missing figure)?

Answers at LAW189

Revision Answers

▶ Legislation

1 – The land areas and adjacent territorial waters under the sovereignty, protection or mandate of the state.

2 – Yes

3 – No

4 – The Pilot-In-Command

5 – Certificate of Registration

6 – Yes

7 – Air Navigation Order

8 – The Aeronautical Information Publication (AIP), also known as the Air Pilot

9 – Monthly

▶ Rules of the Air

10 – Maintain course and speed

11 – Airships give way to balloons and gliders, but not powered aircraft.

12 – You should overtake to the right, and overtaking situation exists while you at an angle of less than 70° to the extended centreline of the other aircraft

13 – Most definitely *yes.* Constant bearing = constant danger!

14 – Left-hand

15 – The lower aircraft has right of way

16 – To the right of the aircraft already landed – you should expect it to turn left.

17 – No

18 – The aircraft commanders

19 – On your left

20 – There is no minimum height. Aerobatics are *not* permitted over a congested area at *any* height

21 – On the left

22 – No, the safety pilot must be a qualified pilot.

23 – Yes. An aircraft must not fly *closer* than 500ft to a person, vessel, vehicle or structure

24 – 1500ft above the highest fixed object within 600m (2000ft) of the aircraft, **or** high enough to glide clear, whichever is higher.

25 – No

26 – No. The land-clear requirement remains, although the pilot is exempt from the 1500ft above the highest fixed object within 600m (2000ft) requirement.

27 – The Pilot-In-Command

28 – Visual Meteorological Conditions: meteorological conditions expressed in terms of visibility, distance from cloud and ceiling, equal to or better than a specified minima.

29 – Pan Pan

30 — 7700

31 — Right-hand circuit

32 — Landing prohibited

33 — Red

34 — Red

35 — 310° (magnetic), marked in white

36 — Emergency Distance Available: The Take Off Run Available plus the stopway distance

37 — The Landing Distance Available (LDA)

38 — The runway is 'damp'

39 — Do not land, wait for permission

40 — Move clear of the landing area

41 — White flashes or white pyrotechnics, switching the navigation lights on and off, switching the landing light(s) on and off

42 — One or two solid and one or two broken yellow lines across the taxiway, the broken line being on the runway side, plus possible marker boards next to the taxiway

43 — orange and white striped markers

44 — This bay

45 — Cut engines

46 — Raise your arm horizontally in front of your face with your fist clenched, then unclench your fist and extend your fingers

47 — The part of the aerodrome provided for the take-off and landing and movement of aircraft, excluding the apron and any maintenance area

48 — Prior Permission Required

49 — Surface level

50 — 2000ft Above Aerodrome Level. The answer is the same for all ATZs; the runway length has no bearing on the vertical limit

51 — Yes. A military ATZ is active during the hours notified in the AIP, most often 24 hours a day, regardless of whether or not the ATC unit is open

52 — **No!** Black signs indicate JET A-1, fuel used in jet engines...

53 — Initially the ATSU with which you are in contact, then the interceptor aircraft on 121.5

▶Division of Airspace and Air Traffic Services

54 — Uncontrolled, advisory airspace

55 — A, B C, D and E

56 — A CTR

57 — Terminal Control Area, a CTA established where several routes merge in the vicinity of one or more major airfields

58 — Class A

59 – The objectives of the Air Traffic Services as set out in ICAO annex 11 are to:

Prevent collisions between aircraft

Prevent collisions between aircraft on the manoeuvring area and obstructions on that area

Expedite and maintain an orderly flow of air traffic

Provide advice and information of the safe and efficient conduct of flights

Notify organisations of aircraft in need of search and rescue aid, and assist such organisations

60 – An alerting service is provided to:

All aircraft receiving an ATC service

As far as practical, all aircraft having filed a flight plan or known to the ATS

Any aircraft known or believed to be subject to unlawful interference

61 – ICAO annex 11 states that aircraft within a Flight Information Region (FIR) will be provided with a flight information service and alerting service

62 – An Air Traffic Control Unit

63 – An Aerodrome Flight Information Service

64 – No

65 – 1500m (which is not a lot really)

66 – No. However radio contact with the controlling ATSU is highly recommended

67 – No. Conditions must be the VMC minima or better to permit VFR flight

68 – Flight visibility is the visibility forward from the cockpit of an aircraft in flight

69 – An odd flight level + 500, e.g. FL35, FL55, FL75, etc.

70 – Only for IFR flights. VFR flight are *recommended* to fly the correct quadrantal, for obvious reasons

71 – **NO**! Terrain clearance is the pilot's responsibility. If you hit the mountain, it will hurt you more than it hurts anyone in Air Traffic...

72 – No. The pilot is responsible for obtaining a clearance through an ATZ

73 – Class D airspace

74 – Class F airspace

▶Rules of the Air and Air Traffic Services

75 – Contact the departure ATSU. ICAO recommend that in this instance the old plan should be cancelled and a new one filed

76 – Yes! You must inform the ATSU at the intended destination within 30 minutes of your ETA there

77 – With the appropriate parent ATSU

78 – Altitude, measured from Mean Sea Level

79 – Transition Altitude

80 – FL050

81 – Aerodrome QNH

82 – The QNH of an aerodrome beneath that TMA or CTA

83 – QFE

84 – QNH

85 – 3 minutes

86 – A special air report, to the ATSU you are in contact with a soon as possible (e.g. by radio)

87 – An Air Traffic Control service for controlled flights in control areas

88 – If a pilot in command receives an air traffic control clearance that is not suitable he should request, and if practicable obtain, an amended clearance

89 – Approach Control Service

90 – The situation when the radar position of a particular aircraft is seen and identified on a radar display

91 – An Approach Control Service reduce the normal separation minima in the vicinity of aerodromes if:

adequate separation can be provided by the aerodrome controller when each aircraft is continuously visible to this controller;

each aircraft is continuously visible to the pilots-in-command of the other aircraft and the pilots can maintain their own separation;

the pilot-in-command of a following aircraft has the leading aircraft in sight and can maintain separation

92 – Aerodrome Control Service

93 – When an aircraft requests taxying permission it is normally given:

the runway in use;

the surface wind direction and speed;

the QNH altimeter setting

94 – A service provided to notify appropriate organisations regarding aircraft in need of search and rescue aid, and assist such organisations as required

95 – An air traffic advisory service

▶ Aircraft Registration

96 – The state of registry

97 – 30cm

98 – The aircraft's registration, the aircraft type, the airframe serial number and the name and address of the registered owner(s)

99 – At all times

100 – A fireproof metal identification plate showing at least the nationality and registration mark of the aircraft

101 – A 'Flying Machine'

▶ Airworthiness of Aircraft

102 – By issuing it with a Certificate of Airworthiness (C of A)

103 – Only if the permission of the state whose territory is to be overflown is obtained

104 – The C of A may be invalidated

105 – The C of MR will show the date of issue, the date or flying hours at which the next review must take place, and the signature of the issuing licensed aircraft maintenance engineer

106 – The 14th December (i.e. six months)

107 – Repairs, modifications, maintenance

108 – Yes

109 – In the Pilot's Operating Handbook / Flight Manual (POH/FM) and on placards in the cockpit

▶JAA Regulations

110 – 5 years

111 – Medical

112 – You must seek advice from the authority or an AME without delay

113 – Two years

114 – 21 days

115 – All solo, dual instruction or Pilot-In-Command (PIC) flight time flown in the same category of aircraft for which the licence or rating is sought

116 – The place where a person normally lives for at least 185 days a year for personal and occupational reasons. If a person does not have occupational ties, personal ties showing close links to the place where he or she is living may be sufficient to prove normal residency

117 – 16 years

118 – No

119 – 10 hours

120 – 10 hours

121 – 90 days

122 – 3km

123 – No

124 – The hours between the end of evening civil twilight and the beginning of morning civil twilight. Civil twilight ends in the evening when the centre of the sun's disc is six degrees below the horizon and begins in the morning when the centre of the sun's disc is six degrees below the horizon

125 – One year

126 – To pass a proficiency check four months before the expiry of the rating (it should be no more than three months)

127 – No

128 – 7th March 2002, although in practice most pilots keep all their logbooks for life

▶Operation of Aircraft

129 – A licensed crew member charged with duties essential to the operation of an aircraft during flight time

130 – The aircraft commander

131 – The aircraft commander

132 – At all times when at the controls

133 – No

134 – Only if they are safety matches

135 – No

136 – In the aircraft's POH/FM

137 – A Heading Indicator

138 – Accessible life jackets, accessible liferaft(s) and flares

139 – Two-way communications radio to maintain communication with the appropriate radio station, although this requirement may be waived if the appropriate ATC units permits it in relation to a particular flight

140 – Yes, you have right of way

141 – It is airship, it is head-on to you

▶Search and Rescue

142 – Rescue Co-ordination Centre

143 – A situation where uncertainty exists regarding the safety of an aircraft and its occupants

144 – A Rescue Co-ordination Centre

145 – Record the details of the message, inform the appropriate ATSU and – at his discretion – proceed to the position given in the distress message

146 – 121.5

147 – An X at least 2.5m (8ft) in size

▶Accident and Incident Investigation

148 – An engineer seriously injured whilst an aircraft is manoeuvred by tractor in a maintenance hanger

149 – The Pilot-In-Command, or the aircraft operator if the commander is unable to, to the AAIB and the local Police Authority

150 – To the AAIB

151 – By the quickest possible means – by radio if possible

▶Noise Abatement

152 – In the AIP or commercial flight guide

▶Contravention of Regulations

153 – With ink or indelible pencil

154 – Within a reasonable time

Revision Answers

UK Procedures

▶The Aeronautical Information Service

155 – GEN

156 – Pink

157 – No

158 – Yes

▶Airspace Restrictions and Hazards

159 – It is a restricted area, extending from ground level to 2200ft AMSL

160 – When notified by NOTAM

161 – No. You should avoid the danger area because it may be active

162 – In the ENR section of the AIP

163 – You must leave the area (without descending) by the shortest route

164 – Across the whole of the UK up to 2000ft AGL

165 – 3000ft AAL

166 – Yes. Danger areas such as rifle ranges, whose upper limit does not exceed 500ft AGL are not shown on these charts, but are listed in the AIP

167 – 300ft AGL

168 – 492ft AGL (150m)

Air Law Appendix
ICAO Definitions

Aerial Work	An aircraft operation such as agriculture, construction, photography, surveying, observation and patrol, search and rescue, advertisement etc.
Aerodrome Control Service	An air traffic control service for aerodrome traffic.
Aerodrome Control Tower	A unit to provide air traffic control service to aerodrome traffic.
Aerodrome Traffic Circuit	The specified path to be flown by aircraft operating in the vicinity of an aerodrome.
Aerodrome Traffic	All traffic on the manoeuvring area of an aerodrome and all aircraft flying in the vicinity of an aerodrome.
Aeroplane	A power-driven heavier-than-air aircraft, deriving its lift principally from aerodynamic reaction against fixed surfaces.
Air Traffic Control Clearance	An authorisation for an aircraft to proceed under conditions specified by an air traffic control unit
Aircraft	Any machine that can derive support from the reactions of the air, other than the reaction of the air against the earth's surface.
Alert phase	A situation where apprehension exists regarding the safety of an aircraft and its occupants.
Alerting service	A service provided to notify appropriate organisations regarding aircraft in need of search and rescue aid, and assist such organisations as required.
Alternate Aerodrome	An aerodrome to which an aircraft may proceed when it becomes impossible or inadvisable to proceed to or land at the aerodrome on intended landing.
Approach Control Service	An air traffic control service for arriving and departing controlled flights.
Approach sequence	The order in which two or more aircraft are cleared to approach to land at an aerodrome.
Area Control Service	An Air Traffic Control service for controlled flights in control areas.
Commercial Air Transport Operation	An aircraft operation involving the transport of passengers, cargo or mail for remuneration or hire.
Control Areas	Controlled airspace extending upwards from a specified limit above the earth.
Controlled Flight	A flight which is subject to an air traffic control clearance.
Dangerous Goods	Articles or substances capable of posing a significant risk of health, safety or property when transported by air.

Distress phase	A situation where there is reasonable certainty that an aircraft and its occupants are threatened by grave and imminent danger or require immediate assistance.
Ditching	The forced landing of an aircraft on water.
Emergency phase	A generic term covering an uncertainty, alert or distress phase.
Flight Crew Member	A licensed crew member charged with duties essential to the operation of an aircraft during flight time.
Flight Information Service	A service provided for the purpose of giving advice and information useful for the safe and efficient conduct of flights.
Flight Time	The time from the moment an aircraft first moves under its own power for the purpose of taking-off until it comes to rest at the end of the flight.
General Aviation Operation	An aircraft operation other than a Commercial Air Transport Operation or Aerial Work.
Incident	An occurrence, other than an accident, associated with the operation of an aircraft which affects or could affect the safety of operation.
Instrument Meteorological Conditions (IMC)	Meteorological conditions expressed in terms of visibility, distance from cloud and ceiling, less than a specified minima.
Minimum Fuel	A situation where an aircraft's fuel has reached the state where little or no delay can be accepted.
Night	The hours between the end of evening civil twilight and the beginning of morning civil twilight. Civil twilight ends in the evening when the centre of the sun's disc is six degrees below the horizon and begins in the morning when the centre of the sun's disc is six degrees below the horizon.
Overtaking	An overtaking situation exists while the overtaking aircraft is approaching another from the rear within an angle of less than 70° from the plane of symmetry of the aircraft being overtaken.
Pilot-In-Command	The pilot responsible for the operation and safety of the aircraft during Flight Time.
Radar approach	An approach where the final approach phase is conducted under the direction of a radar controller.
Radar contact	The situation when the radar position of a particular aircraft is seen and identified on a radar display.
Radar identification	The situation when the radar position of a particular aircraft on a radar display is positively identified by an air traffic controller.

Radar vectoring	The provision of navigational guidance to aircraft, in the form of specific headings, based on the use of radar.
Rescue Co-ordination Centre	A unit responsible for promoting the efficient organisation of a search and rescue service and co-ordinating search and rescue operations within a search and rescue region.
Search and Rescue Region	An area of defined dimensions within which a search and rescue service is provided.
Serious Incident	An incident involving circumstances indicating that an accident nearly occurred.
Serious Injury	An injury sustained by a person in an accident and which:
	Involves 2nd or 3rd degree burns, or any burns affecting more than 5% of the body surface
	Involves injury to any internal organ
	Involves lacerations causing severe haemorrhage, nerve, muscle or tendon damage
	Involves verified exposure to infectious substances or harmful radiation
	Requires hospitalisation for more than 48 hours, commencing within seven days of the date of injury
	Results in a bone fracture (except simple fractures of fingers, toes or nose)
State of registry	The state on whose register an aircraft is entered.
Traffic Avoidance Advice	Advice provided by an ATSU specifying manoeuvres to assist a pilot to avoid a collision.
Traffic Information	Information issued by an ATSU to alert a pilot to other known or observed air traffic which may be in the proximity of the flight or its intended route, and to help the pilot to avoid a collision.
Uncertainty phase	A situation where uncertainty exists regarding the safety of an aircraft and its occupants.
Visual Meteorological Conditions (VMC)	Meteorological conditions expressed in terms of visibility, distance from cloud and ceiling, equal to or better than a specified minima.

Air Traffic Services

The objectives of the Air Traffic Services are to:
- Prevent collisions between aircraft
- Prevent collisions between aircraft on the manoeuvring area and obstructions on that area
- Expedite and maintain an orderly flow of air traffic
- Provide advice and information of the safe and efficient conduct of flights
- Notify organisations of aircraft in need of search and rescue aid, and assist such organisations

Alerting Service

An alerting service will be provided to:

1 All aircraft receiving an ATC service

2 As far as practical, all aircraft having filed a flight plan or known to the ATS

3 Any aircraft known or believed to be subject to unlawful interference.

Control Zone

A Control Zone should extend at least 5nm from the centre of the airfield in the directions from which approaches may be made.

Flight Plans

If a flight plan has been submitted, and a departure delay of more than 30 minutes then occurs, a new flight plan should be submitted and the old one cancelled.

Air Law Appendix
JAR Glossary

Class Rating	A rating to fly single-pilot aeroplanes not requiring a type rating
Proficiency Check	A demonstration of skill to revalidate or renew a rating, including oral questions as the examiner requires.
Renewal	Administrative action taken after a rating has lapsed to renew the privileges of that rating for a set period, upon completing specified requirements.
Revalidation	Administrative action taken within the period of validity of that rating that allows the holder to continue to exercise the privileges of that rating for a further set period, upon fulfilling specified requirements.
Single-Pilot Aeroplanes	Aeroplanes certified for use by one pilot.
Skill Test	A demonstration of knowledge and skill for initial licence issue, rating issue or renewal.
Solo flight time	Flight time during which a student pilot is the sole occupant of the aircraft.
Type Rating	A rating to fly a specific type of aeroplane, normally (but not always) an aeroplane not covered by a class rating.

Air Law Appendix
JAR Abbreviations

CRE	Class Rating Examiner
CRI	Class Rating Instructor
FCL	Flight Crew Licensing
FE	Flight Examiner
FI	Flight Instructor
FTO	Flight Training Organisation
JAA	Joint Aviation Authorities
JAR	Joint Aviation Requirements
ME	Multi-engine aeroplanes
MEP	Multi-engine Piston aeroplanes
PPL (A)	Private Pilot Licence (Aeroplane)
SE	Single-engine aeroplanes
SEP	Single-engine Piston aeroplanes
SPA	Single-pilot Aeroplane
TR	Type Rating

Communications introduction

I know that you think you heard what you thought I said; however; I don't think you realise that what I said is not what you thought you heard

(RAF flight safety poster ©1973).

The Aim Of The Communications (RT) Section

It's not an uncommon scenario. During an early flying lesson, the student pilot goes through the starting procedures and is ready to taxy. At this point the instructor presses a small button hidden somewhere in the cockpit and transmits something along the lines of:

"Golf Michaelangelo whispering klingons, situation over bar the frying pan apron, free quest hair field de part-sure in formation hand taxy destruction. Over."

While the student is still trying to get a grip on the meaning of this, a stream of similar nonsense materialises out of the ether and into the student's headset. This obviously has some significance to the instructor, because she/he nods meaningfully and makes some notes on a pad. Then some form of reply goes back:

"Rogers got that. Queue and ache ones hero two trees, quiffy ones hero one time, taxy two runaway in puce zero height, golf whisk-key key low."

This procedure is repeated at regular intervals throughout the flight, while the student thinks something along the lines of "The flying is straight-forward enough, but this radio business is going to need some real hard work". The student is even more bemused when the instructor insists that the authorised language for aviation radio communications is English...

The communications section of the PPL course has two aims. Firstly to demystify the procedures and phrases used on the radio – after which the whole procedure becomes far more understandable – and secondly to equip you to pass the simple written and practical test necessary for the grant of a Flight Radio Telephony Operator's licence.

The basics of radio phrases and procedures are easy enough once you understand the standard phrases and conventions used. It's not unlike learning the basics of another language; once you can use a simple phrase ("I'd like a beer please") and can anticipate the sort of reply you are going to receive ("Here it is, that will be two pounds please") a lot of the fear goes out of the process. If you have an air-band radio, listening to everyday conversation on aviation frequencies is very useful and to some extent can save you trying to learn radio procedures and learn to fly the aircraft simultaneously.

Use Of This Publication

The first four chapters of this publication 'Pre-flight, General operating procedures, Air Traffic Service Units, Callsigns, Abbreviations, General procedures' cover the basics and ensure that you can start using the radio under the guidance of your instructor.

The next three chapters 'Departure procedures, En-route procedures, Arrival/traffic pattern procedures' deal more with the specific phraseology used in various stages of the flight. Work through these chapters as your flying course progresses and you use the radio more and more

The last two chapters 'Communications failure and Emergency procedures' deal with events which one hopes occur rarely in everyday flying. Nevertheless you should fully understand these procedures before you start your solo cross-country flights, and to pass the FRTO exams you will have to be word-perfect on the emergency procedures in particular.

General Points

Under CAA regulations you can use the radio while a student pilot. However, once you have a PPL, you can only use the radio if you hold a valid FRTO licence. It therefore makes sense to pass the RT exams before the completion of your PPL course.

This publication concentrates on radiotelephony (RT) procedures applicable to the VFR pilot i.e. a student pilot or a pilot without instrument qualifications. For this reason, phraseology and procedures relating specifically to IFR operations (flight in airways, instrument approaches etc.) are not covered here. Bear in mind also that RT procedures and phrases do change from time-to-time, so it is worth keeping up-to-date with current usage.

Pilots, controllers and so on are mostly referred to throughout this book by the pronoun 'he'. This has been done purely to avoid the cumbersome and repetitive use of 'he or she'. I ask for the understanding of female readers; the English language has not yet arrived at a generally accepted resolution of what is obviously an unsatisfactory position.

A final point at this stage. Once you know the standard RT phrases and procedures, it pays to stick to them. Few things are more frustrating to pilots and controllers alike than a 'Walter Mitty' character who monopolises the RT with long monologues about his flight, himself in general and his favourite non-standard phraseology. We've all heard them, and you will too. Most pilots prefer to treat the RT as an aid to the safety of their flight, not an excuse to hear their own voice, and their fellow RT users are grateful for that. After all, wouldn't you prefer to be flying an aeroplane rather than talking about it?

Pre-Flight

Communications

Pre-flight

▶ Introduction to VHF Radio

▶ Use of the AIP

▶ Use of Aircraft Radio Equipment

▶ Revision

Communications

▶Introduction to VHF Radio

The vast majority of civil aeronautical radio communications take place in what is known as the VHF ('Very High Frequency') band. In a formal technical sense, 'VHF' implies frequencies between 30 and 300MHz; the "Hz" is a unit of frequency, and one MHz (or *Mega*hertz) is a frequency of one million cycles per second. Within this range, the section between 118 and 137MHz is allocated for aeronautical communications. Small airfields may have a single frequency allocated to them, whereas larger aerodromes and airports may use several for different services (e.g. ground movement, tower, approach etc.). At an exceptionally busy airfield such as London Heathrow, a specific service may be available on more than one frequency. Frequencies are usually quoted in a form such as "124.15" (or as an air-traffic controller would say, "one two four decimal one five"), where the portion to the left of the decimal point refers to MHz and the digits to the right of the decimal point refer to *kilo*hertz or thousands of Hz. The abbreviation for the latter is "kHz". Frequency allocations in the civil aeronautical VHF band as used by General Aviation (GA) are spaced 25kHz apart, so the frequencies immediately adjacent to 124.15MHz would be 124.125 and 124.175MHz. However, frequencies used in Airways and upper airspace (mostly the preserve of airliners and the like) are now being allocated with an 8.33kHz spacing. There is specific phraseology to be spoken when using 8.33 frequency spacing, which is described later.

LEFT> Aeronautical VHF frequencies are quoted in MHz and decimals of MHz (i.e. kHz)

RIGHT> At present, most aeronautical VHF frequencies are allocated in 25kHz steps

MHz	kHz
124	**.150**

124.125
124.150
124.175
124.200
124.225

The range of VHF communications is a function of the fact that at frequencies above about 70MHz, radio waves behave very much like light rays; that is, they travel in straight lines and can be blocked by obstacles. In consequence, it is often said that the range of a VHF radio system is 'line-of-sight', implying that in order to communicate, the stations must be able to see each other. In actual fact this is not strictly true; VHF radio waves travel slightly beyond the visible horizon as a result of refraction in the troposphere. This has the effect of slightly bending them back towards the earth. However, the line-of-sight assumption is reliable and conservative. Look out from an aircraft on a perfectly clear day, and any point you can see should be within VHF communication range.

As you might intuitively expect, the higher an aircraft is above the ground, the further the theoretical range to a ground-based receiving station (because the visible horizon is further away). For example, if an aircraft is flying at an altitude of 2000ft, it can in principle contact a ground station at least 56nm away. If the aircraft is at 10,000ft, the theoretical range is 125nm. Having said that, it is worth mentioning that VHF radio range is also slightly affected by other factors such as the sensitivity of the receivers involved, the power of the transmitters and the siting and height of the ground transmitter's antenna above the local terrain.

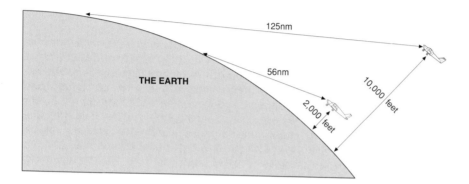

125nm

THE EARTH

56nm

10,000 feet

2,000 feet

The higher an aircraft flies, the greater the range of VHF communications

Because the range of VHF communications is restricted by the line-of-sight principle, more than one ground station can use the same frequency provided there is a degree of geographical separation. Such frequency sharing is necessary in any event, because there are far more VHF ground stations than separate frequencies available for them. At the time of writing, for example, RAF Marham Lower Airspace Radar Service (LARS) and Plymouth Military LARS use a frequency of 124.15MHz. By virtue of their distance from each other (Norfolk and Devon respectively) interference is not usually a problem.

Occasionally VHF transmissions travel a good deal further than would be expected. There are two main reasons for this.

A phenomenon known as 'tropospheric ducting' or 'duct propagation' is caused by the temperature inversion sometimes associated with a persistent anticyclone. These ducts can disperse VHF signals over distances of anything up to 500nm or so at low level. Ducting can lead to unexpected results; you may call a ground station a short distance away and be unable to make contact with it, but hear transmissions from another station which is several hundred miles away. Ducts can persist for several days, and are usually responsible for the widespread interference to television reception which can take place during October or November.

A different and little-understood phenomenon is called 'sporadic E', which in European latitudes occurs in May and June each year. It can cause VHF signals to be reflected by ionized clouds of metallic material at altitudes of 90-100km and travel anything up to 1000nm or so. The onset of Sporadic E is very sudden, and it typically lasts only a matter of minutes.

Communications

Apart from these occasional circumstances, VHF is considered to be unaffected by other weather conditions that can cause static on lower frequencies. You may hear some interference if you fly in the vicinity of a large and heavily charged cumulo-nimbus cloud (i.e. a thunderstorm). However, in a light aircraft, interference to radio reception under these circumstances is likely to be the least of your concerns. For completeness, it should be added that intense magnetic storms or aurora can occasionally cause problems with VHF reception, especially in the more northerly latitudes.

▶ Use of the AIP

Before you can use the aircraft's radio to talk to someone, you need to know what frequency to tune it to. The primary reference for aeronautical radio communications frequencies in the UK is the Aeronautical Information Publication (AIP). This can be checked when planning a flight, and the appropriate frequencies noted. In the AD section the frequencies for each licensed airfield are listed as part of the airfield entry, together with the type of service, frequency and hours of watch. This information can change and new frequencies can be introduced, so you should always check pre-flight bulletins and NOTAMs for amendments or temporary changes. The ENR section of the AIP contains radio frequency information, particularly in respect of danger and restricted areas, Military Aerodrome Traffic Zones (MATZs), the Lower Airspace Radar Service (LARS) and airways. Contact frequencies are also found on aeronautical charts, which can be useful if you need a quick reference when you are airborne. However, there is a greater risk of information from these being out-of-date. Although charts are regarded as remaining valid for up to two years, some frequencies will undoubtedly change within this period. Commercial flight guides also carry frequency information, and may be the only source for many unlicensed airfields.

Cambridge	
APP	123.60
RAD	124.975
VDF	123.60
TWR	122.20
NDB	CAM 332.50*
ILS/DME	I-CMG 111.30 Rwy23**
	*on A/D, range 15nm
	**on A/D

Cambridge radio frequency information box as it appears in the 'UK VFR Flight Guide'

Given that several different ground stations may use the same frequency, it is sensible not to plan to contact an airfield at extreme range because you may cause unnecessary interference to a different station operating on the same frequency. Frequency channels at an international airport are usually 'protected', which means that they are guaranteed to be free from interference under normal circumstances as follows:

Tower: up to a range of 25nm and a height of 4000ft

Approach: up to a range of 25nm and a height of 10,000ft

At other airfields, the CAA recommends that communications should be restricted to the immediate vicinity of the airfield, and heights below 1000ft; and in any case not more than 10nm from the airfield nor above 3000ft.

En-route frequency channels, such as those used for communication in controlled airspace, are normally protected to the limits of the unit's area of responsibility.

▶ Use of Aircraft Radio Equipment

As you might expect, aircraft radios are like any other sort of radios insofar as they come in various different models and can be very basic, extremely sophisticated or anything in between. In general terms, however, the controls tend to be fairly standard, as follows:

On/Off Switch: Sometimes combined with the volume control. There is not very much to say about this switch, although one point is worth noting. It is standard practice to switch off *all* items of aircraft avionics before starting the engine(s), and again before closing down the engine(s). The reason is that the starter motor of an engine can generate very large voltage surges in the aircraft's wiring, which could damage electronic circuitry if it happened to be switched on at the time.

A radio with a separate off/on switch and volume control

Volume: This control alters **only** the received volume **not** the power of the signal transmitted from the radio. A common error in relation to the volume control is to turn the volume down for some reason, then forget to turn it back up again. The result is that the aircraft does not receive other radio transmissions but its own transmissions still go out as normal. The volume control is rotated *clockwise* to *increase* volume, *anti-clockwise* to *decrease* volume.

A radio with a combined off/on/volume control

Most volume controls rotate clockwise to increase volume, anti-clockwise to decrease volume

Frequency Selection: Rotary switching of some sort is normally used to select frequency. It is quite common for the frequency-setting control to consist of two concentric knobs. The outer selects MHz (e.g. 124, 125, 126 etc.) and the inner selects kHz (.15, .17, .20 etc.). Rotary controls of this type rotate *clockwise* to *increase* frequency and *anti-clockwise* to *decrease* frequency. The kHz selector usually operates on a continuous basis, so that for example you could change frequency from 119.97 to 120.02 with one step of each knob. In the case of some radios, you may need to operate a separate switch to select 25kHz spacing, or it may be necessary to pull and twist a part of the frequency-selection dial.

1 The outer dial of the frequency control selects MHz – 120, 121, 122 etc.

2 The inner dial of the frequency control selects kHz – .80, .82, .85 etc.

Communications

More modern radios may have a memory, for retaining up to three commonly used frequencies, and some have a 'flip-flop' feature. With this, the next frequency to be used is selected in advance without altering the existing frequency in use. When the time comes, you press the flip-flop button and the standby frequency becomes the active frequency.

1 On this radio the frequency control changes the 'standby' frequency

2 To select 25 kHz spacing, the kHz control is pulled out

3 To change the standby frequency to the in-use frequency, the 'flip-flop' button is pushed once

Squelch: The squelch control is used to adjust the level at which the receiver mutes in the absence of a signal. In use, you rotate the control so that the loud background hiss heard when a station stops transmitting just disappears. At this setting, the receiver should be as sensitive to incoming transmissions as possible without producing a constant background noise when there are none. If required, the squelch can be turned fully up to check the receiver's volume setting; set the volume so that the hiss is at a comfortable level. Many radios have an automatic squelch facility together with a test facility for checking the receiver volume.

Intercom: Virtually all modern aircraft are fitted with an intercom, which allows direct communication between those wearing a headset. Speech on the intercom is only heard by those in the aircraft; it is not transmitted on the frequency in use. The volume of most simple intercom systems is not adjustable by the pilot. Some aircraft, however, have more elaborate intercoms, with on/off and volume selection.

Audio Selector Box: An aircraft with several radio sets may be fitted with an Audio Selector Box. This allows the pilot to control which radios he is listening to or transmitting on. Once the radios have been turned on and set-up as required, the pilot uses the audio selector box switches to choose which radio is used for various functions. The box also allows the pilot to direct the radio output to headphones or the aircraft's speaker.

Two examples of an audio selector box. Both work in much the same way

LEFT> This audio box is set so that radio 'COM1' will transmit

RIGHT> This audio box is set so that radio 'COM2' will transmit

Each radio has its own switch on the audio selector box. This switch is used to select which radio to listen to, and routes the audio output from that radio to the speaker or headsets. A separate switch dictates which radio will transmit. An audio selector box can disconcert the unwary, and it is necessary to pay special attention to the manner in which it is set up. Otherwise you may find yourself listening to one radio but transmitting on another, which is probably set to a different frequency – to the considerable confusion of all concerned. The more sensible boxes feature an 'Auto' position, which ensures that the radio selected for transmission is automatically selected for reception as well.

Hand-Held Microphone: It is thankfully rare for hand-held microphones to be used in modern training aircraft. Using such a device can be inconvenient (requiring the pilot to take one hand from the controls to hold and operate it) and the high level of noise inside a light aircraft can make a radio conversation from the radio speaker difficult to hear. The microphone is operated from a PTT (Press To Talk) switch normally found on the front or side of the microphone unit.

Despite these reservations, many pilots tend to carry a hand-held microphone for use in the event of a headset failure or if headsets are not available. Airline pilots also commonly use microphones when in the cruise, since even the lightest headset can become uncomfortable during a long flight. Of course airliner cockpits also tend to be a good deal quieter than those of most light aircraft. If you have to use a hand-held microphone, try to speak across it rather than directly into it for best results.

Headsets: Headsets are normally used in most modern aircraft. The headset consists of two main features: a set of small speakers (headphones) mounted in some form of sound-absorbent material and lightly held over the pilot's ears; and a microphone held in front of the pilot's mouth with a boom. The headset frees up the hands and reduces the noise levels heard by the pilot, making it easier to hear and understand the radio. In fact, given the high noise levels inside many light aircraft, it is worth remembering that a headset will also offer significant hearing protection.

Many modern headsets have their own volume control, and some even have a separate volume control for each ear. Headsets are connected to the intercom via one or two standard sockets. Where there are two, as in most light aircraft, they are of different sizes so that the microphone plug cannot be inadvertently plugged into the headphone socket and vice-versa. When inserting or removing the headset plugs, **always** take care to grip the plug itself rather than the wires. Otherwise the wires inside the plug can be pulled loose.

When wearing a headset, you make a transmission by pressing a spring-loaded PTT switch which is usually located on the control wheel or control column. When the PTT switch is pressed, the microphone is live and transmitting on the selected frequency. Unlike a telephone conversation, only one person can talk on a radio frequency at a time. While one station is transmitting, no other is able to. If two stations accidentally transmit simultaneously, the result is a high-pitched squeal heard by everyone else on that frequency.

One minor point you might like to ponder is that someone recently worked out that up to 230 separate infections and diseases are transmissible via a headset. For this reason alone you might like to consider buying your own quite early in your flying career!

Communications

When the pilot completes his message, the PTT is released and the transmission ends. It occasionally happens that a PTT sticks in the transmitting position. If this happens:

a) everything said on the intercom or within the cockpit is transmitted.

b) nobody else can transmit on the frequency.

'Permanent transmit' can also occur if the headset plugs are not fully pressed home.

The consequences of a stuck PTT vary from the highly entertaining (depending what is being said in the aircraft) to the dangerous (if a busy frequency is blocked for some time).

▶ Revision

Revision questions are printed at the end of each chapter in this book. The aim of the revision questions is to enable you to test your knowledge of the chapter subject, and help you retain the principal elements of each subject.

Attempt the revision questions once you are satisfied that you have understood and learnt the main points of each chapter. You should aim for a 'success' rate of around 80%.

1 As an aircraft flies higher, what is the effect on the range of VHF communications?

2 Which sections of the AIP contains information on aeronautical radio frequencies?

3 What frequency is selected if a radio is set to 125.17?

4 When the PTT is depressed, who will receive the transmission?

   Answers at RT101

General Operating Procedures

▶ **The Phonetic Alphabet**

▶ **Transmission of Numbers and Transmission of Time**

▶ **Transmitting Technique**

▶ **Revision**

Communications

▶The Phonetic Alphabet

A standard phonetic alphabet in which each letter is given a name and specific pronunciation has been developed. The phonetic alphabet is internationally recognised, even when English is not being spoken.

Letter	Phonetic Word	Pronunciation
A	Alpha	**AL** FAH
B	Bravo	**BRAH VOH**
C	Charlie	**CHAR** LEE
D	Delta	**DELL** TAH
E	Echo	**ECK** OH
F	Foxtrot	**FOKS** TROT
G	Golf	GOLF
H	Hotel	HOH **TELL**
I	India	**IN** DEE AH
J	Juliett	**JEW** LEE **ETT**
K	Kilo	**KEY** LOH
L	Lima	**LEE** MAH
M	Mike	MIKE
N	November	NO **VEM** BER
O	Oscar	**OSS** CAH
P	Papa	PAH **PAH**
Q	Quebec	KEH **BECK**
R	Romeo	**ROW** ME OH
S	Sierra	SEE **AIR** RAH
T	Tango	**TANG** GO
U	Uniform	**YOU** NEE FORM
V	Victor	**VIK** TAH
W	Whiskey	**WISS** KEY
X	X-ray	**ECKS** RAY
Y	Yankee	**YANG** KEE
Z	Zulu	**ZOO** LOO

The phonetic alphabet is used in RT communications where letters are to be specifically transmitted. For instance, a registration of G-ABCD would be transmitted as:

GOLF – **AL** FAH **BRAH VOH CHAR** LEE **DELL** TAH

A standard pronunciation has also been developed for numbers.

Number	Pronunciation
0	**ZERO**
1	**WUN**
2	**TOO**
3	**TREE**
4	**FOWER**
5	**FIFE**
6	**SIX**
7	**SEVEN**
8	**AIT**
9	**NINER**
Decimal	**DAYSEEMAL**
Hundred	**HUN DRED**
Thousand	**TOUSAND**

So runway 24 would be transmitted as Runway TOO FOWER. In this context, note that runway designators are always transmitted as separate digits; it is always Runway Two Four, never Runway twenty-four.

The phonetic alphabet, and the correct pronunciation of phonetic words and numbers, will quickly become second nature. You will find that those involved in aviation tend to use the phonetic alphabet even in face-to-face situations. Learning it is a question of practice and usage, and perhaps listening to aircraft on an air-band radio if you have access to one. This latter can also provide you with plenty of examples of aeronautical radio usage (both correct and incorrect). Another quick way to learn the phonetic alphabet is to convert car number-plates into the phonetic alphabet and correct pronunciation whilst driving.

▶Transmission of Numbers and Transmission of Time

Each digit of a number is transmitted SEPARATELY in the following cases:

Case	Example	Transmitted As
aircraft callsigns	N17B	NOVEMBER WUN SEVEN BRAH VOH
altimeter setting	1014mb	WUN ZERO WUN FOWER millibars
flight levels	FL45	Flight Level FOWER FIFE
headings	Heading 080	Heading ZERO AIT ZERO
wind speed/direction	290/19	TOO NINER ZERO degrees, WUN NINER knots
transponder codes	Squawk 7436	Squawk SEVEN FOWER TREE SIX
frequencies	118.6	WUN WUN AIT DAYSEEMAL SIX

Exception: FL100 is transmitted as Flight Level WUN HUN DRED

Numbers containing hundred or thousands can be transmitted by pronouncing the digits of the number together with the word HUN DRED or TOUSAND as appropriate, in the following instances:

Case	Example	Transmitted As
altitude	9000ft	NINER TOUSAND feet
height	1500ft	WUN TOUSAND FIFE HUN DRED feet
cloud height	cloud ceiling 25,000ft	cloud ceiling TOO FIFE TOUSAND feet

When a radio frequency is transmitted, the word "decimal" is included – as already shown. If the radio frequency is a multiple of 25kHz, the last digit is NOT transmitted. So:

Example	Transmitted As	
118.625	118.62	WUN WUN AIT DAYSEEMAL SIX TOO
128.175	128.17	WUN TOO AIT DAYSEEMAL WUN SEVEN

If the radio frequency is a multiple of 8.33kHz, it will be referred to as a 'channel', and every digit is spoken, hence:

Example	Transmitted As	
135.010	Channel 135.010	CHANNEL WUN TREE FIFE DAYSEEMAL ZERO WUN ZERO

In aeronautical communications, time is always referred to in relation to UTC (a French acronym for 'Co-ordinated Universal Time') which for practical purposes is what used to be known as GMT or ('Greenwich Mean Time'). UTC incorporates the 24-hour clock, where 0001 hours is the first minute of the day and 2400 hours (midnight) the last. In the UK there is not normally more than an hour's difference between UTC and local time, although in other countries the difference can obviously be much larger. In conversation (and occasionally on radio) UTC is also sometimes referred to as 'Zulu' or just Z. So 15:25Z is the same thing as 15:25UTC.

Where no confusion will arise, time is transmitted in minutes only:

airborne at ZERO AIT (08 or eight minutes past the hour),

 landed at FOWER NINER (49 or forty-nine minutes past the hour).

Where confusion might arise, the hour should be included:

 This airfield closes at WUN SIX ZERO ZERO (1600 hours, or 4 o'clock).

In the interests of clarity (and to save several rain forests!) this publication will from now print just the appropriate letter or number in RT exchanges, and you should assume that the correct phonetic word and pronunciation applies.

▶Transmitting Technique

There are several simple techniques to use and common errors to avoid when using the radio. The use of proper techniques and avoidance of mistakes will make life easier for you and those you are communicating with. The essentials of good radio telephony (usually shortened to RT) are:

▷ Check that the radio frequency and volume are correctly set before transmitting.

▷ Listen-out before transmitting, and do not interrupt an existing conversation.

▷ Decide on your message content before starting to speak (**engage brain before opening mouth**). Avoid hesitations such as ers and ums.

▷ Maintain an even rate, volume and tone of speech.

▷ Avoid clipping the beginning or end of your transmissions (e.g. by beginning to speak before fully depressing the PTT, or releasing the PTT before fully completing your message).

▷ Avoid excessive courtesies and non-operational chat (e.g. Good morning Sir: its a fine day: I wonder if you would be so kind: thats my pleasure: did you see the football last night – who won? Thank you very much that's greatly appreciated, have a nice day...).

▷ Adhere to standard phraseology.

▷ When using a hand microphone, do not turn your head away from it while speaking.

▷ Do not hold the microphone or microphone boom of a headset while transmitting.

▷ Do not have the microphone too close to your lips when talking.

At first sight, such a list looks decidedly daunting. Indeed, it is said (not entirely in jest) that using the radio can at first seem more of a challenge to the novice pilot than flying the aeroplane. Learning to use RT is not unlike learning a new language, and it should be approached one step at a time – starting with the essentials and introducing more detailed procedures as your experience, knowledge and confidence grow. Here are a few simple tips which will make your life easier when first using the radio:

▷ Before pressing the PTT, rehearse what you are going to say and consider the sort of reply you expect.

Compose your message before
starting to speak to avoid hesitation

▷ If you are going to be given information which must be read back – such as an altimeter setting – be ready to write it down as you hear it. Do *not* try to memorise a route clearance or important information. Always write it down on a kneepad or something similar.

▷ Do not be rushed into transmitting before you have decided on the message content, or before you have digested a message just received. Sometimes the greatest difficulty in a foreign language is the speed of the talker. By the time you have worked out one part of the message, you have missed the rest – and RT can be the same, at least in the early stages. Get the speaker to slow down, or repeat the part of the message that you did not understand.

▷ Concentrate at first on listening-out for your own call-sign in the general radio traffic. As RT comes to you more easily, you can listen more generally to build up a picture of the general situation (situational awareness).

▷ Avoid excessive courtesies and non-standard phraseology;

KEEP IT SIMPLE, KEEP IT SHORT.

▶ Revision

5 What is the phonetic word for Q?

6 What is the correct pronunciation of the number 9?

7 Are the digits of an altimeter setting transmitted separately or as one number?

8 How would an altitude of 5000ft be transmitted?

9 What is the standard time reference for RT communications?

Answers at RT101

Air Traffic Service Units

Communications

Air Traffic Service Units

▶ **Introduction**

▶ **Types of ATSU**

▶ **Revision**

▶Introduction

A ground station providing some type of air traffic service is called an 'Air Traffic Service Unit' or ATSU. It is important to appreciate that not all ATSUs are equal. They differ in the kinds of service they can offer, their access to facilities and communications and the qualifications of the person providing the service. Whereas an ATSU will have little interest in the exact qualifications a pilot holds, or the equipment in his aircraft, a pilot must establish the nature of the ATSU with which he is communicating.

▶Types of ATSU

There are three types of ATSU.

– Air Traffic Control Unit (ATC Unit)

This is a place from which instructions and advice can be issued. An Air Traffic Control Unit will be manned by air traffic controllers who hold a full Air Traffic Controller's licence. An air traffic controller is a professional who will have completed a course in air traffic control and procedures, passed various exams and completed various licence validations. The air traffic controller and the air traffic control unit will be licensed and closely regulated by the CAA, in much the same way that an airline and its flight crew are. The specific point to appreciate is that **clearances** – permissions or instructions to do something – may *only* be issued by an ATC Unit.

– Aerodrome Flight Information Service (AFIS)

An Aerodrome Flight Information Service (AFIS) is provided at an aerodrome primarily for the safe and efficient conduct of flight within the Aerodrome Traffic Zone – ATZ. An AFIS is provided by a Flight Information Service Officer (FISO) – someone who will have undergone a short course of training to a CAA syllabus and who is regulated by the CAA. However, due to the less comprehensive nature of their training and equipment, FISOs can only issue instructions to aircraft and vehicles on the ground. To aircraft about to take-off and those in flight they issue information concerning the aerodrome and guidance to assist pilots in avoiding collisions. Note: helicopters 'hover taxiing' are treated as aircraft on the ground for the purpose of an AFIS.

– Air/Ground Stations (A/G)

An air/ground service is a rudimentary service provided by a person who holds a certificate of competence. A certificate of competence will normally be automatically issued to somebody who already has some form of CAA radio licence – for example, a pilot with an FRTO licence. Alternatively a certificate of competency is issued if the applicant passes a simple written and practical test, similar to that which a pilot has to pass to be granted an FRTO. Although the operator of an A/G service must be authorised by the CAA, he or she obviously cannot provide the level of service which an ATC unit or an AFIS station can offer. The operator of an A/G station is essentially limited to giving information regarding an aerodrome, and details of any known traffic.

From the foregoing it is obvious that a pilot needs to know what type of service an ATSU is able to provide. The type of service an ATSU is offering is indicated quite simply by its callsign:

Type of ATSU	Callsign
Air Traffic Control Unit	Control, Radar, Approach, Director, Tower, Ground.

for example; Manchester **Tower** provides an Air Traffic Control service at Manchester Airport.

Aerodrome Flight Information Service	**Information**

for example, Wolverhampton **Information** provides an Aerodrome Flight Information Service at Wolverhampton airfield

Air/Ground	**Radio**

for example, Welshpool **Radio** offers an air/ground service at Welshpool airfield.

These callsign suffixes are found in the AIP, and are also used in the initial contact between an aircraft and an ATSU; for example:

Wolverhampton **Information**, this is G-BUXO

G-BUXO this is Wolverhampton **Information**, pass your message.

The pilot should pay attention to this exchange to determine the service being provided. If the pilot uses the wrong callsign suffix, or no suffix, the ATSU should state the correct callsign, for example:

Welshpool this is G-MPWT

G-MPWT this is Welshpool **Radio**, pass your message.

Having established the nature of the service being offered, the pilot will notice different phraseology (with different meanings) being used. For example, when an aircraft is ready to take-off, the three types of ATSU might give the following typical replies if they know of no reason why the aircraft should not take-off:

Air Traffic Control Unit	G-SUIT is **cleared take-off**
Flight Information Service	G-TEWS, **take-off at your discretion**
Air/Ground station	G-AYRI, **no known traffic.**

Because of the importance of the callsign suffix in indicating the ATS being offered, it is an offence to use an inappropriate callsign, e.g. an air/ground station cannot use the callsign **tower**.

Communications

Through-out this book, where different ATSUs use significantly different phraseologies, examples will be given.

The precise level of service provided by an ATSU can vary temporarily or permanently, or may alternate on a regular basis. For example, an airfield might provide an ATC service during the week but only an AFIS at weekends.

▶Revision

10 What type of ATSU can give clearances to an aircraft in flight?

11 What is the callsign suffix of an AFIS unit?

Answers at RT101

Callsigns, Abbreviations, General Procedures

▶ Callsigns

▶ Spoken Abbreviations

▶ Omission of Words and Phrases

▶ Categories of Message

▶ Revision

Communications

▶ Callsigns

Once satisfactory two-way communication has been established with an ATSU, it is normal practice for both parties to drop the use of the ATSU callsign and suffix in an ongoing exchange:

✈ Manchester Approach, this is G-BEWR

♟ G-BEWR this is Manchester Approach, pass your message

✈ G-BEWR is a Cessna 172.....

♟ G-BEWR report your position?

✈ 5 miles south of Crewe, G-BEWR

However, an aircraft may only abbreviate its callsign after the ATSU has done so. The way in which a callsign is abbreviated depends on the type of callsign. Most light aircraft use their registration as the radio callsign, which can be abbreviated as follows:

CALLSIGN	ABBREVIATION
G-FAYE	G-YE
N36841	N841

✈ Biggin Hill Approach, **G-BGRR**, request runway in use

♟ **G-RR**, runway in use 21

✈ Runway in use 21, **G-RR**

Other callsign formats and permissible abbreviations are as follows:

CALLSIGN	ABBREVIATION
The aircraft operator designator followed by the aircraft's registration	
Neatax G-LEAR	**Neatax AR**
The operator's designator followed by the flight identification	
Speedbird 8341	**No abbreviation permitted**
The aircraft type followed by the aircraft's registration	
Spitfire G-AIST	**Spitfire ST**
The aircraft type only (especially military aircraft at air displays, etc)	
Tornado	**No abbreviation permitted**

Aircraft cannot change their callsign in flight unless instructed to do so by an ATSU. An ATSU may instruct an aircraft to change its callsign if there is the danger of confusion with another aircraft on the frequency. An ATSU may request an aircraft to use its full callsign when there is another aircraft with a similar callsign on the same frequency e.g. if both G-DASH and G-BGSH are on the same frequency simultaneously:

Coventry Tower, G-DASH

G-DASH use full callsign

G-SH downwind

G-BGSH use full callsign

When two-way communications are established, callsigns should be used thus:

1. ATSU to aircraft:
aircraft callsign + message or reply

G-XY, report your position?

2. Aircraft to ATSU:
-To reply: message/read back of information + callsign

Overhead Brentwood, G-XY

-To initiate a new message: callsign + message/information

G-XY is overhead Brentwood

An aircraft in the HEAVY wake-turbulence category will use the word "HEAVY" after its callsign in initial contact with an ATSU, for example:

Birmingham Approach,
Britannia 941 **Heavy**

If an ATSU wishes to broadcast a message to all aircraft on the frequency, it will preface its call with the words "All stations", for example:

All stations, Southend Tower, this airfield will be closing in 30 minutes

Aircraft do not have to reply to this type of general broadcast unless the ATSU specifically requests them to.

When information is passed to a specific aircraft, it can be acknowledged in one of two ways; by giving the aircraft's callsign:

G-MU, reported cloudbase at Norwich 800ft

G-MU

or by giving the receiving stations callsign together with the word 'Roger'.

G-MU, Roger

The word Roger and other words of the same general type are explained in the following chapter.

It should also be mentioned at this stage that certain instructions or information must be read back. Again this point is explained in detail in the following chapter.

▶ Spoken Abbreviations

Some abbreviations in common aviation usage can be heard on the radio as their constituent letters, rather than in phonetics. Examples of such common abbreviations are:

Abbreviation	Meaning
ATIS*	Automatic Terminal Information Service (pronounced "Ay-tis")
ATC	Air Traffic Control (in general)
ATZ	Aerodrome Traffic Zone
CAVOK*	Visibility, cloud and present weather better than certain prescribed conditions (pronounced "Cav-okay")
CB*	Cumulo Nimbus (pronounced "Cee-bee")
DF	Direction Finding
ETA	Estimated Time of Arrival
FIR	Flight Information Region
FIS	Flight Information Service
IFR	Instrument Flight Rules
IMC	Instrument Meteorological Conditions
LARS*	Lower Airspace Radar Service
MATZ*	Military Aerodrome Traffic Zone
MET*	Meteorology or Meteorological
PAPI*	Precision Approach Path Indicator
POB	Persons On Board
QDM	A magnetic track **to** a point (e.g. a heading to steer assuming zero wind)
QFE	The altimeter pressure setting to indicate **height** (above a fixed point on the surface)
QNH	The altimeter pressure setting to indicate **altitude** (above mean sea level)
SSR	Secondary Surveillance Radar
TMA	Terminal Control Area
UHF	Ultra High Frequency (used at military airfields)
UTC	Co-ordinated Universal Time
VASI*	Visual Approach Slope Indicator (pronounced "Var-Zi")
VDF	VHF Direction Finding
VFR	Visual Flight Rules
VMC	Visual Meteorological Conditions
VOLMET*	Meteorological information for aircraft in flight

* These abbreviations tend to be spoken as a single word.

As with many other activities, aviation is notorious for its large number of abbreviations and specialised words. Beginners sometimes feel that aviation language is designed for the express purpose of excluding them, which is not meant to be the case. Nevertheless, it is important never to use an abbreviation unless you are absolutely sure what it means. Equally, if somebody uses an abbreviation you do not completely understand, do not hesitate to query it. This is an essential principle of RT communications. **Rather than carrying on in doubt, ask for clarification of a message, or any part of it, that you did not understand.** Or, to put it another way:

If in doubt – shout!

Obviously the word "shout" should not be taken in its literal sense; you do not need to scream into the microphone every time you do not understand a radio message. A simple request for clarification is enough. More on this subject later.

▶Omission of Words and Phrases

Certain words or phrases, usually those relating to units of measurement, can be omitted if no confusion will result:

Phrase	Context
Surface	In relation to the surface wind
Degrees	In relation to wind direction
Knots	In relation to wind speed
Visibility	
Cloud	} In relation to a MET report
Height	
Millibars	In relation to pressure settings of 1000mb or more

Examples:

> ☗ G-CF, wind 310/15

– G-CF the surface wind (here) is from 310 degrees, strength 15 knots.

> ☗ 6000 metres, scattered at 2500

– Visibility is 6000 metres, cloud amount is scattered, base 2500ft above ground level.

> ☗ G-FC, the QNH is 1011

– The QNH is 1011 millibars.

Again, it is important that no confusion should result from the omission of these words. If in doubt, request a clarification. For example, altimeters in most American-registered aircraft use inches of mercury as a pressure setting, not millibars (and some can use both). A pilot using such an altimeter would want to establish precisely whether he was being given a pressure setting in millibars or inches of mercury.

▶Categories of Message

Clearly, within the day-to-day business of RT communications, some messages are more important than others and so should take priority. The following is the order of precedence for RT messages, starting with the most important:

Distress messages

Urgency messages

Direction Finding communications

Flight Safety messages

Meteorological messages

Flight Regularity messages

▶Revision

12 When can an aircraft abbreviate its callsign?

13 What is the permitted abbreviation of the callsign 'Britannia 832B'?

14 What words would an ATSU use to initiate a broadcast to all aircraft on the frequency?

15 When can the word "millibars" be dropped in RT communications?

Answers at RT101

Departure Procedures

▶ **Standard Phraseology**

▶ **Items Requiring Read-Back**

▶ **Radio Check**

▶ **Booking Out**

▶ **Airfield Data and Taxy Instructions**

▶ **Departure Clearance/Departure Instructions**

▶ **Taxying Instructions, Holding Instructions, Take-off Instructions**

▶ **Immediate Take-Off**

▶ **Conditional Clearances**

▶ **Over and Out**

▶ **Roger**

▶ **A Complete Departure Sequence**

▶ **Revision**

Communications

▶Standard Phraseology

Let's start to look at using the radio in practice. First of all, here is a list of some standard phraseology. These are words used by both pilots and ATSU operators. They have standard meanings as follows:

Standard Phraseology	Meaning
Acknowledge	Confirm that you have received and understood this message
Affirm	Yes (shortened from "affirmative")
Cleared	Authorised to proceed under the specified conditions
Correct	That is correct
I Say Again	I repeat for emphasis or clarity
Negative	No, or That is not correct, or Permission is not granted
Out	This exchange is ended and no response is expected
Over	This transmission is ended and I expect a response
Read Back	Repeat all, or a specified part, of the message; exactly as you received it
Request	I want to know, or I want to obtain
Roger	I have received all of your last transmission

From here on, 'Standard Phraseology' will be introduced in stages. Do not think it is that the standard phraseology shown here is ONLY used in departure procedures, merely we are introducing some of the most common phrases first. After all, nobody learns a new language by trying to memorise a dictionary, and learning RT is no different. By the end of the Communications section all recognised standard phraseology that is relevant to the VFR PPL will have been introduced. If you wish to look-up a word or phrase, there is a complete list of standard phraseology as an appendix.

▶ Items Requiring Read-back

There are certain instructions or items of information given to a pilot that are particularly vital to get right. These include items such as altimeter settings and level or heading instructions – which are obviously central to the safety of a flight; or items which keep you in step with what other aircraft are doing, and which could cause problems for you and others if you didn't follow them properly. These items are "read back" – that is to say, after the operator on the ground has given you the instruction or information, you repeat it back to him. So the dialogue might go:

> ▼ G-MJ cleared to cross Runway 08

> ✈ Cross Runway 08, G-MJ

Some items requiring read-back:

1 Runway in use

2 Clearance to land/take-off/backtrack, cross, enter, or hold short of, an active runway

3 Altimeter Settings

4 Airways or route clearances

5 Taxy instructions

You must also read back any other message if an ATSU requests you to.

▶ Radio Check

You can check the serviceability of the radio by making a transmission requesting a 'Radio check'. This can be done at the beginning of the flight as the first transmission, or at any other time. A radio check takes the following form:

Identification of station being called/Aircraft identification/"Radio check"/Frequency being used.

> ✈ Fairoaks Information, G-AVWL,
> **radio check** 123.42

In reply the ground station will grade the **readability** of the aircraft's transmission on a scale between one and five:

> ▼ G-AVWL, Fairoaks Information,
> **readability 4**

Readability Scale	Definition
1	Unreadable
2	Readable now and then
3	Readable but with difficulty
4	Readable
5	Perfectly readable

It is not necessary for the pilot to reply with the readability of the ATSU's transmission, but many do as a matter of course.

If an ATSU is having difficulty hearing your messages (or vice-versa) the readability of the transmissions may be passed as information:

> ▼G-AYOZ, readability 3

▶Booking-out

At some airfields it is standard practice to book-out over the radio. Check before flight whether or not this procedure is in use at the airfield you are about to depart from. If the ATSU cannot accept a booking-out over the radio, it can be a long walk back to the briefing office...

▶Airfield Data and Taxy Instructions

Apart from the radio check, the first contact with an ATSU at an airfield is usually to request some essential airfield information. This is normally done using the phrase "Request departure information". The ATSU will reply with the following:

Runway in use

Surface wind

Aerodrome QNH

Significant meteorological conditions (if appropriate)

✈ Leicester Radio, G-BJYG
request departure information

🛎 G-YG, **runway 28, surface wind
260/10, QNH 1012**

In reply, you *must* read back the runway in use and pressure setting (see the items requiring read-back at the beginning of this chapter).

✈ G-YG, **runway 28, QNH 1012**

In addition, some airfields may give the circuit direction or other essential information

✈ Shawbury Tower, G-WIZZ
request departure information

🛎 G-ZZ, runway 19, right-hand,
surface wind 200/12, QNH 1003

Remember that some airfields have parallel runways in the same direction (e.g. 27 Left and 27 Right) and also that some airfields will want you to use one side or other (or even the centre) of a wide grass strip. It is obviously important not to confuse circuit direction with a runway designator.

🛎 G-VB, runway 23 right, left-hand,
surface wind 240/15, QFE 1001

The usual maxim applies – if there is any confusion, request clarification. Or:

If in doubt – shout!

✈ Say again runway in use and
circuit direction G-VB

🛎 G-VB, runway in use 23 right,
circuit direction left-hand

Do not hesitate to query any instruction or information you do not understand. Always remember that whatever flavour of air traffic service exists at a particular airfield – whether a fully-fledged ATC Unit or a small A/G station – it is there to help you. The air traffic controller (or FISO or air/ground radio operator) will be more than happy to repeat or clarify a message to prevent any ambiguity.

At larger airfields there may be a recorded broadcast of aerodrome and current weather information, updated at least every thirty minutes – this broadcast is known as 'ATIS' (Automatic Terminal Information Service) and is described more fully later. Each 'issue' of the ATIS broadcast is given an identification letter and a time, e.g. "This is Newcastle Information Zulu, time 0949...". On initial contact with the ATSU you should confirm that you have received the relevant ATIS broadcast and so already have the departure information.

– Requesting Taxy

A request for taxy instructions will be answered in one of several ways, depending on which type of ATSU you are talking to:

ATC unit or AFIS:

G-LN, request taxy

G-LN taxy to the holding point runway 06 via the eastern taxiway

Air/Ground unit

G-LN, request taxy

G-LN runway 06

You can request the airfield information and taxy instructions in one call:

Sywell Information, G-NICK request departure information and taxy instructions

G-CK Sywell, taxy holding-point runway 03, surface wind 050/5, QNH 1025

G-CK taxy to holding point 03, QNH 1025

▶ Departure Clearance/Departure Instructions

A departure clearance or departure instructions describe the routing for the aircraft to follow after take-off, and any special instructions. **It is NOT a clearance to take-off.** Departure clearances are normally issued at airfields within controlled airspace, where an aircraft is leaving the zone on a specified route at (or below) a specified altitude.

Because controllers know that a pilot needs to write down the clearance, they will normally prompt him or her that it is about to be delivered. In any case, controllers will not issue departure clearances to pilots whilst they are lining-up on the runway or engaged in complicated taxying manoeuvres. Remember that a departure clearance is one of the items which **must** be fully read-back by the pilot, the aircraft's full callsign should be used, even if it already been abbreviated by ATC.

G-DP, are you ready to copy departure clearance ?

Affirm G-DP

G-BBDP is cleared to leave the Liverpool zone via Chester, VFR, not above 1500 feet Liverpool QNH 1035.

Departure Procedures

Roger, cleared to leave the
Liverpool Zone via Chester, VFR,
not above 1500 feet Liverpool
QNH 1035, G-BBDP

G-DP read-back correct

Because it is essential that the departure clearance is not misinterpreted as clearance to take-off, a controller may reiterate the holding instruction:

G-DP ready for departure

G-BBDP hold position. Your
clearance is to leave the
Liverpool control zone...

When reading back the clearance the pilot confirms the instruction to continue holding.

This point is vital, so it is worth repeating. **A departure clearance is NOT a clearance to take-off**.

It has to be stressed that an accurate read-back is essential, and ATC will not issue a take-off clearance until they have received your read-back. If you do not read back the clearance, the controller will prompt you to. Whilst you are reading back the clearance, the controller will check to be sure that you have copied it correctly. Should the clearance be different from the one you were expecting (which may happen on occasions) or if there is some aspect of it you do not understand, do not hesitate to query it. The usual maxim applies:

If in doubt – shout!

Incidents have occurred because a pilot blindly followed a clearance, despite suspecting that it might be incorrect.

▶Taxying Instructions, Holding Instructions, Take-off Instructions

When an aircraft is given an instruction to hold at a runway holding point, that instruction must be read back and strictly adhered to:

G-UN, taxy to holding point F,
runway 09

Taxy to holding point F,
runway 09, G-UN

Alternatively an ATSU might want you to stop, or remain at your present position

G-UN **hold position**

Holding, G-UN

Communications

The instruction to hold remains in force until the ATSU issues a further instruction. Even if you think it is safe to move off, you must continue to hold until authorised to proceed.

Occasionally an aircraft may have to cross an active runway to reach another part of the airfield. In this case the ATC unit will issue a specific clearance, and may require a report from the aircraft when it has cleared the runway:

➤ G-AY at holding point C for runway 24

♜ G-AY, **cross runway 24, report vacated**

➤ **Cross 24**, G-AY

➤ G-AY **runway vacated**

♜ G-AY roger, continue to the flying club

➤ Continue to the flying club G-AY

Alternatively an air/ground station may just report its known traffic

➤ G-AY at holding point C for runway 24

♜ G-AY I have no known traffic

Then it is up to the pilot to decide whether it is safe to cross the runway.

Particular care should be used when in the vicinity of the runway in use. Poor R/T procedure here is the cause of heart-stopping moments for controllers and pilots alike. Most instructions regarding an active runway require a read-back.

At the risk of stating the obvious, you must **not** enter or cross an active runway **unless positive permission has been given and acknowledged.** If you are not sure, do not be afraid to check.

At larger airfields there may be more than one holding point for each runway, or extra holding points for use during low-visibility conditions. You must be absolutely clear as to which point you have been cleared to.

Even when cleared to enter or cross a runway, you should visually check that it is safe to do so. Controllers are generally very good, but they are also human and can make occasional mistakes like the rest of us. Remember that the ultimate responsibility for the safety of the aircraft always rests with the pilot-in-command.

Departure Procedures

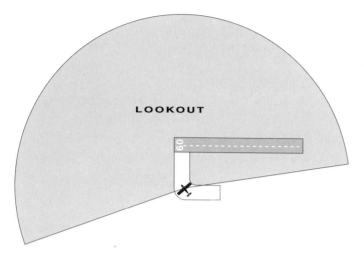

Usually a light aircraft will taxy to the specified holding point, and after completing the pre-take-off checks satisfactorily, the pilot reports that he is ready to go. The phraseology used is "ready for departure". Note that the words take-off are **not** used at this stage.

➤ G-RD **ready for departure**

♜ G-RD hold position

➤ Holding G-RD

An aircraft may be given an instruction to enter the runway, line-up on the centreline, and hold at that new position – "line up and wait":

➤ G-RD ready for departure

♜ G-RD **line up and wait**, vehicle crossing the runway

➤ **Line up and wait** G-RD

Sometimes it may be expedient for air traffic control to line-up more than one aircraft at once, either at different points on the same runway or on crossing runways. This will only be done under the following circumstances:

– it is daylight

– all the aircraft will be continuously visible to the controller

– all the aircraft are on the same frequency

– the pilots are advised of the aircraft ahead of them in the departure sequence, and the position/runway from which they will depart

– following aircraft are able to keep those ahead in sight

Once a pilot has reported ready for departure, and if the ATSU knows of no reason why the aircraft should not go, the words "take-off" can be used for the first time, by the ATSU:

> G-ST ready for departure

> G-ST **cleared take-off**
> runway 15, surface wind 170/8

> **Cleared take-off** 15, G-ST

*note that there is no need to read back the wind information.

Different phraseology will be used by an AFIS unit:

> G-ST **ready for departure**

> G-ST **take-off at your discretion**,
> surface wind 170/8 over

> Taking-off, G-ST

An air/ground unit will merely pass on details of any known traffic:

> G-ST **ready for departure**

> G-ST **no known traffic**, surface
> wind 170/8

Remember that the word "take-off" will first be used by the ATSU, *not* the pilot.

No matter what type of ATSU exists at the airfield, the final decision on whether or not to take-off rests solely with the pilot – that is, you. Hence the requirement for good airmanship at this point. Even after receiving a clearance to enter, cross, or take-off on a runway, you should *always* visually check that the runway, approach paths and departure paths are clear. As with other aspects of RT, do not expect other people to take decisions for you. You are the captain of the aircraft.

▶Immediate Take-Off

An ATC Unit may issue a clearance for an *immediate take-off*. If the pilot accepts the clearance he should:

1   From the holding point, taxy on to the runway immediately and begin
    the take-off without stopping.

2   If already on the runway, begin the take-off without delay.

> G-VC, cleared immediate take-off

> Cleared immediate take-off,
> G-VC

Departure Procedures

▶Conditional Clearances

A controller may also offer a *conditional clearance*. To give a conditional clearance the format is: Aircraft callsign/the condition/ the instruction.

> ▜ G-VC/after the landing
> Warrior/line-up and wait runway 31

For a pilot to be able to accept such a clearance, he must obviously be able to identify the object of the condition; in this case the Warrior. If there is any doubt in your mind for instance, if you are not sure exactly what a Warrior looks like, **do not** accept the clearance and hope for the best. Ask for clarification:

> ▜ G-NU, after the landing Chipmunk,
> line-up and wait runway 31

> Say again aircraft type, G-NU

> ▜ The Chipmunk is the red and
> white single-engine low-wing
> tailwheel aircraft on one-mile finals.
> G-NU, after the Chipmunk has
> landed, line-up and wait runway 31

> After the landing Chipmunk,
> line-up and wait 31, G-NU

From what has been said so far, you will have realised that before reporting ready for departure you should have a good view of the active runway and the approach paths. By doing this you will be able to respond quickly if given a conditional instructional or an immediate take-off clearance.

Should you have to abandon a take-off for some reason, you should report when possible

> [callsign] **stopping**.

Alternatively, if ATC wish to cancel a take-off clearance, having already given one, the following phraseology would be used:

> ▜ G – PO **hold position**. Cancel I
> say again cancel take-off.
> Acknowledge

> **Holding**, G – PO

▶Over and Out

Out – this exchange is ended and no response is expected.

Over – this transmission is ended and I expect a response.

Much used and abused in black-and-white movies, these two possible endings to a transmission are mostly omitted in an ongoing exchange. Where they are used, it is usually to emphasise that one party does or does not expect or want a reply.

Communications

For example, after issuing a clearance to a pilot a controller may finish the transmission with the word "over", to emphasis that the clearance DOES require a read back.

> ☗ G-LK, taxy to holding point A for runway 01, **over**

> ➤ Taxy to holding point A for runway 01, G-LK

Alternatively, if – for example – a controller is transmitting the surface wind to an aircraft on short finals, he might finish the transmission with the word "out" to emphasise that the aircraft need not acknowledge:

> ☗ G-JR, surface wind 180/25, **out**

When you appreciate the meanings of the words "over" and "out", you will appreciate why pilots never say "over and out" after a radio transmission. The only people who do are badly advised actors.

▶ Roger

Be particularly clear in your mind about the correct meaning of the word 'roger'. It merely signifies that you have received all of the last transmission. It does not necessarily imply that you have understood a word of it, or have any intention of complying with an instruction or clearance! The word 'roger' should never be used when you mean to say "yes" (or even "affirm"). It should also never be used in place of a full read-back; or to confirm an instruction.

►A Complete Departure Sequence

Southampton tower, G-IDEA request radio check on 118.2

G-IDEA Southampton tower, readability 5

G-IDEA Roger, request departure information and taxy instructions

G-EA, taxy to holding point A, runway 02, QNH 998 millibars

Taxy to holding point A for runway 02, QNH 998 millibars G-EA

G-EA are you ready to copy departure clearance?

Affirm G-EA

G-IDEA hold position. Cleared to leave the Southampton control zone at Romsey, VFR, not above 1500ft, Southampton QNH 998 millibars, over

Holding. Cleared to leave the Southampton control zone at Romsey, VFR, not above 1500ft, QNH 998 millibars, G-IDEA

G-EA read-back correct. Report ready for departure

G-EA ready for departure

G-EA, after the landing F27, line up and wait 02

After the landing F27, line up and wait 02, G-EA

G-EA cleared take-off 02, surface wind 350/10

Cleared take-off, G-EA

▶Revision

16 What is the meaning of the word 'affirm'

17 Which of the following items does *not* need to be read back?

Runway in use

Altimeter setting

Surface wind

18 What is the readability of a transmission that is graded "readable but with difficulty"?

19 What is a departure clearance?

20 An aircraft has been instructed to hold position. When may it proceed?

21 What is the ATC instruction meaning that the aircraft should enter the runway, line-up on the centreline and hold at that position?

22 At an airfield with an AFIS unit, you report ready for departure. What phraseology will the AFIS officer use to indicate that he/she is not aware of any reason why you may not take-off?

23 If an ATC unit instructs you to take-off immediately, is it mandatory to comply with this instruction?

24 What is the standard format used by ATC for a conditional clearance?

25 What is the meaning of the word 'out'?

26 What is the correct meaning of the word 'roger'?

Answers at RT102

En-Route Procedures

▶ Standard Phraseology

▶ Items Requiring Read-Back

▶ Frequency Changing

▶ Establishing Contact – Passing Details

▶ Air Traffic Services

▶ Radar and Non-Radar Services

▶ Level and Position Reporting

▶ Airspace Classifications

▶ ATZs

▶ MATZs

▶ Lower Airspace Radar Service (LARS)

▶ Danger Areas

▶ Use of Transponder

▶ VHF Direction Finding (VDF)

▶ VOLMET And ATIS

▶ Avoiding Confusion

▶ An En-Route Sequence (non-radar)

▶ An En-Route Sequence (radar)

▶ Revision

Communications

▶Standard Phraseology

Having got airborne, we can now consider some aspects of RT usage which will crop up in the course of the flight proper. Here is some more standard phraseology:

Standard Phraseology	Meaning
Approved	Permission for proposed action is granted
Changing to	I intend to call [unit] on [frequency]
Climb	Climb and maintain
Contact	Establish radio contact with [unit], (they have your details)
Descend	Descend and maintain
Free-call	Call [ATSU] (they do not have your details)
Monitor	Listen out on [frequency]
Pass your message	Proceed with your message
Report	Pass requested information
Standby	Wait and I will call you
Wilco	I understand your message and will comply with it 'Wilco' is an abbreviation for 'will comply'

▶Items Requiring Read-back

In addition to those on RT 29

6   Level instructions

7   Heading instructions

8   Speed instructions

9   VDF information

10   Frequency changes

11   Type of radar service

12   SSR (transponder) operating instructions

and any other message when requested to by an ATSU

▶Frequency Changing

You must not change frequency without informing the ATSU you are currently talking to. Usually the ATSU will advise you to change frequency, but you can make the request if you wish. In either case the callsign and frequency of the next ATSU to be called is usually given.

> G-DP **contact** Liverpool
> Approach on 119.85

> **Contact** Liverpool
> Approach on 119.85 G – DP

There are two items worth noting here. By using the word "contact", the controller is indicating that the next frequency to be called has the aircraft's flight details. Also, a frequency change *must* be read-back.

> Liverpool approach, G-BBDP

> G-DP roger, report at Chester

> Wilco G-DP

Note that the implication of this exchange is that the ATSU already has the flight details. Note also the use of the word "wilco" to indicate that the pilot understands and will comply with the instruction. The ATC instruction did not require a read-back.

Alternatively, an ATSU may suggest the most suitable unit to call next, and indicate that they have *not* passed on the flight details

> G-DP abeam Chester

> G-DP roger. Suggest you
> **free-call** Shawbury 120.775

> Roger, **changing to**
> Shawbury on 120.775 G-DP

Of course, you can request a frequency change, or indicate that you intend to change frequency.

> G-EN **request frequency**
> **change** to Brize Radar 134.3

> G-EN roger, **frequency change**
> **approved**

To reiterate, the most important point about changing frequency is that you should **never** do so without first informing the ATSU you are presently talking to. Apart from the obvious point of courtesy, it is worth bearing in mind that an ATSU is duty-bound to provide an alerting service to any aircraft whose details it knows. An alerting service means that if the pilot transmits a emergency message, or if the ATSU has some reason to believe the aircraft may be in trouble (e.g. if contact with the aircraft is lost), the appropriate authorities will be informed.

If an aircraft disappears from a frequency, the ATSU has no way of knowing whether the pilot has merely changed frequency unannounced or if there is a problem. At best the ATSU will have to telephone other ATSUs to see if the aircraft has changed to their frequency. At worst, if the aircraft cannot be traced, a totally unnecessary search-and-rescue operation could be initiated. Both are avoidable if the pilot takes the simple precaution of confirming any frequency change with the ATSU.

▶ Establishing Contact — Passing Details

When en-route, and first establishing contact with an ATSU, the pilot should be careful to comply with the reply given, e.g.

> Birmingham Approach this is G-BFPB, over

> G-BFPB, Birmingham Approach, **standby**

'Standby' means just that — wait. No acknowledgement is required; wait and the ATSU will call you back. Few things are more frustrating to a controller than a pilot who, having been instructed to standby, replies with a recital of his flight routing, intentions, requests and other items of general interest! Naturally the instruction "standby" does not imply that any clearance or service is given to the pilot.

It might be worth remembering that the pilot can also instruct an ATSU to standby if they happen to call at an awkward moment.

When the ATSU does invite you to "Pass your message" you should give your flight details in a clear and concise manner. Probably the most commonly used mnemonic for passing flight details is TP HAIR:

T - aircraft **T**ype

P - **P**oint of departure, present **P**osition

H - **H**eading

A - **A**ltitude/height/flight level, with altimeter setting if appropriate

I - **I**ntentions i.e. estimate, routing, destination, flight rules (VFR/IFR) etc.

R - **R**equest — type of service required etc.

This mnemonic should provide all the information the controller needs; you will be prompted if further information is required. Remember — before making the call, think through the content of your intended message. To avoid hesitations whilst you are transmitting, engage brain before opening mouth…

We can now begin to put the various ingredients together. We will assume that we are in a Cessna 152, registration G-BGLH, on a VFR flight from Hawarden to Shoreham. As we pass Telford we call the ATSU at Wolverhampton Business Airfield, near Wolverhampton:

Wolverhampton Information,
this is G-BGLH

G-BGLH Wolverhampton
Information, **standby**

G-BGLH Wolverhampton
Information, **pass your message**

G – BGLH
[Type]...is a Cessna 152...
[Position]...point of departure
Hawarden overhead Telford...
[Heading]...160
[Altitude]...at 2800 feet on
QNH 1032...
[Intentions]...ETA overhead
Wolverhampton airfield at 25, VFR
destination Shoreham...
[Request]...request Flight
Information Service...
...over

The ATSU now has the details it needs about the flight. It can offer a service and pass relevant information to the aircraft as the situation warrants.

G – LH roger, Flight Information
Service. Wolverhampton
QNH 1031, report overhead the
airfield

QNH 1031, wilco, G – LH

This exchange raises the issue of what we mean by a 'Flight Information Service'. For an answer we need to digress briefly and look more closely at the various Air Traffic Services available.

▶Air Traffic Services

It is a common misconception amongst non-pilots that if a pilot is talking to somebody on the ground, his aircraft is automatically being tracked by radar. By implication, there is an ever-vigilant controller somewhere who is watching over the aircraft and clearing a path through the skies for it. In reality this is not true. Not all ATSUs have radar, and even those that do may not be always able to offer a radar service to all comers. For example, a radar unit offering an approach service will give priority to aircraft using that airfield, and may not be able to offer radar assistance to aircraft in uncontrolled airspace.

Communications

Broadly speaking, there are four types of air traffic service; the official definitions are a little formal and need reading carefully, but here they are:

1.) Air Traffic Control Service

This service can be an aerodrome, approach or area control service, with or without the assistance of radar.

It is provided to: Prevent collisions between airborne aircraft

Assist in preventing collisions between aircraft on the aerodrome

Assist in preventing collisions between aircraft and obstructions on the aerodrome

Expedite and maintain an orderly flow of air traffic.

2.) Air Traffic Advisory Service

This service has the same purpose as an Air Traffic Control Service for aircraft flying outside controlled airspace (Classes F & G). It operates in the same way as an Air Traffic Control Service, and aircraft are assumed to be complying with the ATSUs instructions unless they state otherwise. This service can be radar or non-radar but, because of the uncontrolled nature of these classes of airspace, pilots should be aware that there is an increased chance of encountering traffic not known to the ATSU.

3.) Flight Information Service

This service provides information useful to the safe and efficient conduct of a flight, which may include weather reports, conditions at airfields etc. A controller may seek to identify a flight for monitoring or co-ordination, but this on its own does not imply that a radar service is being provided. **The pilot remains responsible for separation.**

4.) Alerting Service

This service is designed to notify the appropriate authorities (e.g. search and rescue services etc.) in the event that an aircraft needs assistance, and aid the appropriate authorities in search and rescue activities.

Armed with this information, we can look more closely at the en-route air traffic services available. It is necessary first of all to decide within what type of airspace you are flying and whether you are flying VFR or IFR. A VFR flight normally proceeds on the basis that the pilot is looking out for other aircraft and taking responsibility for navigation, terrain clearance and avoiding conflicting traffic. The basic principle of VFR flight is 'see and avoid'. Regardless of the service offered, if you are flying VFR you should always operate on a "see-and-avoid" basis. Even if you are receiving a radar service, you should never relax your lookout. Neither should you assume that navigation and terrain clearance have suddenly become the responsibility of the controller. If you hit something, it will hurt you more than it hurts him.

When making initial contact with an en-route ATSU, it is sensible to request the type of service required. Only when this is confirmed by the ATSU can you assume you are receiving a specific service.

▶ Radar and Non-Radar Services

Air traffic services can also be divided into *radar* and *non-radar*. The definitions look like this:

Radar Services

In controlled airspace (Classes A, B, C, D and E) a Radar Control Service may be offered. This service is an air traffic control service providing radar separation from other aircraft, radar vectoring, navigation assistance and full ATC services.

When flying in uncontrolled airspace (Classes F and G) two types of radar service are available:

1. **Radar Advisory Service (RAS).**

    This is an *Air Traffic Radar Service* which is only available to aircraft operating IFR. When providing this service the controller will pass information on any known conflicting traffic and **advise** on avoiding action, which the pilot is expected to comply with. If the pilot is not qualified to fly IMC, he should not accept an RAS where the controller's instructions might take the aircraft into IMC. The pilot can decide not to take the controllers' advice on avoiding action, but if he chooses to do this he must inform the controller and the pilot becomes responsible for taking avoiding action. The pilot must advise the controller before changing heading or level. The pilot is responsible for terrain clearance, although sometimes a controller may decline to give a radar service if an aircraft is flying lower than the Minimum Safety Altitude.

2. **Radar Information Service (RIS).**

    This is also an *Air Traffic Radar Service*, but it is available to aircraft in VMC or IMC, operating VFR or IFR. Under a RIS the controller will only provide traffic **information**; the pilot will have to decide on what avoiding action to take. When receiving a RIS the pilot is wholly responsible for separation from other aircraft, whether or not the controller has given traffic information. The pilot should advise the controller before changing level or route (although a pilot may request a RIS when manoeuvring to avoid this requirement). Often a RIS is offered when the controller is unable to give a RAS. Again the pilot remains responsible for terrain clearance.

To establish a service, you should request the type of service required. The controller will then positively identify the aircraft on radar. However, you should not assume that you are receiving a service until the controller positively states what type of service he is able to offer. Generally the controller will try to offer a RAS, unless that is not practical or if the pilot specifically requests a RIS.

The type of radar service being provided by the ATSU is another item that must be read back by the pilot. For example, assume a Cherokee G-DIAT on a flight from Bristol (Lulsgate) to Bembridge on the Isle of Wight. The initial contact with an ATSU to request a RAS might go something like this:

Yeovilton Approach, G-DIAT

G-DIAT, Yeovilton Approach, pass your message

G-DIAT is a Piper Cherokee,
point of departure Bristol,
overhead Radstock heading 150,
2800ft Bristol QNH 1017,
estimate Compton Abbas at 08,
VFR, destination Bembridge,
request Radar Information Service

Roger G-AT, **you are identified** overhead Radstock, **Radar Information**, Portland QNH 1016.

Radar Information, Portland QNH 1016, G-AT

To identify an aircraft on radar, the controller has various options including – as in the example above – a position report over a notified 'Visual Reference Point' or VRP. Alternatively the controller might request the aircraft to turn onto a specific heading (normally 30° left or right), and he can then identify the aircraft by observing the turn on radar. If the radar unit is equipped with SSR (Secondary Surveillance Radar) identification may be made by the use of the aircraft's transponder.

The provision of a radar service obviously requires radar, with all its electronic idiosyncrasies. Contrary to popular belief, even modern high-performance ground-based radars have several limitations and they certainly cannot be relied on to detect all airborne traffic. For example, a low-flying aircraft may merge into the ground return – in effect a shadow cast by the radar signal being reflected from hilly terrain lying between the radar head and the aircraft – and become invisible as far as the radar operator is concerned. Certain weather conditions (heavy rain, snow, hail etc.) can also cast a radar shadow within which an aircraft's contact may be lost, although modern radar can often see through weather clutter. A contemporary radar system may have circuitry to remove from the display any blip travelling more slowly than a preset speed. This feature is intended to delete clutter from birds and so on, but it may also delete some very slow-moving aircraft such as gliders, hang-gliders, microlights etc. Certain objects such as hot-air balloons or aircraft built predominantly of wood or GRP may not show up well on radar either. An aircraft may also be lost from the radar display if it passes overhead the radar antenna, or when it is at the edge of coverage. Additionally, from the controller's point of view, an area of high traffic density (not all the constituents of which may be talking to him) will make the provision of a radar service difficult.

The moral of all this is clear. Even when you are receiving a radar service, *maintain a good lookout of your own*. As more than one pilot has found out, even within controlled airspace a radar service does not necessarily **guarantee** separation from all other aircraft, particularly those not known to the controller.

En-Route Procedures

If a controller suspects that he will not be able to provide a full service, he may offer a limited service:

> ☗ G-XK, **limited traffic information** all round due to high traffic density

When a controller passes information to an aircraft regarding possible conflicting traffic, the following form is usually used:

– the relative bearing of the conflicting traffic in terms of the clock code*

– distance from the conflicting traffic

– flight direction of the conflicting traffic

– relative speed of the conflicting traffic, or aircraft type and level if known

*if the aircraft receiving the radar service is in a turn, the relative position will be given in terms of a cardinal point e.g. South, Northeast etc.

For example:

> ☗ G-JN, traffic left 11 o'clock range 8 miles, heading east, a Tornado at FL50 under my control

Additionally, the relative direction of the traffic may be given, using one of the following terms:

Closing

Converging

Crossing left to right

Crossing right to left

Diverging

Manoeuvring

Opposite direction

Overtaking

Parallel

Same direction

A controller may also describe the relative speed of the other traffic e.g. slow-moving, high speed.

> ☗ Channex 149, unknown traffic 12 o'clock range 3 miles, crossing left to right, high speed

The traffic will be described as 'unknown' if the controller does not have its flight details (it's not a UFO!).

As already discussed, the limitations of radar mean that traffic may suddenly appear on a controller's radar screen with no prior warning. This is particularly the case with military fast-jet aircraft climbing from low level. Such unknown traffic is often described as 'late sighting' or 'pop-up traffic':

> ☗ Skydive UT, pop-up traffic right
> 2 o'clock range 2 miles height
> unknown, diverging

When the controller advises a heading/height change to maintain separation from other traffic, he may use the phrase "avoiding action". An avoiding-action instruction should be complied with **immediately**, and acknowledged once the manoeuvre is complete, since it is only used by a controller when urgent action by the pilot is needed:

> ☗ Aerial 02, **avoiding action** turn
> right heading 210, pop-up traffic
> 11 o'clock range 1 mile,
> manoeuvring, height unknown,
> slow-moving

The pilot initiates the required turn as soon as he hears the instruction, then acknowledges

> ☗ Aerial 02 roger, turning

As an aircraft approaches the limit of an ATSU's radar coverage, the ATSU may advise the aircraft "[aircraft callsign], you will shortly be leaving radar cover". When the aircraft leaves the frequency, or if the unit can no longer offer a radar service, the pilot will be advised "[aircraft callsign], radar service terminated".

Before leaving the subject of radar service, there is one common situation which can be a little disconcerting the first time it happens. When there are lots of other aircraft about, the controller may give several successive changes of heading or route for traffic avoidance – which naturally take you off your carefully pre-planned route. As you leave his area of responsibility, you hear the time-honoured phrase "Resume your own navigation". At which point you may realise that you are, as they say, "temporarily uncertain of position". What should happen is that the controller will give your position and a heading and range to your next waypoint. If you are certain that you know exactly where you are and where you are going, fine. If you are not, do not hesitate to ask the controller for your present position, and perhaps the track and distance to your next waypoint. Remember that the controller is there to provide a service to you, not to make you feel foolish.

If in doubt – shout!

Non-Radar Services

Without radar, the level of service that can be offered to the pilot is obviously more limited.

Flight Information Service (FIS)

A FIS provides information useful to the safe and efficient conduct of a flight i.e. information relating to other aircraft known to the ATSU ("known traffic"). A FIS may also be able to pass information on meteorological conditions, airfield services and availability, facilities etc.. Remember that traffic information is based on known traffic only, and in uncontrolled airspace there is a far greater chance of encountering aeroplanes that are not in contact with the same ATSU as yourself – or for that matter, are not speaking to any ATSU at all.

Class G airspace is often referred to as the 'open FIR'. Each FIR (Flight Information Region) has a dedicated FIS to cover large blocks of airspace, and radio contact is usually available on several different frequencies according to which sector of the FIR you happen to be in. This type of FIS uses the callsign of the FIR (e.g. in the London FIR it is 'London Information' and so on.) and it is provided from an Area Control Centre or ACC. An ACC is a central unit whose primary purpose is to provide ATC to aircraft flying in the airways system over a large area. In the UK there are two ACC's – London and Scottish. As well as providing an en-route FIS, an FIR controller will have access to other information and is also a good contact point for obtaining clearance for airways joining and crossing clearances, accepting airborne flight plans etc.. However, the heavy workload of the FIR controller means that many pilots choose to obtain an FIS from en-route ATSU's instead. An FIS can be provided by any ATSU, at its discretion.

Procedural Service

This is an air traffic *advisory* service in *uncontrolled* airspace, and an air traffic *control* service in *controlled* airspace, which maintains standard separation between participating aircraft. This service is most often given to aircraft using an advisory route, but may also be given in controlled airspace when a radar service is not available.

Alerting Service

This is the most basic level of ATS, which is automatically provided by any ATSU to an aircraft of whose details it is aware. If the aircraft transmits an emergency message, if the aircraft is overdue, or if the ATSU has some reason to believe an aircraft is in difficulties, the ATSU is responsible for alerting the appropriate authorities. The life-saving potential of this service is obvious. If flying over water or sparsely populated terrain, you should always endeavour to maintain contact with an ATSU if only to receive an alerting service.

Generally speaking, an ATSU will be providing more than one service to an aircraft. For example, when receiving a RAS or RIS, the aircraft is also by implication receiving a FIS and an alerting service.

▶ Level and Position Reporting

Where it is compulsory to make a position report, it takes the following format:

Aircraft callsign

Position

Time

Level

Next position and ETA

Communications

Compulsory position reporting is rare nowadays, although a pilot may be asked to report at an on-request reporting point. Reporting points are generally found in association with controlled airspace (such as airways) and on advisory routes. For a VFR flight it is more common for the pilot to report at a given geographical location such as a VRP, in which case a full position report is not required.

The aircraft's level can be referred to in terms of height (based on QFE) altitude (based on QNH) or flight level (based on 1013mb/hPa). As a reminder, the three altimeter settings are summarised below. If you are still in any doubt about the exact nature of the different altimeter setting procedures, revise the altimeter-setting chapter of the Aviation Law section before going any further.

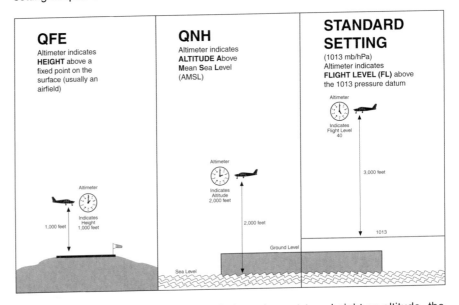

The three types of altimeter pressure setting

When passing instructions regarding climb or descent to a height or altitude, the word TO is always used e.g.

G-RD **descend to** altitude 1500ft, Manchester QNH 1009

Descending to altitude 1500ft, Manchester QNH 1009, G-RD

When messages relate to flight levels the word TO can be omitted e.g.

G-XY **climb** Flight Level 50

Climbing Flight Level 50 G-XY

A climb instruction means to climb and maintain a given level. A descent instruction means to descend and maintain the given level.

Pilots are normally expected to comply with a climb or descent instruction as soon as it is issued. However, if the ATSU uses the words "when ready", the timing of the manoeuvre is at the discretion of the pilot. In this instance the pilot will report when commencing the climb or descent e.g.

G-MA, when ready descend to height 1000ft, Hawarden QFE 997 millibars*

When ready descend to height 1000ft, Hawarden QFE 997 millibars G-MA

G-MA leaving altitude 2500ft descending to height 1000ft

*NOTE; the word millibars is used because the pressure setting is below 1000 millibars.

In exceptional circumstances an aircraft may be asked to expedite (i.e. accelerate) the climb or descent, or to make an immediate (i.e. start this instant) climb or descent. These instructions may be given to maintain separation from other traffic. For example, to an aircraft already established in a descent:

Omega 03, **expedite** descent to altitude 2500ft

Expedite descent to altitude 2500ft, Omega 03

or to an aircraft in level flight

Aztec Air LF, descend **immediately** Flight Level 70

In this instance, the priority is to initiate the instruction, then acknowledge

Descending Flight Level 70, Aztec Air LF

Normally controllers will assume that an aircraft is climbing or descending at not less than 500 feet per minute. If the aircraft's actual or anticipated rate of climb or descent is less than 500fpm, the pilot should advise the controller.

Before leaving this section, it must be emphasised that you must *never* allow yourself to be in any doubt as to the height/altitude/level you should be climbing to/descending to/ maintaining. Neither should there be any doubt as to the correct altimeter pressure setting. Accidents have occurred because pilots have been reluctant to query an instruction or information, even though they suspected there was something wrong. The usual maxim applies; here it is again in case you have forgotten...

If in doubt – shout!

When transferring from a QNH setting to airfield QFE setting, the difference in millibars will be approximately the airfield elevation divided by 30 (because one millibar equals approximately 30ft in height). For example, if an airfield has an elevation (its vertical distance above mean sea level) of 300ft, the difference between the airfield QNH and the airfield QFE will always be about 10 millibars. Any major discrepancy from this estimated difference should be queried.

▶ Airspace Classifications

What follows is examined in more detail in the aviation law section. Nevertheless you need to have at least a working knowledge of airspace classifications to get the best out of ATC.

Airspace is divided into seven classes, designated A to G.

Classes A-E are **controlled** airspace. In brief, to fly in Class A, B, C, or D airspace, ATC clearance is required *before* entering the airspace, the pilot must remain in radio contact whilst in the airspace and must obey ATC instructions. In Class E airspace, pilots undertaking IFR flights must obtain ATC clearance before entering the airspace and otherwise behave as for classes A-D; pilots undertaking VFR flights are *recommended* to contact ATC, but it is not mandatory.

The principle of obtaining a clearance to enter controlled airspace is a most important one to appreciate. Merely establishing contact with an ATSU governing a piece of controlled airspace *does not* imply that the aircraft has been cleared to enter controlled airspace. Such a clearance will be specifically granted to the pilot when appropriate. Imagine an aircraft on a flight from Netherthorpe (near Sheffield) to Coventry. The pilot wishes to pass through the East Midlands Control Zone, which is class D airspace:

> East Midlands Approach, G-BTMA

> G-BTMA East Midlands Approach, pass your message

The pilot can now proceed with the standard TP HAIR call, the **R**equest being for clearance through the control zone:

> G-BTMA is a Cessna 172 from Netherthorpe, overhead Heanor heading 180, at 2000ft Barnsley QNH 1003, estimate Long Eaton at 36, destination Coventry request VFR clearance Long Eaton to Shepshed

> G-MA roger, East Midlands QNH 1005, report at Long Eaton

> East Midlands QNH 1005, wilco, G-MA

The important point about this exchange is that *the aircraft has not received any clearance to enter the zone.* Upon reaching Long Eaton (a notified entry/exit point for the East Midlands control zone) the pilot will report his position, and then he may (or may not) be given a clearance to transit through the zone.

Why might G-BTMA not be given a clearance through the East Midlands zone? Basically because there might be other traffic with higher priority. If you are planning a flight to pass through controlled airspace, you should always bear in mind that a clearance through such airspace may not be forthcoming if circumstances do not permit. Controlled airspace is established around major airfields for a good reason (and has been known to be removed if an airfield's traffic does not warrant it) and an en-route aircraft will not be given priority over an aircraft arriving or departing, especially if the aircraft in question is an airliner making an instrument approach or departure. On the other hand, it does not hurt to ask – especially if routing through a control zone or control area will aid the safety or expediency of your flight. Not long ago the CAA reminded those operating control zones that clearance for en-route aircraft to enter a zone should only be refused if traffic or other considerations make it necessary, and not as a matter of course.

Incidentally, when flying within controlled airspace, bear in mind that a separate clearance to enter an ATZ in or close to a control zone may be necessary.

To fly in controlled airspace, a pilot may be offered a Special VFR (SVFR) clearance. It is up to the pilot whether to accept an SVFR clearance (equally it is offered at the discretion of ATC) and you should be aware of certain limitations and obligations relating to SVFR flight. If a pilot accepts a SVFR clearance:

1. The pilot must comply with ATC instructions.

2. The pilot is responsible for terrain clearance, maintaining the required flight visibility, remaining clear of cloud, remaining clear of ATZs (unless cleared to enter by the relevant ATSU) and flying within the limitations of his licence.

3. The pilot must ensure that at all times the aircraft can land clear of a built-up area in the event of an engine failure.

Classes F & G are **uncontrolled** airspace. Flight in Class F and G airspace is not subject to ATC clearance, although it may be advisable to contact an appropriate ATSU. Remember, however, that even in uncontrolled F & G airspace there are certain areas where contact with an ATSU is **mandatory** before you enter them (such as an active Aerodrome Traffic Zone–ATZ); and other areas where contact with an ATSU is **advisable** (e.g. a Military Aerodrome Traffic Zone or MATZ), Areas of Intense Aerial Activity (AIAA), an Advisory Route (ADR), or an advisory radio area such as the Boscombe Down Advisory Radio Area. The word "advisable" is used strictly in the legal sense. Nobody in their right mind would fly through a busy MATZ and steadfastly refuse to contact the controller merely because radio contact is not a legal requirement.

▶ATZs

Aerodrome Traffic Zones are areas of standard dimensions around an active airfield; revise the relevant chapter of the Air Law section if you've forgotten the details. ATZs do not have an airspace classification of their own but adopt the classification of the airspace they are located within, i.e. an ATZ in the open FIR is regarded as Class G airspace. However, an aircraft must not fly within an active ATZ unless the pilot has the permission of the ATC unit, or has contacted the AFIS unit or the Air/Ground radio station for information. An ATZ is active at government (i.e. military) airfields during notified hours (usually 24 hours a day) or during the hours of radio watch at other airfields.

▶MATZs

Military Aerodrome Traffic Zones are established around most military airfields in the UK and tend to have standard dimensions. A MATZ should not be confused with the separate ATZ established at a military aerodrome. Although it is not mandatory to establish radio contact or to receive permission to enter a MATZ (see preceeding remarks) it is there for a reason and pilots should take advantage of the service offered. Bear in mind that – as at civilian airfields – you may not enter into the active ATZ of a military aerodrome without permission.

Details of MATZs and the MATZ penetration service are found in the ENR section of the AIP. Wherever possible the MATZ controller will offer a RAS or RIS. Pilots are advised to contact the MATZ 15nm or 5 minutes flying time (whichever is greater) before the MATZ boundary to request MATZ penetration. The recommended phraseology or the initial call is:

"[controlling aerodrome] this is [aircraft callsign] request MATZ penetration."

When asked to pass his message, the pilot can use the standard TP HAIR call.

Often two or more military airfields may have a combined MATZ (CMATZ), in which case one ATSU may be designated as the controlling authority. Within the MATZ, aircraft normally set the aerodrome QFE, as instructed by ATC.

In the case of a combined MATZ the lowest value aerodrome QFE for the CMATZ may be used. This is referred to as the 'Clutch QFE'.

Military controllers sometimes use different phraseology from civilian controllers (i.e. wait instead of standby) and may be operating more than one frequency simultaneously. So:

Shawbury, this is G-BJAP, **request MATZ penetration**

▼Aircraft transmitting on VHF, **wait**

is not uncommon when first contacting a MATZ.

Most military aviation communication takes place in the UHF (225-380MHz) band, and there is considerable use of common frequencies (i.e. frequencies available at all airfields). Two VHF frequencies provided at almost all military airfields are 122.1 for tower and 123.3 for talkdown (radar approach), although there may well be others in addition.

▶Lower Airspace Radar Service (LARS)

LARS is a service available in Class F and G airspace, up to FL95, from participating units. For full details of coverage, see the ENR section of the AIP.

A LARS unit will be able to offer a RAS or RIS service normally within 30nm of the airfield. Because the areas of service mostly overlap, it is usually possible for the pilot to be offered a hand-over to the next unit en-route, thereby reducing the pilot's workload. The pilot will be told to contact the next unit and that ATSU will already have his flight details.

Most LARS units provide a service within approximately 30nm of the ATSU.

Few LARS units are available 24 hours a day; the majority are located at military airfields where the radio hours of watch tend to be between 0800 and 1700 Monday-Friday, so it is not unusual to find LARS unavailable at weekends or during public holidays. The initial call should be in the same format as the initial call to a MATZ, e.g.

[ATSU callsign], this is [aircraft callsign], request Lower Airspace Radar Service

When asked to pass your details, you can give a standard TP HAIR message.

If you are unable to establish contact after three consecutive calls, you should assume that the service is not available. Remember to check pre-flight bulletins and NOTAMs, since military airfields may close for up to a week at certain times of the year.

▶ Danger Areas

Danger areas are designed to protect aircraft from activities which are dangerous to aircraft. This is another seemingly obvious fact, but it does not stop aircraft regularly entering active danger areas unannounced and running the risk of being fired at, having near-misses with military aircraft, getting tangled in target towing lines, dropped on by parachutists, etc. None of these things are conducive to a peaceful and pleasant flight, and all tend to generate an unwelcome amount of paperwork.

In the ENR section of the AIP, you will find details of the Danger Area Crossing Service or Danger Area Activity Information Service (DACS or DAAIS) which is available for certain Danger Areas. Details are also printed on aeronautical charts.

A DACS may be able to offer a clearance to cross a danger area, but will not necessarily be able to give any traffic information. A DAAIS can only advise on the present activity status of a danger area; it is then up to you to decide whether it is safe to cross it. *A DAAIS cannot issue a clearance to cross a danger area.*

The initial call to a DACS unit should take the following form:

[DACS unit] this is [aircraft callsign] request Danger Area Crossing Service for [danger area]

The initial call to a DAAIS unit should take the following form:

"[DAAIS unit] this is [aircraft callsign] request Danger Area Activity Information Service for [danger area]"

It is worth knowing that military controllers sometimes refer to an active danger area as "hot", and an inactive one as "cold" but, of course, if in doubt ask for clarification:

If in doubt – shout

If you are unable to contact a DACS/DAAIS you *must* play safe and keep well clear of the area. Always assume that a Danger Area is active unless someone clearly tells you otherwise.

▶ Use of Transponder

Despite its name, Secondary Surveillance Radar (SSR) is not really a radar system. It is an electronic interrogator which obtains information from the transponder carried on board an aircraft. In its most elementary form, SSR displays to the controller the four-figure number set on the transponder. This is positioned next to the aircraft's position on the radar screen and universally referred to by controllers as the 'squawk'. When using Mode C the controller's display will also show the aircraft's flight level. Usually in the case of commercial flights, the ATC computer is programmed to convert the four-figure squawk into the aircraft's callsign. The basic controls and functions of the transponder are:

TEST   this button or switch setting is used to test the transponder. When it is operated, the reply light should illuminate.

STBY   the transponder should be set to standby when it is switched on but not required to send a code. *Always set the transponder to standby before changing the code.*

ON   the transponder will give its set number to the radar unit. This is Mode A.

ALT   where a transponder is fitted with Mode C, this mode will give the aircraft's flight level (based on 1013mb/hPa) to the radar unit. Some units are able to process this read-out further and convert the screen display to show the aircraft's altitude based on the actual QNH. If a transponder is fitted with Mode C, this should always be selected unless instructed otherwise.

IDENT   when this button is pressed (on instruction from ATC) the aircraft's transponder return will flash on the radar screen.

A typical transponder unit. The four-figure code is selected using the dial under each window. The "Ident" button is usually under the ident light – which illuminates when the transponder is interrogated by ground based SSR:

The code '7326' set on the transponder, in this case with Mode C selected.

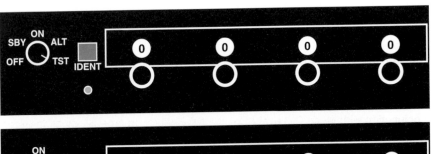

The most common standard SSR phrases are:

Standard Phraseology	Meaning
Squawk [code and mode]	Set this mode and code
Squawk standby	Set the transponder to the standby position
Squawk Charlie	Set the transponder to mode C
Squawk ident	Operate the ident button on the transponder
Confirm squawk [code]	Confirm the code and mode you have set on the transponder
Re-cycle [code][mode]	Set the transponder to standby, then re-select the assigned code and mode
Verify your level	Check and confirm your level (used to verify the Mode C flight level/altitude read-out the controller is seeing)

Note that SSR operating instructions require a read back.

G-DH, squawk 7326

Squawk 7326 G-DH

G-DH squawk standby

Squawk standby, G-DH

The assignment of a code does not mean that a radar service is being provided. If it is, the controller will notify this in a separate message. When leaving a frequency the controller may request you to squawk standby. This means he will be free to assign the code to another aircraft.

Radar units have blocks of transponder codes allocated for their use, but four are common throughout the world. These are:

7000   the standard conspicuity code, to be used outside controlled airspace if no other code has been allocated to the aircraft

7700   the emergency code – signifies the aircraft is in difficulties

7600   the radio failure code – the aircraft has experienced a communications failure

7500   the hi-jack code – the aircraft is being subject to unlawful interference

The conspicuity code (7000) should used when flying in the Open FIR (Class G airspace), unless an ATSU has given you a code to squawk. The transponder is normally set to standby when remaining within an ATZ (e.g. when flying circuits) unless an ATSU requests otherwise. All the above codes should be used in conjunction with Mode C if available. **DO NOT** select an emergency code except in an actual emergency.

Not all aircraft are fitted with a transponder, and indeed not all radar units have SSR capability. However, SSR coverage over the UK is very good, and a radar unit somewhere is almost certain to be receiving your squawk if your transponder is operating.

One final word on the subject of SSR phraseology. It has become a frequent (and dangerous) practice amongst some pilots to use the non-standard phrase "coming down" e.g.

G-CK squawk 5439

5439 coming down G-CK

The problem is that this could easily be construed by someone else (perhaps with the callsign 5439) as a descent instruction – with disastrous results. This is a good example of why non-standard phrases should not be used. As with several others, this one is mostly used by a 'Walter Mitty' pilot wishing to convey how clever he is. It doesn't work. This particular phrase is a pet hate of many pilots and controllers, for good reason.

▶ VHF Direction Finding (VDF)

In these days of radar and sophisticated navigation systems, the principle of radio direction-finding (DF) can seem old-fashioned. When a station transmits, a DF instrument indicates the direction from which the transmission is coming. This information can be passed to an aircraft either as its *bearing from* the DF station or its *track to* the station.

In years gone by, DF was commonly used for en-route navigation as well as for making an instrument approach to an airfield. Nowadays, the use of DF for en-route navigation is very rare and very few DF stations can offer an en-route navigation service. Several airfields still have DF-based approach procedures, but it is fair to say that these are rarely used except for training purposes. However, VDF is a simple and inexpensive system sometimes found at an airfield that does not have radar, and it still has its uses for guiding a pilot to an airfield.

The AD section of the AIP will detail any radio frequencies at an airfield that can offer a VDF service. VDF does not normally take place on a dedicated frequency, but is usually available on one or more of the approach frequencies. Once in contact with an ATSU offering a VDF facility, you must specify the type of service required. To do this use the appropriate Q code:

QDM   The magnetic track TO the VDF station; in other words the magnetic heading for the aircraft to steer to reach the VDF station, assuming no wind.

QDR   The magnetic bearing of the aircraft FROM the VDF station, the reciprocal of the QDM.

QTE   The true bearing FROM the VDF station – in other words the QDR corrected for magnetic variation.

When the VHF station passes DF information to an aircraft, it will be qualified as one of the following classes:

A   Accuracy +/- 2°

B   Accuracy +/- 5°

C   Accuracy +/- 10°

D   Accuracy worse than class C

VDF can be used by a controller to verify the bearing of an aircraft from the airfield, or it can be requested by a pilot to confirm the correct direction to the airfield. Once in contact with an ATSU with VDF facilities, the pilot requests the required information in the form of the relevant Q code. In this example we assume that the aircraft is already in contact with the ATSU:

G-BPRX, request QDM,
G-BPRX over

The aircraft's full callsign must be transmitted at the end of any request for DF. The use of the word over is intended to give the controller extra time to get a reasonable reading on the DF instrument:

G-RX, standby for QDM

G-RX, transmit for DF

Transmitting for DF, G-BPRX
over

G-RX your QDM is 320, class C

QDM 320 class C, G-BPRX

When a pilot is receiving a series of QDMs it is not usual for the ATSU to give the class of bearing each time, unless it has changed.

Communications

Although the use of DF is not common nowadays, you should be aware that VDF can help you find an airfield if you are uncertain of position (i.e. lost) or flying in marginal weather conditions. *In extremis*, VHF/DF can also be used for approach purposes in IMC via the (infamous) VDF let-down. Military controllers can offer the much more useful Controlled Descent Through Cloud (or QGH) procedure, in which the DF information is interpreted by the controller rather than the pilot. This obviously leads to a much reduced workload.

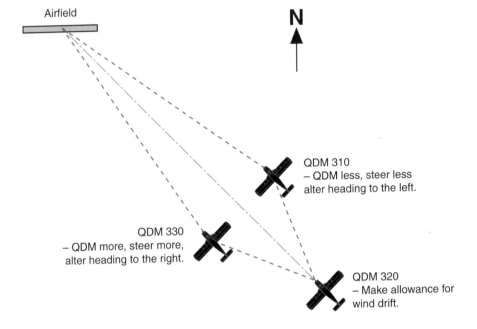

It is necessary to obtain a series of QDM's to check that you are maintaining a constant track to an airfield.

►VOLMET and ATIS

These recorded meteorological broadcasts take two forms:

VOLMET   Meteorological information for aircraft in flight

ATIS   Automatic Terminal Information Service

The VOLMET service broadcasts a set of METARS (weather-at-the-time reports, usually referred to as "actuals") for a set list of major airfields. It is used by pilots flying en-route, to check the current weather at one of the airfields referred to in the VOLMET broadcast. A VOLMET sequence will normally cover a set geographical area. In the UK there are four civilian VOLMET broadcasts on VHF, together with RAF VOLMET in the High Frequency (HF) band. The civil VOLMET broadcasts in the UK are:

London Volmet Main

London Volmet South

London Volmet North

Scottish Volmet

Details of this service (such as the frequency of each VOLMET broadcast and the airfields covered) can be found in the GEN section of the AIP, as well as in commercially produced flight guides.

Several airfields have a dedicated ATIS broadcast, which usually transmits on either a dedicated VHF frequency or is radiated by a VOR close to the airfield. An ATIS broadcasts the actual weather report for the airfield, together with the runway in use and any other relevant information. The broadcast is changed with each new METAR (these are normally observed at 20 minutes and 50 minutes past the hour) and to avoid confusion each new broadcast is given a letter, so that you can check that you have the most up-to-date information.

A typical ATIS broadcast might sound like this:

> This is Manchester Information Victor at 1120. Runway in use 24, radar vectors to the ILS. Surface wind 300 degrees 05 knots, 15 kilometres visibility, nil weather. Cloud scattered at 2500. Air temperature +15, dewpoint +8. QNH 1025, QFE for 24 1015. Northern taxyway India is closed east of taxyway Sierra. On initial contact confirm information Victor received.

When arriving at an airfield which has ATIS, the pilot should listen to the ATIS information before establishing contact with the ATSU. He should confirm receipt of the ATIS in the initial call by quoting the letter:

Manchester Approach, G-BGZE

G-BGZE Manchester Approach, pass your message

(Remember TP HAIR)

> G-BGZE is a PA-38 Tomahawk from Sleap, overhead Whitchurch heading 050 at 2500 feet QNH 1007, estimate Crewe at 25, inbound to Manchester, request VFR clearance to the airfield. **I have information V**

Likewise, ATIS should be checked before departure, and confirmed in the initial call:

> Bristol Tower, G-BURD on the main apron **with information W**, request taxy instructions

In reply the ATSU will confirm the runway and QNH for a positive read-back from the pilot,

> G-BURD roger, taxy for runway 09, QNH 1017

> Taxy for runway 09, QNH 1017 G-BURD

Details of the ATIS services can be found in the AIP and in commercially produced airfield guides.

If you have an air-band radio and live within range of either a transmitter site from which VOLMET is radiated or the local airfield ATIS, you obviously have an additional source of weather or airfield information to hand. If you have an HF receiver, RAF VOLMET is audible everywhere in the UK on 4722kHz and in certain areas also on 11200kHz. Other voice weather broadcasts are also available on HF.

▶Avoiding Confusion

Some more standard phraseology...

Standard Phraseology	Meaning
Break	This is a separation between messages
Check	Examine a system or procedure
Confirm	Have you/I correctly received [message/information]? Did you correctly receive this message?
Correct	That is correct
Correction	An error has been made. The correct message is..
Disregard	Consider that transmission was not sent
How do you read?	What is the readability of my transmissions?
I Say Again	I will repeat (for clarity or emphasis)
Say Again	Repeat all, or a specified part, of your last transmission
Speak Slower	Slow down your rate of speaking
Verify	Check and confirm
Words Twice	As a request: please transmit each word twice
	As information: I will transmit each word twice

Throughout this publication, you will have noticed the considerable emphasis on the principle of clear and unambiguous communication and the necessity of querying any message or instruction you do not fully understand. If communication difficulties arise, either because of poor radio reception/transmission or a misunderstanding between the ATSU and the pilot, it is as important as ever to use standard phraseology to avoid further confusing the situation.

An unwelcome development in RT communications has been that of 'malicious interference', namely unauthorised transmissions from unknown sources, often impersonating ATC and attempting to give false instructions or clearances. Given the availability of 'handheld' airband transceivers, the chances of one falling into the wrong hands – possibly through theft from authorised users – was always there. It has to be assumed that no sane pilot would act so stupidly and recklessly. Fortunately, occurrences seem to be rare, but the possibility only emphasises the importance of using, and expecting to hear, correct phraseology. Furthermore, once again the absolute necessity to query any anything that you do not fully understand or have confidence in is paramount. Experience so far has shown that malicious interference tends to cease when the false instructions are queried.

For example, imagine an aircraft inbound to Hawarden (near Chester). Hawarden has an elevation (AMSL) of 35 feet:

> Hawarden Tower G-RS, request QNH and QFE

> G-RS Hawarden Tower, the QNH is 1022, QFE 1011

There is a pause while G-RS thinks about this (remember 1 millibar is approximately equivalent to 30 feet)

> **Verify** Hawarden QFE, G-RS

> G-RS, **correction**, Hawarden QFE 1021, **I say again** QFE 1021

> QFE 1021 G-RS

In another example, an ATSU might want to check that an aircraft has correctly received a message:

> G-LJ, Runway in use 27, QNH 998 millibars

> Roger G-LJ

The pilot of G-LJ is at fault here. The reply "roger" only means that he has received the last transmission – by using the word "roger" he gives no indication that he has understood the message at all or will take any notice of it. You will remember that items such a runway in use and altimeter setting require a read-back:

> G-LJ **read-back** runway in use and QNH

> Runway 27, QNH 998 millibars G-LJ

> G-LJ, **that is correct**

If an aircraft or ATSU makes a mistake during a transmission, it can be corrected simply:

> Atlantic 05 contact Biggin Approach 119.4, **correction**, contact Biggin Approach 129.4

> Overhead Congleton **correction** overhead Crewe G-ZW

An aircraft with the registration G-ER has just taken off when he hears:

> G-ER cleared to land 27

which is something of a surprise. Perhaps he heard it incorrectly.

> **Say again** G-ER

> G-ER **disregard, break**, G-RE cleared to land 27

Additionally, you must tell the ATSU if for any reason you cannot follow an instruction they have issued. The phrase to use is 'Unable comply', for example:

🗼 G-YM climb Flight Level 70

✈ **Unable comply** due to cloud, G-YM

This is obviously better than attempting to comply with an instruction against your better judgement, or just ignoring it.

Its been said many times in this book that you should never hesitate to query, or request clarification of, any information/message/instruction that you do not understand. The importance of grasping this point cannot be over-stated.

An inexperienced pilot, especially a student pilot, may well be reluctant to query a lordly Air Traffic Controller, or admit that he does not understand something. Bear in mind that many of the people operating an ATSU are pilots themselves, and all of them should be particularly sensitive to the situation of a beginner pilot. Perhaps even more than pilots, ATSU personnel value the importance of clear communication and will patiently repeat or clarify something until both parties are satisfied. In case you've forgotten it – as if you could – the standard maxim *always* applies -

If in doubt – shout!

whether you are talking to a weekend air/ground radio operator at a grass strip or the Senior Tower Controller at London Heathrow.

▶ An En-Route Sequence (non-radar)

G– BOEN is a C-172 flying from Mona (on Anglesey) to Derby airfield:

✈ Liverpool Approach, G-BOEN

🗼 G-BOEN Liverpool Approach, pass your message

✈ G-BOEN is a C-172 from Mona, overhead Rhyl heading 140 at 2500ft Holyhead regional 1014, VFR en-route to Derby request radar information service

🗼 G-EN roger. Flight information service only. The Holyhead regional QNH is 1014, the Barnsley 1015

✈ Flight information service, Holyhead 1014, Barnsley 1015 G-EN

✈ G-EN traffic information is a Mooney, passed Wallasey two minutes ago bound for Dublin, altitude 1500 feet

➤ Traffic copied G-EN

☗ G-EN report abeam Holywell

➤ Wilco G-EN

➤ G-EN abeam Holywell, changing to Hawarden Approach 123.35

☗ G-EN frequency change approved

➤ Hawarden Approach, G-BOEN

☗ G-EN Hawarden Approach, pass your message

➤ G-EN is a Cessna 172 from Mona. south abeam Holywell heading 140 at 2500ft Barnsley QNH 1015. Estimate overhead Hawarden at 35, VFR, destination Derby

☗ G-EN roger, Flight information service, Hawarden QNH 1017. There are two aircraft in the circuit, report overhead Hawarden

➤ Flight information service, Hawarden QNH 1017, wilco G-EN

Note. Although at this altitude the aircraft will not enter the Hawarden ATZ, it is clearly good airmanship to contact Hawarden.

►An En-Route Sequence (radar)

G-BHFS is a Robin flying from Gloucestershire (formerly Staverton) to Cranfield:

➤ Brize Radar this is G-BHFS

☗ Aircraft calling Brize Radar, wait

☗ Aircraft calling Brize Radar, say again callsign and pass your message

➤ G-BHFS is a Robin, from Gloucestershire 5 miles east of Gloucestershire heading 070 passing 2500ft for FL 50, estimate Upper Heyford at 47 IFR en-route to Cranfield, request Radar Advisory Service

G-FS roger, Cotswold QNH 1005, squawk 4356

Cotswold 1005, say again squawk G-FS

G-FS squawk 4356

Squawk 4356 G-FS

G-FS you are identified 7 miles east of Gloucestershire airfield, radar advisory, report reaching FL50

Radar advisory service, wilco G-FS

G-FS maintaining FL50

Roger G-FS

G-FS for separation descend to altitude 2500ft Cotswold QNH 1005

Descend to 2500ft Cotswold QNH 1005 G-FS

G-FS, limited traffic information on your right as you approach Upper Heyford due to traffic density

Roger G-FS

G-FS pop-up traffic 12 oclock, range three miles opposite direction, height unknown, slow-moving. If not sighted turn right, heading 100

Right heading 100 G-FS

G-FS clear of traffic, resume own navigation for Upper Heyford, magnetic track 070, range five miles

Wilco, and maintaining 2500ft G-FS

Roger G-FS

G-FS overhead Upper Heyford, new heading 080

Roger G-FS

G-FS approaching the limit of radar cover, radar advisory service terminated, squawk 7000 free-call Cranfield approach 132.85 correction 122.85

Radar advisory terminated, squawk 7000 changing frequency to Cranfield 122.85 G-FS

▶ Revision

27 What is the correct reply to an instruction to "standby"

28 Is it necessary to read back frequency-change information?

29 What is implied by the word 'contact'?

30 What is implied by the word 'free-call'?

31 What is the meaning of the word 'wilco'?

32 What are the two types of radar service generally available to aircraft in uncontrolled airspace?

33 What is the correct clock code for traffic on your left wing-tip?

34 Is it mandatory to obtain permission to transit the Aerodrome Traffic Zone of a military aerodrome?

35 Where can you find details of the LARS?

36 Should a transponder code be changed when the transponder is set to On?

37 Do SSR instructions require a read-back?

38 What is the SSR conspicuity code?

39 What is a QDM?

40 What level of VDF accuracy is defined as 'class C'?

41 What is the name/abbreviation of a recorded broadcast giving weather and other information for a specific airfield?

42 What is the meaning of the phrase "say again"?

43 Under what circumstances can a pilot request an ATSU to 'say again'?

Answers at page RT102

Arrival/Traffic Pattern Procedures

▶ Inbound to an Airfield

▶ Circuit Joining and Overhead Joins

▶ Standard Circuit Procedures

▶ Orbit and Extend Phrases

▶ Wake Turbulence

▶ Landing Clearance

▶ Touch and Go

▶ Go-around

▶ The Visual Circuit at Military Airfields

▶ Vacating The Runway and Taxy Instructions

▶ Complete Sequence – arriving at an airfield with a
  AFIS

▶ Complete Sequence – visual circuits at an airfield
  with ATC

▶ Revision

▶Inbound to an Airfield

When approaching an airfield inside controlled airspace, it is **imperative** to receive positive clearance to enter controlled airspace. Simply establishing contact with the ATSU does *not* imply that the aircraft is cleared into controlled airspace. The pilot *must* receive and read back an explicit clearance to enter controlled airspace. Even at an airfield in the Open FIR (Class G) it is a requirement to have established contact with the ATSU before entering an active ATZ. Take another look at Airspace Classifications if you're not sure of the fine details.

To reduce the chances of an aircraft's transmission interfering with communications at another airfield using the same frequency, the CAA recommends the following maximum ranges for contacting an airfield ATSU:

At an international airfield

Tower: up to a range of 25nm and a height of 4000ft

Approach: up to a range of 25nm and a height of 10,000ft

At other airfields: communications with a Tower, AFIS or air/ground facility should be restricted to the immediate vicinity of the airfield, and heights below 1000ft; and in any case not more than 10nm from the airfield nor above 3000ft.

In the interests of safety or observing good airmanship, you may well decide to establish two-way communications when beyond these recommended distances.

Many airfields use Visual Reference Points (VRPs). Notified VRPs are marked on topographical aeronautical charts and you can expect to be routed with reference to these points. Occasionally, however, an ATSU may refer to landmarks not depicted on the chart. If you are requested to report at a landmark that you cannot find on the map – do not hesitate to ask for further information:

If in doubt – shout!

An inbound aircraft will be passed the airfield details: runway in use, surface wind, altimeter pressure settings, inbound/outbound aircraft, circuit traffic and any other relevant information such as circuit direction, runway surface state etc. Remember to read back information which requires a read-back, such as the runway in use and the altimeter pressure settings.

Do not hesitate to request the use of a different runway, for instance if there is a strong crosswind on the runway in use. The ATSU will do its best to accommodate this, although there may be a delay if other traffic is using the runway selected by the ATSU.

The surface of the airfield is inspected at least once per day at licenced airfields. Any potential problems (work in progress, temporary obstructions, soft ground etc.) will be relayed to pilots. Surface deposits may be described as dry snow, wet snow or slush. The presence of water on a runway is reported in accordance with the following standard descriptions:

Description	Runway condition
Damp	The surface shows a change of colour due to moisture
Wet	The surface is soaked but no significant patches of standing water are visible
Water Patches	Significant patches of standing water are visible
Flooded	Extensive standing water is visible

Additionally, at a grass airfield, the runway surface may be described as "very wet" when circumstances warrant it. If the description of the surface is based on a report from an aircraft, or as seen from the ATSU (as opposed to that observed during an actual airfield inspection), the following phraseology is used:

Unofficial observation from [the control tower/a preceding aircraft]. The runway surface condition appears to be [condition].

▶ Circuit Joining and Overhead Joins

The ATSU will normally specify circuit joining instructions e.g. join downwind, join base leg, join long finals etc.. Where circuit direction is variable, or if a right-hand circuit is in use, the circuit direction will also be specified. It is obviously important that you are certain of the runway in use, the circuit direction and how you are to join the circuit. When arriving at an airfield do not hesitate to ask for clarification or assistance to join in the correct position for the correct runway. There have been many reported instances of aircraft landing on the wrong runway, a taxyway, or even at the wrong airfield! The culprits are not necessarily inexperienced pilots; many professional crews have been caught out as well. Preparation is the key – know what you are looking for and do not make the view outside fit into the picture you expect to see. As always, the ATSU is there to help you:

If in doubt – shout!

Communications

Smaller airfields may have an overhead join as the standard circuit-joining procedure. This can be easier than joining straight into the circuit at a strange airfield, and is the favoured procedure where radio and non-radio aircraft may be operating together.

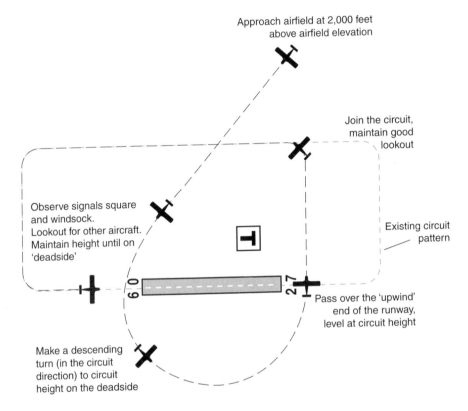

The standard overhead join

Approach airfield at 2,000 feet above airfield elevation

Join the circuit, maintain good lookout

Observe signals square and windsock.
Lookout for other aircraft.
Maintain height until on 'deadside'

Existing circuit pattern

Pass over the 'upwind' end of the runway, level at circuit height

Make a descending turn (in the circuit direction) to circuit height on the deadside

If an airfield has a non-standard overhead join this will be notified in the AIP and/or commercial flight guides such as the UK VFR Flight Guide.

▶ Standard Circuit Procedures

The standard circuit pattern and associated phraseology is shown below:

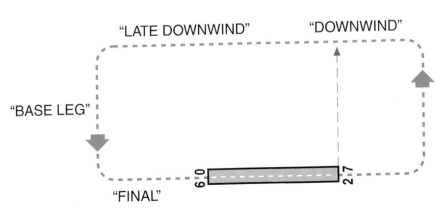

The radio position reports in the standard circuit pattern

"LATE DOWNWIND"   "DOWNWIND"

"BASE LEG"

"FINAL"

Where an ATC unit is in operation, the controller may specify a landing order to maintain traffic separation:

G-GH downwind

G-GH **number 2** follow the Cessna 152 on base leg

The pilot must keep to this landing order. Of course you have to keep the other aircraft in sight throughout to maintain the proper separation.

At an airfield with an AFIS or air/ground unit, the pilots will be passed traffic information and expected to maintain their own separation:

G-EM downwind

G-EM one Tomahawk ahead on base leg.

Pilots should maintain their own separation based on the rules of the air, which you should revise now if they have slipped from your mind...

▶Orbit and Extend Phrases

At times an ATC unit may need to give delaying or expediting instructions to co-ordinate traffic. The two most common instructions are to orbit or to extend the downwind leg. The controller should specify the direction of the orbit (one 360° turn):

G-CD downwind

G-CD, **orbit left** and report again downwind

Wilco G-CD

or

G-CD downwind

G-CD, **extend downwind,** number 2 to the 737 on three-mile finals

Wilco G-CD

▶ Wake Turbulence

When operating in the vicinity of large aircraft, the possibility of wake turbulence should always be recognised.

Aircraft in the heavy wake-turbulence category i.e. a maximum take-off weight of 136,000kg or over, may use the suffix 'Heavy' after their callsign on initial contact.

When the possibility of wake turbulence exists, the ATSU may caution the possibility of wake turbulence and pass the recommended minimum spacing:

> ♜ G-NB number two to the 767 on short finals. **Caution vortex wake**. The recommended spacing is eight miles.*

*Note that for various reasons the UK operates wake-vortex separations which are different from ICAO recommendations.

Responsibility for maintaining proper spacing remains with the pilot of the following aircraft, so you can increase spacing at your discretion.

▶ Landing Clearance

Landing clearance is normally passed to an aircraft when it has reported on finals, and *must* be read back. An aircraft on finals will not be given clearance to land while another aircraft is holding on the runway.

Once established on final approach to the runway, report 'long final' if between 8 and 4 miles from the threshold

A controller may delay giving landing clearance, by using the instruction "continue approach":

> 🛬 G-BB final

> ♜ G-BB continue approach, surface wind 310/15

> 🛬 Continue approach G-BB

In this instance landing clearance has *not* been given. You must wait for landing clearance to be given when you are further down the approach.

When landing clearance is given, it normally takes the following form and is read back:

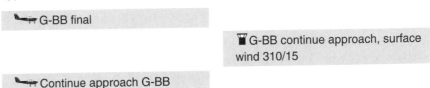

> 🛬 G-ZX final

> ♜ G-ZX **cleared to land** runway 28, surface wind 260/20

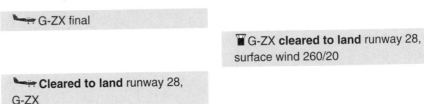

> 🛬 **Cleared to land** runway 28, G-ZX

Arrival/Traffic Pattern Procedures

On occasion, an aircraft might be allowed to land on a runway, behind another aircraft on the same runway – the instruction is "land after". A land after is only offered subject to the following conditions:

1. The runway is long enough to allow adequate separation.

2. It is daylight.

3. The controller is satisfied that the landing aircraft will be able to keep the aircraft ahead in sight at all times.

4. The pilot of the landing aircraft has been warned of the other aircraft.

If the pilot of the landing aircraft chooses to accept a land-after instruction, he becomes responsible for maintaining adequate separation between the two aircraft:

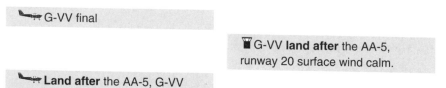

G-VV final

G-VV **land after** the AA-5, runway 20 surface wind calm.

Land after the AA-5, G-VV

At an airfield with an AFIS unit, clearances cannot be issued and so a different phraseology is used when an aircraft reports final:

G-YU final

G-YU **land at your discretion**, surface wind 180/10

Wilco G-YU

At an airfield with an air/ground unit a typical exchange would be:

G-AU final

Roger G-AU, surface wind 090/5

Roger G-AU

When giving a landing clearance (or a land at your discretion message) the surface wind will normally be given. It is not necessary to read back this information. If the ATSU thinks it might be helpful, it may pass further reports of the wind speed and direction; these do not require a reply. Obviously you can request a wind check at any time if it might be useful to you.

▶ Touch And Go

When making a number of take-offs and landings for training it is common to make a 'Touch and Go', i.e. to land, roll along the runway and take-off without stopping. It is useful to notify the ATSU of the intention to do this before making the finals call:

G-CD, downwind, touch and go

The ATSU will also want to know if you are going to make a type of approach and landing which will alter the normal circuit shape e.g. a glide or a flapless approach.

▶ Go-around

A go-around may also be known as a 'missed approach', although this phrase is most often associated with IFR operation.

When making a go-around, you should inform the ATSU when able to do so (remember that the flying of the aeroplane is your no.1 priority):

G-CD, **going around**

G-CD roger

If the go-around is initiated by the ATSU, the instruction will be:

G-CD, **go-around**, I say again **go-around**, acknowledge.

This instruction should be acted on immediately and acknowledged when it is safe to do so:

Going around G-CD

During the go-around the aircraft is positioned to the 'deadside' of the runway

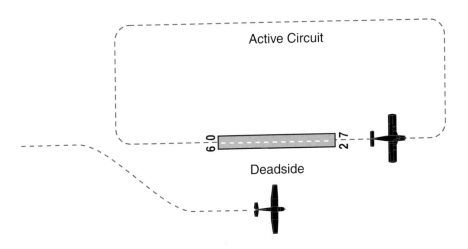

Active Circuit

Deadside

If you are planning to make a go-around it is helpful to notify the ATSU before making the final call.

An aircraft on an IFR approach is expected to follow the published missed-approach procedure after a go-around. An aircraft making a VFR approach is expected to climb on the dead side of the runway, and then continue into the normal circuit pattern.

▶The Visual Circuit at Military Airfields

Military aircraft tend to fly visual circuits with semi-circular crosswind and base legs, as illustrated below:

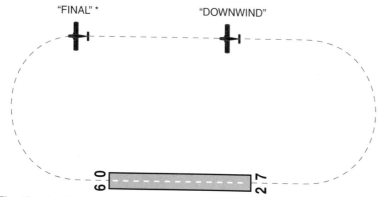

"FINAL" *   "DOWNWIND"

The oval shape of the standard military visual circuit

* The 'final' call is made immediately before turning base leg

There are some differences in phraseology. A touch-and-go may be referred to as a 'roller' e.g.

G-SN downwind to roll

G-SN number one, report finals surface wind 030/15

Additionally a military ATSU may refer to the number of aircraft in the circuit using the phraseology "[number of aircraft in the circuit] in":

G-OC field in sight

Roger G-OC, join downwind left-hand for runway 15, **two in**

At a military airfield the word 'go-around' can be used to instruct an aircraft to fly another circuit. It is common practice to climb back to circuit height on the dead side and report "Dead side" before turning on to the crosswind leg.

▶ Vacating the Runway and Taxy Instructions

The ATSU will not normally give taxy instructions or information until the aircraft is at the end of its landing run. A point or direction to leave the runway may be specified:

> 📡 G-TR, **vacate left** at the **high-speed exit**

> ✈ **Vacate left** at the **high-speed exit**, G-TR

It is worth reiterating at this point that it is the pilot, not ATC, who is ultimately responsible for the safety of the aircraft and those inside it. Sometimes ATC may give you a 'vacate' instruction even before you have landed – e.g. "Vacate first right after landing". If you cannot safely comply with this instruction, *say so.* There is little point breaking the aeroplane in an attempt to comply with an instruction you never thought you could cope with in the first place.

An aircraft may report that it has vacated the runway, and will then be passed taxy instructions. The "runway vacated" call should only be made once the aircraft has cleared the holding-point position as it leaves the runway:

> ✈ G-OK Runway vacated

> 📡 G-OK roger, taxy to the south apron

> ✈ Taxy to the south apron G-OK

More than one pilot has successfully completed a long flight only to get hopelessly lost on the ground at a large airfield. Ask for clarification or assistance before a small uncertainty becomes a major incident.

If in doubt – shout!

▶ Complete Sequence – arriving at an airfield with AFIS

> ✈ Waltham Information, this is G-BOBZ

> 📡 G-BOBZ Waltham Information, pass your message

> ✈ G-BOBZ is a PA28 Warrior, from Thruxton, overhead Henley-on-Thames heading 100 at 2000ft QNH 1025, estimate White Waltham at 37. Inbound, request joining information

G-BZ roger, overhead join for runway 25 left-hand circuit, surface wind 260/10, QNH 1025, QFE 1020, two aircraft currently in the circuit

Runway 25, QNH 1025, QFE 1020 G-BZ

G-BZ has the field in sight, joining overhead

G-BZ roger, report downwind, one Cessna late downwind

Wilco G-BZ

G-BZ downwind

G-BZ roger, report final, one Cessna on one-mile final, one Cherokee on crosswind leg

Wilco, G-BZ

G-BZ final 25

G-BZ land at your discretion, surface wind 250/5

Wilco G-BZ

▶ **Complete Sequence – visual circuits at an airfield with ATC**

G-UD downwind touch-and-go

G-UD roger, continue to final number one

Continue to final G-UD

G-UD final 19 for touch-and-go

G-UD cleared touch and go 19, surface wind 180/10

Cleared touch and go 19 G-UD

G-UD late downwind for flapless touch-and-go

G-UD roger, extend downwind and report before turning base leg. You are number two to a King Air on 4-mile final

Communications

Extend downwind, traffic copied G-UD

G-UD ready to turn base leg, traffic in sight

G-UD report final number two

Report final number 2 G-UD

G-UD final 19 for touch and go

G-UD continue

Continue G-UD

G-UD land after the King Air runway 19, surface wind 200/5

G-UD cleared take-off 19, surface wind 190/10

Land after, 19, G-UD

Cleared take-off 19 G-UD

G-UD downwind for glide approach, to land

G-UD report on base leg, new QFE 1001

Wilco, QFE 1001 G-UD

G-UD base leg

G-UD one orbit right and report again on base leg, one aircraft to depart runway 19

One orbit right, G-UD

G-UD orbit complete

G-UD report final, number one

Report final G-UD

G-UD final to land 19

G-UD cleared to land 19, surface wind 190/15

Cleared to land 19 G-UD

G-UD going around

Arrival/Traffic Pattern Procedures

G-UD Roger

G-UD report downwind

Wilco G-UD

G-UD downwind for glide approach to land

G-UD number two, follow the Seneca on base leg

Number 2 to the Seneca G-UD

G-UD final to land 19

G-UD cleared to land 19, surface wing 190/10

Cleared to land 19 G-UD

G-UD, runway vacated

G-UD taxy to the flying club

Taxy to the flying club, G-UD

▶Revision

44 What radio report could an aircraft make when established on final approach six miles from the runway?

45 What instruction would an ATC unit use to allow an aircraft to land behind another landing aircraft on the same runway?

46 If a pilot chooses to accept a land-after instruction, who is responsible for maintaining separation between the leading and following aircraft?

47 What phraseology would an air/ground station use to indicate that it does not know of any reason why an aircraft should not land?

48 In a military visual circuit, what is a 'roller'?

Answers at page RT103

Communications Failure

Communications

Communications
Failure

▶ Alternative Frequencies

▶ Aircraft Equipment Serviceability Checks

▶ In-Flight Procedures

▶ Light Signals from an ATSU to an Aircraft in Flight

▶ Light Signals from an Aircraft in Flight to an ATSU

▶ Revision

▶ Alternative Frequencies

If you suspect a radio failure while in flight, you should first make some simple checks before assuming a major problem:

1   Is the correct frequency selected ?

2   Should the ATSU being called be open?

3   Is the aircraft in range of the ATSU?

If still unable to make contact, change back to the last frequency in use or – if that is not possible – to an alternative frequency.

If you are still unable to make radio contact, equipment failure is more likely.

▶ Aircraft Equipment Serviceability Checks

The most common pilot-induced errors (finger trouble) can be eliminated by checking the radio volume and the PTT switches:

Many aircraft have a separate 'avionics master switch'

1   If the radio frequency seems especially quiet, check that the volume is correctly set (this can be verified using the squelch control), or make a transmission to the ATSU to check all is OK.

2   Check that none of the PTT switches in the aircraft have stuck in the transmit position (an open mic.). If you have an open mic. everything said on the intercom is being broadcast. As said earlier, this completely blocks the frequency and can be embarrassing.

If checking the above does not clear the problem, a more detailed check of the aircraft equipment is necessary:

1   Check that you do not have an electrical problem. What is the ammeter reading? Has the master switch (or main avionics power switch, if there is one) been switched off? Has a circuit breaker popped?

2   Check that the radio volume is properly set and that the radio is actually turned on. Adjust the squelch control to check volume and receiver sensitivity.

3   If applicable, check that the audio selector box is properly set. Are you using COM1 or COM2? Is the output routed to speaker or headset? Is that correct?

4   Check that the headset leads/microphone leads are secure. If possible try alternative headsets/microphones, alternative radio, standby PTT etc.

Communications Failure

▶In-Flight Procedures

The in-flight procedure in the event of a communications failure will vary depending on the type of flight (i.e. IFR/VFR), the stage of the flight (in the circuit, en-route etc.) and the class of airspace you are currently occupying.

If you happen to be flying IFR in controlled airspace, there are set (and unfortunately rather complicated) procedures laid down. Full details are given in the AIP and also in airways flight guides such as those from Aerad or Jeppesen.

When flying VFR, procedures are less rigid. Generally you should proceed to the last cleared point and then head for the nearest suitable airfield and look for light signals from the ATSU. When arriving at an airfield outside controlled airspace, a standard overhead join will be the favoured option. This will give you plenty of time to check the signals square, look for light signals and integrate into any existing circuit traffic.

If you were approaching controlled airspace at the time of the radio failure, you must not enter controlled airspace unless you had been specifically cleared to do so before the radio failure. If you were not cleared to enter controlled airspace, you should remain clear of it and land at a suitable airfield. One exception to this rule is if you had an SVFR clearance, in which case you must remain clear of controlled airspace even if you had already been granted a clearance to enter.

If the aircraft is equipped with a transponder, the radio communications failure code (7600) should be set.

You might suspect that the transmitter part of the radio is working but not the receiver. In this case you should broadcast your intentions with the message:

[Callsign], **transmitting blind**

in case the transmitter is still working. At scheduled times or positions you should transmit a position report and intentions twice, preceding the message with:

[Callsign], **transmitting blind** due to receiver failure.

Alternatively, the microphone or audio circuitry of the transmitter might fail, leaving it transmitting what is known as carrier wave only. In this case the receiver may well be working. You could then use the speechless code, originated by the military. All you do is to key the PTT switch, as though you were sending Morse code, in accordance with the following:

Number of dots or dashes		Interpretation
One Short	•	Yes or Acknowledged
Two Short	• •	No
Three Short	• • •	Say again,
		– the last transmission was not fully heard
		– the last transmission was not fully understood
		– the last instruction cannot be complied with
Four Short	• • • •	Request homing (heading to steer to reach an airfield)
	(H in Morse)	
One Long	—	Manoeuvre complete
	(two seconds)	
One long, two short, one long		I have another emergency, or a
— • • —	(X in Morse)	greater degree of emergency

The request for homing (• • •) can be used for making initial contact with a controller, although a civilian controller might not recognise it as readily as a military ATSU controller will. When contact has been established, the controller will assign you the callsign "speechless aircraft" if he does not know your identity, and ask some questions which can be answered yes or no.

As a last resort, in the event of a complete communications failure during which you are also uncertain of position, there is a published procedure developed to attract the attention of a radar-equipped ATSU. The pilot should use the radio communications failure transponder code (7600) and attempt to make contact on the emergency frequency 121.50. The aircraft should be flown high enough to ensure terrain clearance and increase the chances of being seen by radar, without entering IMC.

Communications Failure

The basic procedure is to fly a triangular pattern – left or right depending on the nature of the radio problem – to alert a radar ATSU unit to your difficulty. Each leg of the triangle is supposed to be two minutes long if your TAS is below 300kt, and all turns are to be as sharp as practicable. You turn to the *left* if *everything* has failed, and turn to the *right* if only the *transmitter* has failed. If a radar ATSU sees a triangular pattern being flown, it will arrange for a shepherd aircraft to intercept the non-radio aircraft and lead it to a suitable airfield.

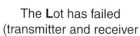

1 minute if average airspeed is over 300kts
2 minutes if average airspeed is under 300kts

Make turns as tight as possible

The radio failure triangles

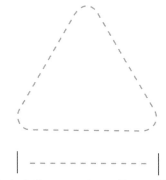

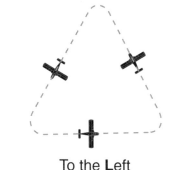

To the **R**ight

The **R**eceiver is working
(receiver only operative)

To the **L**eft

The **L**ot has failed
(transmitter and receiver
inoperative)

This procedure is not the easiest to fly; amongst other things it is necessary to make allowance for the wind in order to 'paint' a good triangle on the radar and not drift downwind. The other minor drawback is that it doesn't seem to work. Several pilots have tried the procedure for real, but have not been rewarded by the promised shepherd aircraft. Flying triangles is one of those ideas that looks fine in text books and official publications, but doesn't seem to stand up to the 'real life' test. In short, if you have a radio failure, do not put all your hopes on this procedure working – you may well have to find your own way home!

Communications

It is worth noting that many pilots now fly with a small hand-held VHF transceiver as a back-up in case the aircraft's own radio(s) fail. There are several recorded occasions where possession of such a unit has allowed a pilot to land safely after the aircraft's radios had failed in IMC conditions. Some of the better transceivers even include a VOR facility, which is not as accurate as the aircraft's own but is better than nothing! For similar reasons there is something to be said for possession of a hand-held GPS receiver, especially if it can operate from internal batteries as well as the aircraft's cigar-lighter socket.

▶ Light Signals from an ATSU to an Aircraft in Flight

Light Signal	FROM AN AERODROME	
	to Aircraft in Flight	to Aircraft on Ground
STEADY RED	Give way to other aircraft and continue circling	Stop
RED PYROTECHNIC LIGHT OR RED FLARE	Do not land; wait for permission	–
RED FLASHES	Do not land; aerodrome not available for landing	Move clear of landing area
GREEN FLASHES	Return to aerodrome; wait for permission to land	**To an aircraft:** You may move on the manoeuvring area and apron **To a vehicle:** you may move on the manoeuvring area
STEADY GREEN	You may land	You may take-off
WHITE FLASHES	Land at this aerodrome after receiving continuous green light and then, after receiving green flashes, proceed to apron	Return to starting point on the aerodrome

▶ Light Signals from an Aircraft in Flight to an ATSU

Light Signal	From an aircraft in flight to an aerodrome
RED PYROTECHNIC LIGHT OR RED FLARE	Immediate assistance is requested
STEADY GREEN GREEN FLASHES OR PYROTECHNIC	**By night:** May I land? **By day:** May I land in a direction different from that indicated by the landing T?
WHITE FLASHES WHITE PYROTECHNIC LIGHTS SWITCHING ON AND OFF LANDING LIGHTS OR IRREGULAR FLASHING OF THE NAVIGATION LIGHTS	I am compelled to land

▶Revision

49 You are inbound to an airfield inside controlled airspace and have received a SVFR clearance to enter the control zone. Before entering the zone you experience a complete radio failure. Can you proceed to the airfield?

50 What is the transponder code to indicate a radio failure?

51 In the speechless code, what is the transmission to request a homing?

Answers at page RT103

Emergency Procedures

▶ Priority Messages

▶ Emergency Frequencies

▶ Emergency Facilities

▶ Distress/Urgency Calls

▶ Relay of Emergency Messages

▶ Maintenance of Silence

▶ Cancellation of Emergency

▶ Uncertainty of Position

▶ Practice Emergencies

▶ Fire Services

▶ Revision

*Emergency
Procedures*

▶ Priority Messages

There are two classifications of emergency.

Distress   The aircraft is threatened by serious and/or imminent danger and requires immediate assistance:

Spoken word – **MAYDAY**

Morse Code ••• — — — •••

Urgency   A condition concerning the safety of an aircraft or other vehicle, or of some person on board or in sight, but not requiring immediate assistance:

Spoken word – **PAN PAN**

Morse Code — •• — — •• — — • •—

A distress (Mayday) message takes priority over *all other radio messages.*

An urgency (Pan Pan) message takes priority over *all messages except a distress message.*

▶ Emergency Frequencies

The pilot of an aircraft which develops an emergency should always attempt to make contact on the frequency currently in use. If this is not possible, the International Aeronautical Emergency Frequency (121.5) should be used. Do not hesitate to make an emergency call if the situation warrants it, since clearly an ATSU cannot begin to offer assistance to you unless it knows you have a problem. An aircraft with an emergency will receive priority over all other aircraft, and all manner of rescue services and facilities can be obtained via an ATSU (shepherd aircraft, SAR services, navigation assistance, weather information, use of normally unavailable airfields etc.).

▶ Emergency Facilities

Several larger ATSUs and some Coastguard stations have facilities to transmit and receive on 121.5, but in the UK a call on this frequency will usually be answered by a Distress and Diversion (D&D) cell. The UK has two D&D cells, one each in the London and Scottish Area Control Centres. Their callsigns are London Centre and Scottish Centre respectively, and in fact the provision of these dedicated D&D cells within an ACC is unique to the UK. The emergency controllers always stress that when they are contacted, they prefer to know exactly what the pilot's actual situation is. It is better to state clearly that you are lost, as opposed to muttering something along the lines of "request confirmation of position". The D&D cells have access to a great many facilities to locate and aid an aircraft with an emergency. There is no charge for use of the service (it is an unfounded rumour that the correct RT terminology is "pass callsign, nature of emergency and credit-card number") and the service is available 24 hours a day, every day of the year. Given the excellent resources at their disposal, it is silly not to make use of D&D if you think they might be able to help you in any way. As anybody who has visited a D&D cell will tell you, it is an exceedingly impressive set-up.

▶ Distress/Urgency Calls

When a distress or urgency call is made, the following format should be used when possible:

1 MAYDAY, MAYDAY, MAYDAY for distress

   or

   PAN PAN, PAN PAN, PAN PAN for urgency

2 Name of the station addressed

3 Aircraft callsign

4 Aircraft Type

5 Nature of emergency

6 Intentions of pilot

7 Position (or last known position); Flight Level/Altitude/Height; Heading

8 Pilot qualifications (e.g. No instrument qualification: IMC rating etc.)

9 Any other useful information e.g. persons on board etc..

If you like mnemonics, it can be remembered as NAAN IPPA.

Although the inclusion of the pilot qualification in a distress message is not an ICAO requirement, it may be helpful to controllers in assisting you. Inexperienced pilots are encouraged to use the word "tyro", as is mandatory in military flying.

The CAA recommends that a pilot with an emergency *always* make either a Mayday or Pan Pan call, rather than a non-specific message about a 'technical problem' or 'temporary difficulty' etc. Specifically, the term 'Fuel Emergency' has no status in the UK; to get priority in this situation the pilot must make an emergency call. If you have an emergency **say so** by making either a Mayday or Pan Pan call, the ATSU can then best help you and if the situation is resolved, the distress or urgency can always be cancelled.

Here is an example of a Mayday call. An aircraft with the callsign of AUTOAIR 3 has experienced an engine failure:

MAYDAY, MAYDAY, MAYDAY

N   Southampton approach...

A   ...this is AUTOAIR 3...

A   ...Piper Malibu...

N   ...with a complete engine failure...

I   ...forced landing at Beaulieu disused airfield...

P   ...current position one mile north of Lymington, altitude 1500 feet, heading 340...

P   ...CPL...

A   ...two POB. (POB = Persons On Board)

Now here is an example of a Pan Pan call. G-DASH has a rough-running engine:

PAN PAN, PAN PAN, PAN PAN

N   Bristol approach...

A   ...this is G-DASH...

A   ...Rockwell Commander...

N   ...with a rough-running engine...

I   ...diverting to Bristol airfield...

P   ...present position one mile west abeam Clevedon, FL50, heading 160...

P   ...PPL...

A   ...three POB...(POB = Persons On Board)

The proper sequence of the distress/urgency call must be memorised to pass the RT licence test. However, in a real-life emergency situation, you must judge the best course of action for the safety of the aircraft and passengers. Making a word-perfect distress call is infinitely less important than **flying the aircraft** and **handling the emergency.** From the Flying Training book you may remember the order of priorities for a pilot:

Aviate   Fly the aeroplane

Navigate   Know where you are, where you are going and what you are doing

Communicate   Converse with the ATSU.

This order of priorities is *never* more important than during an emergency. If it all goes wrong one day, do not allow talking on the radio to become more important than your primary task of **flying the aeroplane**.

To help ATC locate you precisely in an emergency, the transponder emergency code of 7700 should be selected if you are not already using an ATC-allocated squawk.

▶Relay of Emergency Messages

Anybody hearing an emergency call should take the details, in case the message is not received by an ATSU. If an ATSU does not receive the emergency call, you should relay the message, making it clear that you yourself are *not* the aircraft that has the emergency:

> MAYDAY, MAYDAY, MAYDAY
> Leeds Approach,
> G-OAFE. **Have intercepted Mayday call from** G-LOST.
> I say again G-LOST
> PA-28, Engine fire, making a forced landing four miles south of Shipley, altitude 2000ft heading 270, CPL three POB

> G-OAFE, Leeds approach, roger your **relayed Mayday** from G-LOST

If the aircraft you are flying has two radios and one is not being used, it makes sense to set it to 121.5 so that you can keep a 'listening watch' for a possible emergency call. This is particularly relevant if you are flying in a remote or inhospitable region where other aircraft and airfields may be few and far between.

Equally, even if you have force-landed in the middle of nowhere, a call on 121.5 stands a decent chance of being heard and relayed, either by another aircraft or the SARSAT (Search & Rescue Satellite Aided Tracking) system. With a bit of luck, the search-and-rescue services will be on their way before you have to break into the emergency chocolate bars.

▶Maintenance of Silence

Upon hearing an emergency call, all other aircraft on the frequency *must* maintain radio silence **unless they are genuinely able to offer assistance**. The aircraft in the emergency, or the ATSU, can impose silence on all other aircraft or on any one station:

> G-CERT, **stop transmitting**, Mayday

or

> All stations, Lydd Tower, **stop transmitting**, Mayday

Communications

Where possible the ATSU will transfer all other aircraft to another frequency by a general broadcast:

> ▼ Mayday G-COSY. All other traffic contact Luton approach on 129.55, out

▶ Cancellation of Emergency

An aircraft which is no longer in an emergency can cancel the emergency condition e.g.

> ✈ Southampton approach, Autoair 3. **Cancel Mayday**, engine restarted, continuing to Southampton

> ▼ Autoair 3, roger

Likewise the ATSU can transmit a message to indicate that the emergency has ended:

> ▼ All stations, Southend Tower, at time 58 **Mayday traffic Autoair 3 is ended out**

▶ Uncertainty of Position

One common use of 121.5 is for pilots who have become uncertain of position. Since late 1993 an autotriangulation DF service has been in service on this frequency, which greatly aids the location of an aircraft making a transmission on 121.5 if it is over the UK mainland. At the time of writing, the autotriangulation service is available in the area approximately south and east of Manchester, although it is scheduled to be extended to the rest of the UK in due course. When an aircraft transmits in this area on 121.5, various DF stations automatically take a bearing on the transmission and the probable position of the transmitting aircraft is displayed on a wall chart in front of the emergency controller. The system allows D&D to plot your position to within about a mile in very quick time indeed. Old-fashioned DF triangulation is still possible if the aircraft is outside the autotriangulation area, but it has to be carried out manually; the emergency controller contacts various ATSUs by telephone, and they report their bearing to a transmission on 121.5. As you can imagine, manual DF triangulation is very time-consuming and rather less accurate than the autotriangulation system.

So if you are in difficulty, it makes sense to decide to use the service early on and not wait until fuel, weather or daylight remaining become critical.

As a final point, do tell the ATSU or D&D if your aircraft is fitted with a transponder. In most parts of the UK, D&D can use your transponder to plot your position in a matter of seconds and to a very high degree of accuracy.

▶Practice Emergencies

For practice purposes an emergency (Pan) can be simulated, although not a distress (Mayday) situation. This can be a very useful exercise, and also gives the D&D cell some practice (not too often, though, or they may give you a reply along the lines of "you are in the same position as you were this time last Tuesday"). Before transmitting, you should listen out for some time on 121.5 to ensure that an ongoing real emergency is not in progress. A simulated emergency call should be prefixed with the word "practice":

> Practice Pan, Practice Pan, Practice Pan, London centre this is G-JAKE

The emergency controller will indicate that he can accept the practice by inviting the aircraft to continue:

> G-JAKE, this is London Centre, continue with Practice Pan

If the Practice Pan cannot be accepted the aircraft will be instructed to call back at another time.

▶Fire Services

At major airfields, a facility exists for a pilot to communicate directly with the airport's fire services when they are in attendance. This could obviously be a life-saver in certain situations, avoiding the delay and possible confusion involved in relaying messages through the ATSU. The dedicated frequency for this service is 121.6, and it is obviously a good idea to have this as one of the stored frequencies in a portable transceiver if you have one.

▶Revision

52 Does an urgency message take priority over all other radio calls?

53 You are flying a Robinson R22, registration G-DRAI. You are four miles south-west of Coventry airport on a heading of 270° at an altitude of 2000ft. You are a PPL and have one passenger; he suddenly displays a variety of alarming medical symptoms which you construe as a suspected heart attack. You decide to divert directly to Coventry airport, which you have in sight. You are already in contact with Coventry approach; what do you say?

54 You are flying a Cessna 150, G-AMSU. You are two miles to the north of Leicester airfield at 2500ft heading 090 when you experience a complete engine failure. You are a student pilot flying solo, and you decide to land on Leicester's Runway 28. What do you say? (You are already in contact with the air/ground station at Leicester).

55 You are airborne when you hear a Mayday call. What should be your actions?

56 You become lost on a cross-country flight and are unable to contact any of your en-route ATSUs. To whom, and on what frequency, should you make a call for assistance?

57 How might you indicate that you are a student/inexperienced pilot?

Answers at RT103

Revision Answers

▶ **PRE-FLIGHT**

1 – Range increases

2 – The AD and ENR sections

3 – 125.175MHz

4 – Any station within range on the frequency

▶ **GENERAL OPERATING PROCEDURES**

5 – Quebec

6 – Niner

7 – Separately, as in Wun Zero Wun Fower – 1014

8 – Fife Tousand feet

9 – UTC

▶ **AIR TRAFFIC SERVICE UNITS**

10 – Only an Air Traffic Control Unit

11 – [station name] Information

▶ **CALLSIGNS, ABBREVIATIONS, GENERAL PROCEDURES**

12 – Only after the ATSU has done so

13 – No abbreviation of this callsign is permitted

14 – All stations

15 – When the pressure setting is 1000mb or more

▶DEPARTURE PROCEDURES

16 – Yes

17 – Surface wind

18 – Readability 3

19 – A clearance for the aircraft to follow a specified route after take-off. It is *not* a clearance for an aircraft to take-off

20 – Only when authorised to do so by the ATSU

21 – Line up and wait

22 – Take-off at your discretion

23 – No. But if you choose not to, you must inform ATC at once

24 – Aircraft callsign/the condition/ the instruction

25 – This exchange is ended and no response is expected

26 – I have received all of your last transmission. Note that 'roger' must not be used in place of a required read-back.

▶EN-ROUTE PROCEDURES

27 – 'Standby' does not need any acknowledgement

28 – Yes

29 – The ATSU to contact has your details

30 – The ATSU to contact does not have your details

31 – I understand your message and will comply with it

32 – Radar Advisory Service (RAS) and Radar Information Service (RIS)

33 – 9 o'clock

34 – Yes, during the notified hours of the ATZ. Do not confuse the ATZ with the larger MATZ which may be found at a military aerodrome

35 – In the ENR section of the AIP

36 – No. The transponder should first be set to Standby

37 – Yes

38 – 7000

39 – The magnetic track **to** a point or station, or in other words the magnetic heading to steer to reach the point or station, assuming no wind

40 – +/- 10°

41 – ATIS

42 – Repeat all, or a specified part, of your last transmission

43 – At any time if she/he feels it necessary

Revision Answers

►ARRIVAL/TRAFFIC PATTERN PROCEDURES

44 – Long final

45 – Land after

46 – The pilot of the following aircraft

47 – No specific phraseology, other than a report of the surface wind

48 – A touch-and-go

►COMMUNICATIONS FAILURE

49 – No

50 – 7600

51 – •••• (four short dots)

►EMERGENCY PROCEDURES

52 – No. An urgency (Pan Pan) call has priority over all other messages **except** a distress (Mayday) call

53 – Firstly, **Fly the aeroplane.** Then do what is necessary to handle the problem. When you are *absolutely sure* you have the situation fully in hand:

Pan Pan, Pan Pan, Pan Pan, Coventry approach, this is G-DRAI, a Robinson R22 helicopter with a seriously ill passenger. Request immediate diversion to Coventry and ambulance to meet us on arrival. Presently four miles south-west of the airfield at 2000 feet QNH heading 270, PPL, I have the airfield in sight

54 – Firstly, **Fly the aeroplane.** Then do what is necessary to handle the problem. When you are *absolutely sure* you have the situation fully in hand:

Mayday, Mayday, Mayday; Leicester Radio this is G-AMSU, a Cessna 150 with complete engine failure. Intend forced landing runway 28 at Leicester. Presently two miles north of the airfield at 2500 feet heading 090. Student pilot, one POB

55 – Take details of the Mayday, and then *maintain radio silence* unless you can offer assistance

56 – London Centre or Scottish Centre on frequency 121.5 MHz

57 – The use of the word 'Tyro'

Glossary of Standard Words and Phrases

Acknowledge .... Confirm that you have received and understood this message

Affirm .... Yes (shortened from affirmative)

Approved .... Permission for proposed action is granted

Break .... This is a separation between messages

Changing to .... I intend to call [unit] on [frequency]

Check .... Examine a system or procedure

Cleared......................... Authorised to proceed under the conditions specified

Climb........................... Climb and maintain

Confirm......................... Have you correctly received [message/information]? Did you correctly receive this message?

Confirm squawk [code] ...... Confirm the code and mode you have set on the transponder

Contact......................... Establish radio contact with [unit], (they have your details)

Correct .... That is correct

Correction .... An error has been made. The correct message is.....

Descend .... Descend and maintain

Disregard .... Consider that transmission was not sent

Free-call .... Call [ATSU], (they do not have your details)

How do you read? .... What is the readability of my transmissions?

I Say Again .... I will repeat (for clarity or emphasis)

Monitor .... Listen out on [frequency]

Negative .... No, or That is not correct, or Permission is not granted

Out .... This exchange is ended and no response is expected

Over .... This transmission is ended and I expect a response

Pass your message .... Proceed with your message

Re-cycle [code][mode] ...... Set the transponder to standby, then re-select the assigned code and mode

Read Back .... Repeat all, or a specified part, of the message; exactly as you received it

Report .... Pass requested information

Request .... I want to know, or I want to obtain

Communications

Roger	I have received all of your last transmission
Say Again	Repeat all, or a specified part, of your last transmission
Speak Slower	Slow down your rate of speaking
Squawk [code and mode]	Set this mode and code
Squawk Charlie	Set the transponder to mode C
Squawk ident	Operate the ident button on the transponder
Squawk standby	Set the transponder to the standby position
Standby	Wait and I will call you
Verify	Check and confirm
Wilco	I understand your message and will co-operate with it
Words Twice	As a request – please transmit each word twice As information – I will transmit each word twice

Air Law and Communications
combined index

A

index

index

B

C

d

index

D

index

E

index

F

index

index

J

index

L

M

index

N

index

O

P

index

index

O

P

I

index

Q

R

index

index

S

index

index

U

V

index

W

r

notes

notes